Against Automobility

A selection of previous *Sociological Review* Monographs

Theorizing Museums*
ed. Sharon Macdonald and Gordon Fyfe
Consumption Matters*
eds Stephen Edgell, Kevin Hetherington and Alan Warde
Ideas of Difference*
eds Kevin Hetherington and Rolland Munro
The Laws of the Markets*
ed. Michael Callon
Actor Network Theory and After*
eds John Law and John Hassard
Whose Europe? The Turn Towards Democracy*
eds Dennis Smith and Sue Wright
Renewing Class Analysis*
eds Rosemary Cromptom, Fiona Devine, Mike Savage and John Scott
Reading Bourdieu on Society and Culture*
ed. Bridget Fowler
The Consumption of Mass*
ed. Nick Lee and Rolland Munro
The Age of Anxiety: Conspiracy Theory and the Human Sciences*
eds Jane Parish and Martin Parker
Utopia and Organization*
ed. Martin Parker
Emotions and Sociology*
ed. Jack Barbalet
Masculinity and Men's Lifestyle Magazines*
ed. Bethan Benwell
Nature Performed: Environment, Culture and Performance*
eds Bronislaw Szerszynski, Wallace Heim and Claire Waterton
After Habermas: New Perspectives on the Public Sphere*
eds Nick Crossley and John Michael Roberts
Feminism After Bourdieu*
eds Lisa Adkins and Beverley Skeggs
Contemporary Organization Theory*
eds Campbell Jones and Rolland Munro
A New Sociology of Work*
eds Lynne Pettinger, Jane Parry, Rebecca Taylor and Miriam Glucksmann

*Available from Marston Book Services, PO Box 270, Abingdon, Oxon OX14 4YW

The Sociological Review Monographs

Since 1958 *The Sociological Review* has established a tradition of publishing Monographs on issues of general sociological interest. The Monograph is an edited book length collection of research papers which is published and distributed in association with Blackwell Publishing. We are keen to receive innovative collections of work in sociology and related disciplines with a particular emphasis on exploring empirical materials and theoretical frameworks which are currently under-developed. If you wish to discuss ideas for a Monograph then please contact the Monographs Editor, Rolland Munro, at *The Sociological Review*, Keele University, Newcastle-under-Lyme, North Staffordshire, ST5 5BG.

Against Automobility

Edited by Steffen Böhm, Campbell Jones, Chris Land and Matthew Paterson

Blackwell Publishing/Sociological Review

BLACKWELL PUBLISHING
350 Main Street, Malden, MA 02148-5020, USA
9600 Garsington Road, Oxford OX4 2DQ, UK
550 Swanston Street, Carlton, Victoria 3053, Australia

First published 2006 by Blackwell Publishing Ltd

Library of Congress Cataloging-in-Publication Data

Against automobility / edited by Steffen Böhm . . . [et al.].
    p. cm. – (Sociological review monographs)
    "This book started life as a conference at Keele University on "automobility," in September 2002"–P. Includes bibliographical references and index.
    ISBN-13: 978-1-4051-5270-9
    ISBN-10: 1-4051-5270-2
    1. Transportation, Automotive–Social aspects–Congresses.
2. Automobilies–Social aspects–Congresses.   3. Autonomy (Philosophy)–Congresses.
4. Movement (Philosophy)–Congresses.   I. Böhm, Steffen, 1973–

    HE5611.A36 2006
    306.4'819–dc22

                                                          2006018125

A catalogue record for this title is available from the British Library

Set by SNP Best-set Typesetter Ltd, Hong Kong

Printed and bound in the United Kingdom by Page Brothers, Norwich

The publisher's policy is to use permanent paper from mills that operate a sustainable forestry policy, and which has been manufactured from pulp processed using acid-free and elementary chlorine-free practices. Furthermore, the publisher ensures that the text paper and cover board used have met acceptable environmental accreditation standards.

For further information on Blackwell Publishing, visit our website:
http://www.blackwellpublishing.com

Contents

Acknowledgements

This book started life as a conference at Keele University on 'automobility', in September 2002. Thanks are due to Rolland Munro, Director of the Centre for Social Theory and Technology at Keele, also to Tracey Wood for her organizational support. We would like to thank all the participants in the conference, many of whom gave papers which stimulated enormous debate on the occasion. In the process of turning the selection of papers delivered at the conference into the finished book and developing the threads that tie it all together, we thank first of all the authors for their patience and responsiveness to our varying demands for revisions and clarifications. Secondly, we thank the many anonymous referees who helped in judgments on the many papers we had to select from and in guiding authors in revising their work.

We do not want to give the impression that there is anything 'autonomous' in this project, in the sense that it might be the result of individual minds or individualized resistances. Every day, throughout the world, millions engage collectively in presenting possibilities that run against the current regime of automobility, and we will be very happy indeed if the publication of this book contributes to that movement of resistance.

Steffen Böhm, Campbell Jones, Chris Land, and Matthew Paterson
London, Nottingham, Colchester and Ottawa
February 2006

Part One
Conceptualizing Automobility

Introduction: Impossibilities of automobility

Steffen Böhm, Campbell Jones, Chris Land and Mat Paterson

From the automobile to automobility

Automobiles, their production, consumption, meaning and consequences, have vexed and intrigued theorists, governments, businesses, unions, protesters and activists from their inception in the late nineteenth century to the present day. As a figure of the contemporary landscape, the automobile evokes the concerns and thematics of modernity, whether these are the rationalized, automated production line of Henry Ford or the seemingly insatiable appetite for speed and movement that is its counterpoint. Automobiles have thus become a topic about which there is great interest across the social sciences, as well as outside academia. There is consequently a substantial volume of works on the automobile, with varying focuses on history (for example McShane, 1994; O'Connell, 1998; Scharff, 1991), urban development (Kunstler, 1994; Bottles, 1987), environmental politics (Freund & Martin, 1993; Zielinski & Laird, 1996; Whitelegg, 1997; Seel, Paterson & Doherty, 2000), political economy and industrial relations (Luger, 2000; Deyo, 1996; Rupert, 1995), cultural studies (Wernick, 1991; Miller, 2001; Gartman, 1994; Sachs, 1992), or public policy (Dunn, 1998) – these are just a small selection of the existing works.

As undoubtedly important as the *automobile* is, however, the aim of this book is to look beyond the car itself to consider the concept of *automobility* that underlies it. Automobility is one of the principal socio-technical institutions through which modernity is organized. It is a set of political institutions and practices that seek to organize, accelerate and shape the spatial movements and impacts of automobiles, whilst simultaneously regulating their many consequences. It is also an ideological (see Gorz, 1973) or discursive formation, embodying ideals of freedom, privacy, movement, progress and autonomy, motifs through which automobility is represented in popular and academic discourses alike, and through which its principal technical artefacts – roads, cars, etc. – are legitimized. Finally, it entails a phenomenology, a set of ways of experiencing the world which serve both to legitimize its dominance and radically unsettle taken-for-granted boundaries separating human from machine, nature from artifice and so on. Together these apparently diverse strands comprise an understanding of automobility that is irreducible to *the* automobile.

In recent years, 'automobility' has become recognized shorthand for referring to these different meanings, through which to understand their related sets of socio-techno-political practices in all their complexity and interconnections (eg. Rajan, 1996; Shove, 1998; Urry, 2000; Featherstone *et al.*, 2004). In this context, this book seeks both to develop this emerging understanding of the phenomenon we and others call automobility, and to set out an array of distinctive and diverse critiques of this phenomenon. The book draws together a wide variety of international scholars from across a range of academic disciplines to bring their different perspectives to bear on the question. The guiding theme of the volume is this effort critically to rethink and work through the concepts of automobility that have come to dominate contemporary cultures and societies across the globe. Specifically, the volume attempts to *theorize* automobility, in diverse ways, and to *politicize* it. There remains a need to theorize the complex of social and political relations involved in automobility, and there is a crucial importance in recognizing that automobility is fundamentally political – that it entails patterns of power relations and visions of a collective 'good life' which are at the same time highly contestable and contested. Much of the literature which has developed the concept of automobility has, while providing significant additions to our understanding of the phenomenon, eschewed exploration of the specifically political dimensions to automobility (see for example the majority of the contributions to Miller, 1991, or Featherstone *et al.*, 2004).

This twin concern with theory and politics runs through the book. Part I provides diverging views on how we might conceptualize automobility as a social form. Part II asks questions about how automobility is governed – the sorts of rules and forms of rule that have emerged as part of attempts to shape automobility's forms and consequences. Part III asks how automobility has been represented and interpreted within diverse cultural forms – films, advertising, and literature. Part IV asks what comes 'after automobility' – in the sense of forms of autonomy and movement which reject or modify automobility's dominant association with automobiles.

From systems to regimes of automobility

As its name implies, automobility can be understood as a patterned system which is predicated in the most fundamental sense on a combination of notions of autonomy and mobility. Autonomy and mobility are to be understood in the terms of this system as both values in themselves, but also as conjoined – one expresses and achieves autonomy when mobile. Similarly, true mobility can only be achieved autonomously – the distinction between moving and being moved, a passive and decidedly dependent (as opposed to autonomous) state.

These concepts of autonomy and mobility come together around material and symbolic artefacts through which the combination is expressed. In our era, the predominant artefact is the car. In contemporary societies, the car stands in place of automobility itself. It is so thoroughly invested with the constitutive flows of modernity – material, financial, and libidinal – that it has come to appear universal and incontestable. These connections operate in terms of what Laclau and Mouffe (1985) call 'chains of equivalence' in which things which bear no *a priori* relation to each other are made to be the same. These connections become, ironically, 'automatic'. The production and consumption of the automobile becomes the production and consumption of automobility itself.

To refer to automobility as a *system* is to talk of the patterned and structured manner in which a range of social developments have operated to reinforce each other, making the widespread use of automobiles both possible and in many instances necessary. We could describe this system in a variety of ways (for one description see Urry, this volume) but the point here is simply that automobility *is* structured and systemic (see also Shove, 1998). To say that automobility is systemic is to insist that it is not simply the experience of automobile use by drivers, the way in which car use is seen by them to express their control of their own lives (as emphasized by pro-car enthusiasts, such as Lomasky, 1997). It is also the range of images through which the meanings of cars are understood and marketed, the dependences of such use on a range of environmental resources (oil, steel, plastics, etc) and the generation of environmental consequences (noise, air pollution, deforestation, global warming, etc). Perhaps most importantly for the notion of a 'system' is the range of investments involved in what Urry calls a 'machinic complex' which are the conditions of possibility of individual and, more importantly, mass automobile use. Road building and maintenance, traffic regulations, parking arrangements, insurance, criminal justice systems, healthcare, pollution control rules and mechanisms, forward and backward economic linkages (from oil production to garages to maintenance of cars) only serve as a list of the principal elements in this complex which have emerged during the twentieth century to make automobile use possible, to maximize the political and economic benefits such use might bring and to regulate the side effects of such use.

Although automobility is patterned in the way that systems are, at a certain point the language of 'system' loses its value. To speak of a system is to convey the impression of something autopoietic, a set of interlocking features which reinforce each other, and where elements in the system emerge for functional reasons, to 'correct imbalances' or to 'improve performance' of the system as a whole. For example, Urry (2004) talks about automobility as a 'self-organizing non-linear system', and invokes a viral metaphor of the expansion of the car, where cars, once sufficiently established in the 'host body', then create the conditions for their own continued expansion, driving out their competitors. While this may work as a metaphorical description, as an explanation it leaves crucial features out of the picture. The notion of system tends to underplay collective human agency in the production of automobility and to avoid the political questions about the shaping of the automobile 'system'. At the extreme it can create a sense of 'lock-in' where the only possibilities for shaping automobility or of moving away from its dominance arise from within the system itself.

We therefore propose to speak not of a system but of a *regime* of automobility. Speaking of a *regime* allows us not only to emphasize the systemic aspects of automobility but also to bring out the relations of power that make this system possible. At the same time, it attempts to avoid the sense of closure in the notion of system, where its internal relations, feedback mechanisms, create a closed loop reproducing its logics relentlessly. Our intention, then, in this introduction and throughout the volume, is not simply to describe a system of automobility, which might naturalize this system and take it for granted, but to engage in a critique that draws out its political character, its tensions and problems, and the possibilities of moving beyond it.

One element in such a critique is to question the universality of today's regime of automobility. This has two elements. First, cars are typically presented as the embodiment of automobility itself, in universal, transcendent terms. But other modes or regimes of automobility are possible. There are other transport modes which themselves can lay claim to being perhaps more 'real' modes of automobility – apart from walking (see eg, Macauley, 2000), cycling is perhaps the most obvious here, as discussed by Fincham in this volume. There are also modes of mobility which do not in themselves involve bodily travel. A range of information technologies, from the telephone to the internet, themselves create forms of travel which express and embody notions of autonomy, as discussed by Miller and by Latimer and Munro in this volume.

The most basic part of this critique is that there are automobilities that do not depend upon the car. The car is only a particular universality, a particular regime of automobility that is nevertheless universalized, regarded universally as the embodiment of progress. In this sense automobility is a hegemonic project. It is a generalization of particular visions, interests and normativities. But nevertheless, while the car is everywhere, it is also everywhere contested. From the deep protests after the first car related death, of Bridget Driscoll on 17 August 1896 in the UK, the restrictions in car use across many countries, or the anti-car novels in the early twentieth century (of which *The Wind in the Willows* is perhaps the most famous), through to the direct action protests against road building and car culture in the new millennium, automobility has been actively challenged and alternatives promoted. In the face of such adversity those with interests in the development of the system of automobility, and the particular version of automobility embedded in the car, have actively and continuously organized to reproduce it. But this raises the immediate question, how has automobility been politically sustained?

Truth, power, subject

One powerful starting point in taking up these questions would be to follow Michel Foucault's emphasis on the relation of regimes of truth, power and subjectivity. Automobility's regimes of *truth* operate to (re)produce the taken-for-granted character of car driving. They involve a wide range of statements, some of which, of course, are mutually contradictory (and all of which at some level are contested), but which are nevertheless presented as 'natural facts'. Cars are taken, for example, as self-evident embodiments of the following things:

- They are efficient, both for individuals and in social or economic terms; that is, they enable the pursuit of tasks in a manner which involves the least effort to achieve the goals desired, relative to alternatives.
- They are convenient – they enable people to go from A to B directly, at times they choose, and to carry substantial amounts of goods with them.
- They are cheap – the costs of journeys are lower than for alternatives such as the bus or the train.
- They are stylish – they enable the user to express elements of individuality through the car itself, but also to arrive looking smart, untroubled by close contact with others (as on the bus or train) or the exertion of physical effort and thus sweating (as with cycling or walking).
- They are modern or progressive; they represent the 'natural' development of society both to greater mobility and to greater individualization and thus associate their users, and their corollaries, roads, with modernity itself (Berman, 1982).
- They are democratic (see Rajan, this volume) in the sense that they level people – all those on the road are equal.
- They are liberators; not only in the immediate but tautologous sense of embodying individual autonomy but also in that they have helped the development of a politics of freedom and equality (Guattari, 2000). For some, for example, cars made suffrage possible (Scharff, 1991).

Regimes of *power* have also developed as elements in a more overarching regime of automobility. There are obvious and crude elements of power in automobile systems, perhaps the most obvious of which is the brutal power of the Sports Utility Vehicle or SUV, the brutishness of which is analysed by Dery as well as Shukin in this volume. But beyond this there are the perhaps more subtle relations of power that are embodied in the government of automobility. Hence in Part Two of this book we find several analyses of governmentality with respect to automobility (see Bonham, Forstorp and Merriman, all in this volume). Automobility has entailed a plethora of regulatory schemes, regulating speed of travel, the places of travel, direction of travel, where one can park, orders of priority in movement, all designed to regularize the forms of movement in cars. At the same time, the power of cars, fuel efficiency, the sorts of emissions coming out of their exhaust, their safety, is similarly regulated. And for both sorts of regulatory schemes, a whole range of governmental institutions have emerged, engaged in monitoring, shaping, disciplining, drivers (and non-drivers) into behaving in ways consistent with an ordered, regulated, movement of automobiles (arguably, of course, attenuating the 'freedom' of driving to a significant degree). Automobility, exemplifying freedom, has thus gone hand in hand with a deepening of state power. But automobility has also entailed other transformations in power relations. It is entwined with the reorganization of capital's power in the workplace, exemplified by the term 'Fordism' which was a regime of accumulation, structuring growth from the 1910s to the 1970s (at least), but at the same time a particular mode of control of the labour force and culture at large (see Martin-Jones and Shukin, this volume).

The third element involves a regime of *subjectivity*. Again, there are several elements here. Perhaps the most fundamental is the intertwining of automobile discourses with those of individualism, where the two mutually inform and support each other (see especially Rajan and Thacker, this volume). In many respects the subject of automobility is also the subject of the contemporary political arena. Particularly assumed in neo-liberal formations of the subject is the idea that an individual is self-motivating. Whether voting or consuming, the subject should know its own mind and interests and act in accordance with them. The subject so conceived is, or should be, both autonomous from external control and self-moving as opposed to the victim of external influence. A chain of equivalence is constructed whereby to drive is to embody a modernist subjectivity (see Thacker, this volume), and to be in favour of such a subjectivity is to regard driving as unproblematically legitimate (Lomasky, 1997). Such a chain of equivalence creates at the same time a normalization of driving and car ownership – that car driving is what *normal people* do – which both produces and is legitimized by the construction of alternative modes as deviant. 'Margaret Thatcher once said that a man who after the age of 30 finds himself on a bus can count himself a failure in life' (Parris, 2003). Cyclists, for example, are routinely rendered as deviant, both in planning processes which assume their non-existence, and where the car driver is manifestly the 'normal subject', and in more active moral panics such as the one about 'lycra louts' (see Fincham, this volume). Such normalizations frequently involve differentiation of subjectivities around standard categories of class, gender or race. These serve to produce hierarchies of difference among car drivers, with different makes and models serving to signify (and be signified by) different subject positions along these lines, and also serving as sites of resistance to this subjectification, as in the appropriation of BMWs by African Americans serving to signify a certain resistance to such racial hierarchies (Gilroy, 2001), and of course to the policing of such boundaries as these drivers are then harassed for being seen in cars regarded as inappropriate for their 'station'. But these categories also produce such differentiated subjectivities through their intertwining with patterns of car ownership itself – with access to jobs and services structured significantly by access to cars, poverty (itself already gender and ethnically differentiated) is automobilized.

These three principal elements – truth, power, and subjectivity – tend to act in mutually supportive ways. The attribution of deviance to alternatives to the car means that those advocating such alternatives have trouble articulating successfully their own regime of truth regarding cars – we don't believe their statements of 'fact' because they are already regarded as deviant. Regimes of power connected to the governance of automobility produce truth effects about driving or driven subjects, including those concerning the deviance of certain subjects (and of course is reproduced in daily life by the 'brute' power of cars to bully alternatives off the road). But such mutual support doesn't lend itself to interpretation as self-replicating 'system'. Nor can its tripartite components be thought of as clearly separable from one another. Rather it is their interrelations that determine them as components of a regime. But as with other triangular formations, so apparently stable when applied to architectural construction, closer inspection reveals a tendency to multiply their number. Power is productive of subjects and exercised by means of regimes of truth that in turn constitute power.

Antagonisms of automobility

If we are to move beyond the description of the regime of automobility and act against and beyond it, then we need to expose the inconsistencies, contradictions and antagonisms of the present regime of automobility. This might begin by pointing to the obvious 'side-effects' of the automobile: pollution, death and injury, specific formations of geopolitics, the transformation of the urban landscape and modern mindscape. The impossibility of automobility does indeed contain the meaning that if continued, a car-based regime generates widespread problems – ecological collapse, war, widespread death and ill-health and economic dysfunctionality, to name but a few – which cannot be resolved without abandoning the regime itself. In this sense the continuation of automobility is impossible in its current form.

Four specific antagonisms inherent to the current regime of automobility can serve to illustrate its impossibility. One of the most obvious ones is congestion. Once 'universalized', in the sense of a substantial number – in most industrialized countries over 40 percent of adults having regular use of a car – the pursuit of individual mobility becomes collective immobility. In many of the world's largest cities, complete gridlock is an immanent possibility, if not reality, which transport planners have to develop elaborate contingency plans for, and even without gridlock, the economic and social costs of congestion are now very considerable.

A second antagonism, which seems well established and understood today, points to the concerns about ecological sustainability of the contemporary regime of automobility. Automobile use contributes significantly to three principal forms of environmental degradation. It contributes significantly to the depletion of non-renewable resources, notably oil (including production of plastics), rubber, platinum, lead, aluminium and iron (Freund & Martin, 1993: 17–19). It is important in the generation of a range of pollution problems, including urban air pollution, acid rain, global warming, and water pollution from road building and run-off. Finally, it dominates space, especially urban space, accounting for in the extreme case of Los Angeles 67 percent of all space, and has contributed to the radical re-organization of urban space which means towns and cities are now much more spread out, both displacing land from other uses and transforming the use of cars themselves from choice to necessity. There are a range of potential technological fixes for this environmental antagonism, which is built into the regime of automobility, but only the most technologically optimistic (eg, Hawken, Lovins and Lovins, 2000) suggest that it can be resolved by a series of technological fixes.

The dependency on oil, a natural resource which, when burnt, creates vast environmental problems ranging from air pollution to global warming, defines the third antagonism of automobility. The fact that oil is a scarce resource, which has only a finite lifetime (most suggesting a century at best), yet is the single most important fuel for the organization of mass transport, connects the regime of automobility to a host of global geopolitical problems. To satisfy the developed world's thirst for oil, access to cheap oil has to be maintained and enormous amounts of money have to be spent in order to explore, produce, transport, refine and store oil so that it can finally be consumed at a petrol station in Washington, London or Berlin. Automobility is not just a system of car transport; it is a defining geopolitical factor that may even influence governments' decisions to go to war (see Martin-Jones, this volume). In this sense automobility quite literally kills, even though the victims of these wars remain largely invisible to the driver gliding through post-industrial suburbia.

But automobility is not only an invisible killing machine because Western governments go to war to secure access to oil. The car delivers death much more directly, much closer to 'home.' The fourth antagonism, then, is that the regime of automobility cannot be disconnected from the mass 'accident'. Once you have millions of cars, steered by individual drivers, failures of that system are predictable. Annually around 1.2 million deaths are produced directly by the global regime of automobility, that is, by traffic 'accidents', significantly outstripping warfare as the leading cause of violent death (WHO/World Bank, 2004; Dauvergne, 2005). In the OECD countries alone, 107,406 people were killed in car 'accidents' in 2001, approximately one every five minutes (IRTAD/OECD, 2003). Yet these failures of the system remain largely invisible in the sense that they are regarded as 'normality'. The US might go to war because three thousand people die in a horrific attack on two skyscrapers, and a plane crash might make the headline news for a few days; roughly the same number (around 3200) of people are killed in car crashes on a daily basis, but their deaths are not spectacular enough to make it into the news.

What we have got here, then, is not a stable, well-working machinery but a regime that is characterized by fundamental antagonisms. The regime of automobility is impossible because it is inherently fragile. It depends on a range of contingencies for its continued success, including the ability of geopolitical intervention and dominance to secure access to oil, the ability of planners and traffic engineers continually to provide for the mitigation of chronic congestion, the ideological success in rendering thousands of human deaths annually as 'normal' and acceptable, the ability to overcome opposition to road building, the capacity to navigate the fiscal crisis of the state to generate sufficient funds to promote automobile use, and so on. It depends also on the continued capacity to articulate the particularity of the car as the universal form of automobility to shake off alternatives and challengers, from eco-warriors to the internet. Such efforts to shore-up the regime are ubiquitous and occupy significant amounts of time for many politicians, bureaucrats, car company strategists, environmentalists, and others. The government of automobility (pollution control regulations, safety technologies, many road construction schemes, for example) is itself the historical and ongoing legacy of such efforts. Because of the above discussed conceptual impossibility of automobility itself, however, such interventions fail to close the wounds they are designed to 'heal' but either leak round the edges (or through the middle), or generate their own knock-on unintended consequences, their own iatrogenic diseases, and which in turn are articulated as problems requiring their own remedies.

The antagonisms of automobility, then, are not temporary 'bruises' of an otherwise well-working machinery. Instead they are inherent to the 'normal goings-on' of automobility. In other words, automobility, the way it works today, would not be possible without these antagonisms. It has been one of the tasks of this book to expose and oppose these antagonisms in the regime of automobility. What this critique points to is the fact that it is literally impossible to go on with the way modern mass transport has been organized.

Impossibilities of automobility

In addition to these practical antagonisms lies a deeper conceptual impossibility. Automobility is ultimately impossible *in its own terms*. Its impossibility is contained in the very combination of autonomy and mobility. At the point at which a subject attempts to move, the specifics of that movement – the technologies deployed, the spaces which need to be made available, the consequences of the form and place of movement, and so on – require a set of external interventions to render it possible. Cars need roads, traffic rules, oil, planning regulations, and the representation of car driving as autonomous movement involves disguising such conditions. It seems obvious that the more cars are around, the more rules have to be invented (eg, congestion charges and motorway tolls) to allow the regime of automobility to work 'normally', even though this 'normality' might be contradictory to the image of a completely autonomous movement.

The investment of cars with the concept of autonomy thus contradicts these dependencies that are needed to make automobility work. Instead of an autonomous subject that moves freely in space (it is no coincidence that television advertisements show cars on traffic-free mountainous roads with their drivers enjoying the freedom of movement), what we have is a continuously increasing disciplining of drivers. Rajan (1996) has shown this in great detail in relation to air pollution policy in California; in order not to challenge the universal goal of automobile use, legitimized as it was in terms of individual freedom, policymakers intruded ever more intrusively in the manufacture of the cars themselves, in the maintenance regimes owners were forced to operate, in the identification of 'sick cars'. Bonham (this volume) similarly shows the disciplining both of car drivers and of other road users in early twentieth century Adelaide, while Merriman (this volume) shows the necessity of fostering new driving sensibilities in the context of the development of motorways in the UK. At the most extreme, contemporary developments present the possibility of completely automated automobile use, raising fundamental questions about who, or what, is in the driving seat.

Such difficulties and dependencies are, of course, not unique to a regime of automobility built around cars. The representation of any form of mobility as autonomous is similarly impossible. Even walking (at least in modern conditions) requires external labour to construct paths, clear land, etc. But given the sense that the later chapters in the book, in particular Fincham and Miller, posit the possibility of regimes of automobility not premised on cars, the question that remains is whether such regimes are themselves possible. It seems to us that any regime of automobility would be inherently impossible, precisely because automobility as such is conceptually impossible. There will always be dependencies – complete autonomy of movement is an illusion.

The concept of autonomous mobility is riven with antagonisms that have a philosophical heritage harking back to scholastic debates on the possibility of an unmoved prime mover. In this sense the auto-mobile liberal humanist has ascended to take the place of a now dead God. Again the connections proliferate: automobile subjects not only transport themselves efficiently from A to B, but should also be self-motivated, self-starters whose social mobility is a reflection of moral worth and effort (see Bonham, this volume).

In a car it is fairly clear that autonomous mobility is impossible. If it were ever doubted then, in the UK at least, the fuel protests of 2000 made this all too evident, with queues of cars stretching for miles in hope of a gallon of petrol. A car's movement is beyond the control of an individual subject given its systematic interdependencies. Traffic is itself a socially negotiated phenomenon where trajectories cross and intersect in a complex but never independent movement. In the term 'automobile' itself there are also a number of unresolved tensions. It is ambiguous whether the autonomy in movement refers to the machine or the person. Is it the auto that is mobile or moved by the driver? Reflecting a complexification of mind/body dualism, should we consider the motor of movement to be primary (literally the engine), or the increasingly amputated and immobilized body of the driver whose physical movements are minimized whilst the driver's (autonomous?) desire determines the direction and trajectory of movement? To resolve, or sometimes reflect, this tension we have seen the rise of discourses of hybrid subjectivities: cyborgs and 'carsons' (car/persons) who are part machine part human agent but always already socially and technically situated and constituted in their subjectivity as a driver (see Michael, 2001; Lupton, 1999).

But whilst this human-auto hybridity proliferates alongside the wider networks of heterogeneous elements that constitute 'automobility', it is simultaneously hidden by a parallel moment of purification (see Latour, 1993). The complex hybrid network of automobility produces, as one of its effects, the appearance of independent automobility. Whilst the heterogeneous interdependencies that make mobility possible would threaten the apparent autonomy of the subject in motion, this parallel movement of purification enables 'the car' to be dismissed as just a tool or prosthesis to be mastered and controlled by an autonomous subject. To paraphrase Latour, the Gordian knot of hybrid automobility is severed to reinstate a clear separation of subjects and their objects: drivers and their cars are seen as fetishised commodities independent of any social relations. In this sense, 'automobility' is an effect of parallel movements of hybridization and purification. On one hand proliferating heterogeneous rhizomes constituting bodies, rulebooks, licensing authorities, pressure groups, expertise, capital, tarmac and steel; and on the other, their simultaneous sundering into the automobile subject and the objects of the car and traffic system. Without hybridity, auto*mobility* would be impossible. Without purification, *auto*mobility would be impossible. On both counts, *automobility* is impossible.

Beyond automobility

One way of enacting the regime of automobility is to look at the antagonisms that are inherent to this regime and try to address the social, environmental and economic consequences that are produced by its 'malfunctioning'. Take, for example, the introduction of congestion charges in London, an undoubtedly bold scheme that started in early 2003. Charging vehicles for entering city centres is one way to address the growing gridlock that characterizes most big cities on the globe. The protests against this particular scheme in London have been manifold. Commuters complained about the spiralling costs of getting to and from work and the lack of high quality public transport alternatives. Local businesses complained about their increased costs of doing business in London. There will always be a host of social groups that will be affected by the introduction of new governmental measures of control. What seems clear to us, however, is that the introduction of congestion charges points to the inherent antagonisms that characterize the regime of automobility, antagonisms that need to be politically addressed, if the regime as a whole is to continue.

Many insist that individuals should be able to decide for themselves and take things in their own hands, to be responsible for their own destiny. As a corollary, the task of politics is to reduce the interventions of the State and ensure that citizens have as much freedom as possible. The automobile as the vehicle that promises completely autonomous, free movement fits perfectly within such image. It comes as no surprise, then, that despite the serious environmental, social and economic costs due to the 'success' of automobility, dominant political discourses call for cheaper fuel, less taxes, more roads and less 'governing' of automobility. It seems clear that such understanding of the regime of automobility is illusory, precisely because automobility as such, is always already impossible, even on the conceptual level. This is to say that automobility is already an 'open' regime in the sense that it requires enactment to make it work. The task of politics is precisely to 'make up' automobility, that is, to set the limits and thereby gloss over the particular antagonisms of automobility.

What we are describing here is, of course, a reformist model. The politics of particularity aims to reform the regime of automobility by responding to particular failures, breaks and accidents – it makes a regime that is fundamentally impossible possible. The London congestion charge is such a politics of reform. It introduces a new technique for the governance of automobility, which has already changed the face of automobility in London itself: more cyclists are commuting to work, public transport plays a better role and people simply seem to walk more. While we certainly do not want to dismiss the importance of such a political move, the danger of a politics of reform is that it remains at the level of particularity in the sense that it remains geographically and politically a singular event and limited to the 'improvement' of automobility.

The London congestion charge is only a small gesture, precisely because it is not yet embedded in a wider politics of 'regime-change'; a change that would signal a hope of a radically different regime of automobility. It seems to us that one possible signal in urgent need to be sent out is one that entails a radical break from the dependency of automobile life on the unsustainable, environmental and social destruction causing, usage of non-renewable oil resources. How would an automobile society look without oil? This radical, yet so logical, question has been asked by many anti-road protesters, environmentalists and authors (eg, Catton, 1982; Heinberg, 2005; Zuckermann, 1991; www.lifeaftertheoilcrash.net) for many years – and now even progressive governments have caught on (*The Guardian*, 2006). Equally, one could ask: how would a carfree city look (Holtz Kay, 1997)? Cities like Amsterdam, Copenhagen, Freiburg and others show that a mixture of public transport and extensive cycle lane networks can provide an infrastructure that signals a hope in a more sustainable and carfree urban transport future (see Alvord, 2000; Crawford, 2002; see also www.critical-mass.org). Yet, while such provisions are signs of a future beyond the current regime of automobility, what seems to be important is to connect them to a wider, more general, questioning of the impossibility of the regime of automobility itself.

In our view, reforming automobility is not enough. In order radically to change the way automobility works today, it is not sufficient to expose the particular antagonisms of the regime and make it once again, temporarily, 'possible' by introducing new techniques of government. Instead, what is needed is a broadening awareness of the fragility of the entire regime of automobility. When in the year 2000 protests against high fuel prices brought most of the UK almost to a standstill, this fragility of the regime was made clear by a relatively small number of people within a few days: as almost the entirety of social life of the developed world depends on the steady flow of oil, a break of this flow has radical consequences for the normal maintenance of the regime of automobility.

Such breaks in the normal flows of automobility, even if they intended to achieve the opposite, expose the fragility of the regime. It is an act of subversion that has the potential to put into question the entire 'goings-on' of automobility. Such acts do not only aim to engage with a particular antagonism of automobility but to redefine the grounds on which automobility can be thought. Such acts are therefore radically unaccountable; one can never fully foresee their consequences. In our view, this is the task of today: radically to put into question the universality of automobility and engender a space that imagines not only different automobilities that cannot yet be foreseen, but also a social form which recognizes the necessity of disentangling its twin conceptual bases – to delink autonomy from mobility and to put both in context. In this sense, we are proposing interventions that quite literally propose to reconfigure the very co-ordinates of what is perceived as 'possible'. Faced with an antagonistic and impossible regime of automobility, we hope that the essays collected in this volume contribute to the recognition of that impossibility and to the collective possibility of moving beyond it.

References

Alvord, K. (2000) *Divorce Your Car!: Ending the Love Affair with the Automobile*. Gabriola Island, B.C.: New Society Publishers.

Berman, M. (1982) 'Robert Moses: The expressway world' in *All That is Solid Melts into Air: The Experience of Modernity*. London: Verso.

Bottles, S. (1987) *Los Angeles and the Automobile: The Making of the Modern City*. Berkeley, CA: University of California Press.

Catton, W. R. (1982) *Overshoot: Ecological Basis of Revolutionary Change*. Chicago: University of Illinois Press.

Crawford, J. H. (2002) *Carfree Cities*. Amsterdam: International Books, www.carfree.com

Dauvergne, P. (2005) 'Dying of Consumption: Accidents or Casualties of Global Morality?' *Global Environmental Politics*, 5(3): 35–47.

Deyo, F. C. (1996) *Social Reconstruction of the World's Automobile Industry*. London: Macmillan.

Dunn, J. (1998) *Driving Forces: The Automobile, Its Enemies and the Politics of Mobility*. Washington DC: Brookings Institution.

Featherstone, M., N. Thrift and J. Urry (eds) (2004) 'Automobilities' Special issue of *Theory, Culture and Society*, 21(4–5).

Freund, P. and G. Martin (1993) *The Ecology of the Automobile*. Montreal: Black Rose Books.

Gartman, D. (1994) *Auto Opium: A Social History of American Automobile Design*. London: Routledge.

Gilroy, P. (2001) 'Driving while black' in D. Miller (ed.) *Car Cultures*. London: Berg.

Gorz, A. (1973) 'The Social Ideology of the Motorcar' *Le Sauvage*, September-October, http://www.worldcarfree.net/resources/freesources/TheSocialIdeology.rtf, accessed 28 February 2006.

Guattari, F. (2000) *The Three Ecologies*. London: Athlone.

Hawken, P., A. Lovins and L. H. Lovins (2000) *Natural Capitalism: The Next Industrial Revolution*. London: Earthscan.

Heinberg, R. (2005) *Party's Over: Oil, War and the Fate of Industrial Societies*. Clairview Books.

Holtz Kay, J. (1997) *Asphalt Nation: How the Automobile Took Over America, and How We Can Take It Back*. Berkeley, CA: University of California Press.

IRTAD/OECD (2003) 'Fatalities by Road Location' *International Road Traffic Accident Database*, http://www.bast.de/htdocs/fachthemen/irtad/english/we32.html, accessed 6 October 2003.

Kunstler, J. H. (1994) *The Geography of Nowhere: the Rise and Decline of America's Man-made Landscape*. New York: Simon & Schuster.

Laclau, E. (1996) 'Why do empty signifiers matter to politics?' in *Emancipation(s)*. London: Verso.

Laclau, E. and C. Mouffe (1985) *Hegemony and Socialist Strategy*. London: Verso.

Latour, B. (1993) *We Have Never Been Modern*. New York: Harvester Wheatsheaf.

Lomasky, L. (1997) 'Autonomy and Automobility' *Independent Review*, 2(1): 5–28.

Luger, S. (2000) *Corporate Power, American Democracy and the Automobile Industry*. Cambridge: Cambridge University Press.

Lupton, D. (1999) 'Monsters in metal cocoons: 'Road rage' and cyborg bodies' *Body and Society*, 5(1): 57–72.

Macauley, D. (2000) 'Walking the City: an essay on peripatetic Practices and Politics' *Capitalism, Nature, Socialism*, 11(4): 3–43.

McShane, C. (1994) *Down the Asphalt Path: The Automobile and the American City*. New York: Columbia University Press.

Michael, M. (2001) 'The Invisible Car: The Cultural Purification of Road Rage' in D. Miller (ed.) *Car Cultures*. Oxford: Berg.

Miller, D. (ed.) (2001) *Car Cultures*. Oxford: Berg.

O'Connell, S. (1998) *The Car in British Society: Class, Gender and Motoring, 1896–1939*. Manchester: Manchester University Press.

Parris, M. (2003) 'It's big, it's red and it's free. And it will save London' *The Times*, 8 February.

Rajan, S. C. (1996) *The Enigma of Automobility: Democratic Politics and Pollution Control*. Pittsburgh: University of Pittsburgh Press.

Rupert, M. (1995) *Producing Hegemony: The Politics of Mass Production and American Global Power*. Cambridge: Cambridge University Press.

Sachs, W. (1992) *For the Love of the Automobile*. Berkeley, CA: University of California Press.

Scharff, V. (1991) *Taking the Wheel: Women and the Coming of the Motor Age*. New York: Free Press.

Seel, B., M. Paterson and B. Doherty (eds) (2000) *Direct Action in British Environmentalism*. London: Routledge.

Shove, E. (1998) 'Consuming Automobility' Discussion Paper for Project SceneSusTech, Employment Research Centre, Department of Sociology, Trinity College Dublin.

The Guardian (2006) 'Sweden plans to be world's first oil-free economy' 8 February 2006.

Urry, J. (2000) *Sociology Beyond Societies: Mobilities for the Twenty-First Century*. London: Routledge.

Urry, J. (2004) 'The 'system' of automobility' *Theory, Culture and Society*, 21(4): 25–39.

Wernick, A. (1991) '(Re-)imaging technology: The case of cars' in *Promotional Culture: Advertising, Ideology and Symbolic Expression*. London: Sage.

Whitelegg, J. (1997) *Critical Mass: Transport, Environment and Society in the Twenty-First Century*. London: Pluto.

WHO/World Bank (2004) *World Report on Traffic Injury and Prevention*. Geneva: World Health Organization.

Zielinski, S. and G. Laird (eds) (1995) *Beyond the Car*. Toronto: Steel Rail Publishing.

Zuckermann, W. (1991) *The End of the Road: World Car Crisis and How We Can Solve It*. Post Mills, VT: Chelsea Green.

Inhabiting the car

John Urry

What was central now was the fact of traffic. (Raymond Williams, quoted in Pinkney, 1991: 55)

Introduction

One billion cars have been manufactured during the last century. There are currently over 700m cars roaming the world, a figure expected to double by 2015 (Shove, 1998). And world car travel is predicted to triple between 1990 and 2050 (Hawken *et al.*, 1999). The car, however, is rarely discussed in much contemporary social science including that of globalization, although its specific character of domination is as powerful as television or the computer normally viewed as constitutive of global culture (but see Miller, 2000; Featherstone *et al.*, 2004). Indeed contemporary 'global cities', and cities in general, remain primarily rooted in and defined by automobility, as much as they are by these other technologies.

Much social analysis has been remarkably static and concerned itself little with the various mobilities that move into, across and through cities and countrysides (although see Lynd and Lynd, 1937; on sociology's neglect of the automobile, see Hawkins, 1986). Where such mobilities have been taken into account, it is to lament the effects of the car on the city or to argue that a culture of speed replaces older cultures of the 'urban' (Virilio, 1997). Social analysts have mainly concentrated upon the mobility of walking and especially *flânerie*, while the movement, noise, smell, visual intrusion and environmental hazards of the car are seen as largely irrelevant to deciphering the nature of contemporary life.

But automobility is as constitutive of the modern as are the more general processes of urbanization (as le Corbusier understood in the 1920s). Such an automobility comprises six components that in their *combination* generates the 'specific character of domination' that it exercises across the globe (Sheller and Urry, 2000). Automobility is:

- the quintessential *manufactured object* produced by the leading industrial sectors and the iconic firms within twentieth century capitalism (Ford, GM,

Rolls-Royce, Mercedes, Toyota, VW and so on); the industry from which Fordism and Post-Fordism have emerged

- the major item of *individual consumption* after housing which provides status to its owner/user through its sign-values (such as speed, home, safety, sexual desire, career success, freedom, family, masculinity, genetic breeding); is easily anthropomorphized by being given names, having rebellious features, seen to age and so on; and disproportionately preoccupies criminal justice systems
- an extraordinarily powerful *machinic complex* constituted through its technical and social interlinkages with other industries, car parts and accessories; petrol refining and distribution; road-building and maintenance; hotels, roadside service areas and motels; car sales and repair workshops; suburban house building; retailing and leisure complexes; advertising and marketing; urban design and plannning
- the predominant global form of 'quasi-private' *mobility* that subordinates other 'public' mobilities of walking, cycling, travelling by rail and so on; and it reorganizes how people negotiate the opportunities for, and constraints upon, work, family life, leisure and pleasure
- the dominant *culture* that sustains major discourses of what constitutes the good life, what is necessary for an appropriate citizenship of mobility and which provides potent literary and artistic images and symbols (ranging from E. M. Forster to Scott Fitzgerald, John Steinbeck, Daphne du Maurier and J. G. Ballard: see Bachmair, 1991; Graves-Brown, 1997; Eyerman and Löfgren, 1995; Pearce, 1999)
- the single most important cause of *environmental resource-use* resulting from the range and scale of material, space and power used in the manufacture of cars, roads and car-only environments, and in coping with the material, air quality, medical, social, ozone, visual, aural, spatial and temporal pollution of a more or less global automobility (Whitelegg, 1997)

I use 'automobility' here to capture a double-sense. On the one hand, 'auto' refers reflexively to the humanist self, such as the meaning of 'auto' in autobiography or autoerotic. On the other hand, 'auto' refers to objects or machines that possess a capacity for movement, as expressed by automatic, automaton and especially automobile. This double resonance of 'auto' is suggestive of how the car-driver is a 'hybrid' assemblage, not simply of autonomous humans but simultaneously of machines, roads, buildings, signs and entire cultures of mobility (Haraway, 1991; Thrift, 1996: 282–84). In the following I outline an analysis of 'auto' mobility that explores this double resonance, of autonomous humans *and* of autonomous machines only able to roam in certain time-space scapes. I consider how automobility is a complex amalgam of interlocking machines, social practices and especially ways of *inhabiting*, dwelling within, a mobile, semi-privatized and hugely dangerous auto-mobile capsule. The car is not simply a means of covering distances between A and B.

In the next section I consider how automobility makes instantaneous time and the negotiation of extensive space central to how such social life is configured, as people dwell in, and socially interact through, movement within their cars. In subsequent sections I elaborate various ways of inhabiting the car.

Flexibility and coercion

Inhabiting the car permits multiple socialities, of family life, community, leisure, the pleasures of movement and so on, which are interwoven through complex jugglings of time and space that car journeys both allow but also necessitate. These jugglings result from two interdependent features of automobility: that the car is immensely flexible *and* wholly coercive. I elaborate some of the temporal and spatial implications of this simultaneous flexibility and coercion for social life.

Automobility is in some respects a source of freedom, the 'freedom of the road'. Its flexibility enables the car-driver to travel at speed, at any time in any direction along the complex road systems of western societies that link together most houses, workplaces and leisure sites. Cars therefore extend where people can go to and hence what as humans they are literally able to do. Much of what many people now think of as 'social life' could not be undertaken without the flexibilities of the car and its availability 24 hours a day. It is possible to leave late by car, to miss connections, to travel in a relatively time-less fashion. People find pleasure in travelling when they want to, along routes that they choose, finding new places unexpectedly, stopping for relatively open-ended periods of time, and moving on when they desire. They are what Shove terms another of the 'convenience devices' of contemporary society, devices that make complex, harried patterns of social life just about possible, at least of course for those with cars (1998; and see Pearce, 1999).

But at the same time, this flexibility and these rights are themselves necessitated by automobility. The 'structure of auto space' forces people to orchestrate in complex and heterogeneous ways their mobilities and socialities across very significant distances. The urban environment, built during the latter half of the twentieth century for the convenience of the car, has 'unbundled' territorialities of home, work, business, and leisure that had historically been closely integrated and fragmented social practices that occurred in shared public spaces (Sassen, 1996). Automobility divides workplaces from homes, so producing lengthy commutes into and across the city. It splits homes and business districts, undermining local retail outlets to which one might have walked or cycled, thereby eroding town-centres, non-car pathways, and public spaces. It also separates homes and various kinds of leisure sites, which are often only available by motorized transport. Members of families are split up since they will live in distant places necessarily involving complex travel to meet up even intermittently. People inhabit congestion, jams, temporal uncertainties and health-threatening city environments, as a consequence of being encapsulated in a privatized, cocooned, moving capsule. Automobility simultaneously disables those who are not car-drivers (children, the sight impaired, those without cars) by making their every-day habitats dangerously non-navigable (Kunstler, 1994).

Automobility thus coerces people into an intense flexibility. It forces people to juggle tiny fragments of time so as to deal with the temporal and spatial constraints that it itself generates. Automobility is a Frankenstein-created monster, extending the individual into realms of freedom and flexibility whereby inhabiting the car can be positively viewed, but also constraining car 'users' to live their lives in spatially-stretched and time-compressed ways. The car, one might suggest, is more literally Weber's 'iron cage' of modernity, motorized, moving and privatized.

Automobility thus develops 'instantaneous' time to be managed in highly complex, heterogeneous and uncertain ways. Automobility involves an individualistic timetabling of many instants or fragments of time. The car-driver thus operates in instantaneous time that contrasts with the official timetabling of mobility that accompanied the railways in the mid-nineteenth century (Urry, 2000). This was modernist clock-time based upon the public timetable or what Bauman terms 'gardening' rather than 'gamekeeping' (1987). As a car-driver wrote in 1902: 'Traveling means utmost free activity, the train however condemns you to passivity . . . the railway squeezes you into a timetable' (cited in Morse, 1998: 117). The objective clock-time of the modernist railway timetable is replaced by personalized, subjective temporalities, as people live their lives in and through their car(s) (if they have one). This helps to produce a reflexive monitoring of the self. People try to sustain 'coherent, yet continuously revised, biographical narratives . . . in the context of multiple choices filtered through abstract systems' such as automobility (Giddens, 1991: 6). Automobility coerces people to juggle fragments of time in order to assemble complex, fragile and contingent patterns of social life, patterns that constitute self-created narratives of the reflexive self.

The shortage of time resulting from the extensive distances that increasingly 'have' to be travelled means that the car remains the main means of highly flex-ibilized mobility. Also compared with the car other forms of mobility in the city are relatively inflexible and inconvenient, judged by criteria that automobility itself generates and generalizes. In particular, inhabiting the car enables *seam-less* journeys from home-away-home. It does away with the stationary pauses necessitated by 'stations', apart from the occasional stop at the petrol station. And this is what contemporary travellers have come to expect.

The seamlessness of the car journey makes other modes of travel inflexible and fragmented. So-called public transport rarely provides that kind of seam-lessness (except for first class air travellers with a limousine service to and from the airport). There are many gaps between the various mechanized means of public transport: walking from one's house to the bus stop, waiting at the bus stop, walking from the bus station to the train station, waiting on the station platform, getting off the train and waiting for a taxi, walking though a strange street to the office and so on until one returns home. These 'structural holes' in semi-public space are sources of inconvenience, danger and uncertainty. And this is especially true for women, older people, those who may be subject to racist attacks, the disabled and so on. There are gaps for the car-driver involving semi-public spaces, such as entering a multi-storey car park or walking though strange streets to return to one's car. They are less endemic, however, than for other kinds of travel, although they illustrate how all forms of mobility are punctuated by pauses – pauses to refuel, repair, park overnight, clean the machine and/or its 'driver'.

As personal times are desynchronized from each other, so spatial movements are increasingly synchronized to the rhythm of the road. The loose interactions and mobilities of pedestrians give way to the tightly controlled mobility of machines, that (hopefully!) keep on one side of the road, within lanes, within certain speeds, following highly complex sign-systems and so on. Driving requires 'publics' based on trust, in which mutual strangers are able to follow such shared rules, communicate through common sets of visual and aural signals, and interact even without eye-contact in a kind of default space or non-place available to all 'citizens of the road' (Lynch, 1993).

Automobility also dominates how non-car-users inhabit public spaces. Car-drivers are excused from normal etiquette and face-to-face interactions with all those others who are inhabiting the road. Car-travel interrupts the taskscapes of others (pedestrians, children going to school, postmen, garbage collectors, farmers, animals and so on), whose daily routines are obstacles to the high-speed traffic cutting mercilessly through slower-moving pathways and dwellings. Junctions, roundabouts, and ramps present moments of carefully scripted inter-car-action during which non-car users of the road constitute obstacles to the hybrid car-drivers intent on returning to their normal cruising speed deemed necessary in order to complete the day's complex tasks in time. To inhabit the roads of the west is to enter of world of anonymized machines, ghostly presences moving too fast to know directly or especially to see through the eye.

Simmel makes points relevant to the nature of this *inhabiting*. *Contra* much contemporary social theory he considers that the eye is a unique 'sociological achievement' (Simmel, 1997: 111). Looking at one another is what effects the connections and interactions of individuals. Simmel terms this the most direct and 'purest' interaction. It is the look between people (what we now call 'eye-contact') which produces extraordinary moments of intimacy since: '[o]ne cannot take through the eye without at the same time giving'; this produces the 'most complete reciprocity' of person to person, face to face (Simmel, 1997: 112). The look is returned, and this results from the expressive meaning of the face. What we see in the person is the lasting part of them, 'the history of their life and . . . the timeless dowry of nature' (Simmel, 1997: 115). He further argues, following notions of the possessive gaze, that the visual sense enables people to take possession, not only of other people, but also of diverse objects and environments often from a distance (Simmel, 1997: 116). The visual sense enables the world of both peoples and objects to be controlled from afar, combining detachment and mastery. It is by seeking distance that a proper 'view' is gained, abstracted from the hustle and bustle of everyday experience.

Automobility precludes both of these achievements of the eye. Especially for the non-car user roads are simply full of moving, dangerous iron cages. There is no reciprocity of the eye and no look is returned from the 'ghost in the machine'. Communities of people become anonymized flows of faceless ghostly machines. The iron cages conceal the expressiveness of the face and a road full of vehicles can never be possessed. There is no distance and mastery over the iron cage; rather those living on the street are bombarded by their hustle and bustle and especially by the noise, fumes, tastes and relentless movement of the car that can never be mastered or possessed (Urry, 2000: ch. 4). To inhabit a road full of cars is to be in an environment where the visual sense is overwhelmed by other senses.

More generally: 'Modernist urban landscapes were built to facilitate auto-mobility and to discourage other forms of human movement . . . [Movement between] private worlds is through dead public spaces by car' (Freund and Martin, 1993: 119). Large areas of the globe now consist of car-only environments – the quintessential non-places of super-modernity (Augé, 1995). About one-quarter of the land in London and nearly one-half of that in LA is said to be devoted to car-only environments. And they then exert an awesome spatial and temporal dominance over surrounding environments, transforming what can be seen, heard, smelt and even tasted (the spatial and temporal range of which varies for each of the senses). Such car-environments or non-places are neither urban nor rural, local nor cosmopolitan. They are sites of pure mobility within which car-drivers are insulated as they 'dwell-within-the-car'. They represent the victory of liquidity over inhabiting the 'urban'.

One such non-place is the motel that 'has no real lobby, and it's tied into a highway network – a relay or node rather than a site of encounter between coherent cultural subjects' (as would be found in a hotel) (Clifford, 1997: 32). Motels 'memorialize only movement, speed, and perpetual circulation' since they 'can never be a true *place*' and one motel is only distinguished from another in 'a high-speed, *empiricist* flash' (Morris, 1988: 3, 5). The motel, like the motor-way service stations, represents neither arrival nor departure but the 'pause', consecrated to circulation and movement and demolishing particular senses of place and locale. This 'sense of sameness and placelessness' is accompanied by a 'social organization of space that helps to further auto-dependence and to mask any realistic alternatives to automobility' (Freund and Martin, 1993: 11). Morse describes the freeway not as a place but as a vector, as direction, as 'in-betweens' where magnitude is measured in minutes rather than miles (1998).

Dwelling in the car

So far I have considered how, as a moving private-in-public space, automobility involves punctuated movement 'on the road' and produces new temporalities and spatialities. In this section I consider in more detail just what kind of place of dwellingness the car is – what is involved in inhabiting what Morse calls an 'iron bubble' (1998)?

First, domesticity is reproduced through social relations such as the 'back-seat driver' or the common dependence upon a partner for navigation and map reading. Moreover, a variety of services have become available without leaving the car, as the 'drive-in' becomes more of a feature of everyday life. Since the 1950s drive-in movie and the drive-in 'automat', more recent US car-dwellers have been treated to the conveniences of drive-through banking, drive-through car washes, drive-through safari theme parks, and even drive-through beer distributors (not to mention drive-by shootings and drive-up mail delivery). Thus fragments of time are increasingly compressed into taskscapes that keep people inside their cars, while the 'coming together of private citizens in public space' is lost to a privatization of the mechanized self moving through emptied non-places.

Further in each car the driver is strapped into a comfortable if constraining armchair and surrounded by micro-electronic informational sources, controls and sources of pleasure, what Williams calls the 'mobile privatization' of the car (Pinkney, 1991: 55). The Ford brochure of 1949 declared that 'The 49 Ford is a living room on wheels' (Marsh and Collett, 1986: 11; the VW camper is described as a 'Room with a View').

Features such as automatic gearboxes, cruise control, and CD-changers 'free' drivers from direct manipulation of the machinery, while embedding them more deeply in its peculiar sociality. Protected by seatbelts, airbags, 'crumple zones', 'roll bars' and 'bull bars', car-dwellers boost their own safety while leaving others to fend for themselves in a 'nasty, brutish and short' world of millions of moving and crashing iron cages. As Adorno wrote as early as 1942: 'And which driver is not tempted, merely by the power of the engine, to wipe out the vermin of the street, pedestrians, children and cyclists?' (1972: 40; Bull, 2004).

Dwelling at speed, car-drivers lose the ability to perceive local detail, to talk to strangers, to learn of local ways of life, to stop and sense each different place. Sights, sounds, tastes, temperatures and smells get reduced to the two-dimensional view through the car windscreen and through the rear mirror, the sensing of the world through the screen being the dominant mode of contemporary dwelling (Morse, 1998). The environment beyond that windscreen is an alien other, kept at bay through the diverse privatizing technologies incorporated within the car. These technologies ensure a consistent supply of information, a relatively protected environment, high quality sounds and increasingly sophisticated systems of monitoring. They enable the hybrid of the car-driver to negotiate conditions of intense riskiness on high-speed roads (roads are increasingly risky because of the reduced road-space now available to each car). And as cars have increasingly overwhelmed almost all environments, so everyone is coerced to experience such environments through the protective screen and to abandon streets and squares to these omnipotent metallic iron cages.

The car is a room in which the senses are necessarily impoverished. Once in the car there is almost no kinesthetic movement from the driver. So although

23

automobility is a system of mobility *par excellence* it necessitates the minimum of movement once one is strapped *into* the driving seat. Eyes have to be constantly on the look-out for danger, hands and feet are ready for the next manoeuvre, the body is gripped into a fixed position, lights and noises may indicate that the car-driver needs to make instantaneous adjustments, and so on. The other traffic constrains how each car is to be driven, its speed, direction, its lane and so on.

The driver's body is itself fragmented and disciplined to the machine, with eyes, ears, hands, and feet, all trained to respond instantaneously and consistently, while desires even to stretch, to change position, to doze or to look around are suppressed. The car becomes an extension of the driver's body, creating new subjectivities organized around the extraordinarily disciplined 'driving body' (Hawkins, 1986; Morse, 1998). A Californian city planner declared as early as 1930 that 'it might be said that Southern Californians have added wheels to their anatomy' (quoted in Flink, 1988: 143). The car can be thought of as an extension of the senses so that the car-driver can feel its very contours, shape and relationship to that beyond its metallic skin. As Ihde describes: 'The expert driver when parallel parking needs very little by way of visual clues to back himself into the small place – he "feels" the very extension of himself through the car as the car becomes a symbiotic extension of his own embodiedness' (1974: 272). An advert for the BMW 733i promised the 'integration of man and machine . . . an almost total oneness with the car' (quoted in Hawkins, 1986: 67).

The machinic hybridization of the car-driver extends into the deepest reaches of the psyche. A kind of libidinal economy has developed around the car, in which subjectivities get invested in the car as an enormously powerful and mobile object. There is a sexualization of the car itself as an extension of the driver's desires and fantasies (see Sheller, 2004, on automotive emotions). The car takes part in the ego-formation of the driver as competent, powerful, and masterful (as advertisers have shamelessly deployed). Various 'coming-of-age' rituals revolve around the car, with car-sex itself becoming an element of fantasy in everything from music videos to 'crash culture' (Ballard, 1995). The body of the car provides an extension of the human body, surrounding the fragile, soft and vulnerable human skin with a new steel skin, albeit one that can scratch, crumple and rupture once it encounters other cars in a crash. The car is both all-powerful and simultaneously feeds into people's deepest anxieties and frustrations, ranging from the fear of accident and death to the intense frustration of being stuck behind a slow vehicle while trying to save precious fragments of time. Within the private cocoon of glass and metal intense emotions are released in forms that would otherwise be socially unacceptable.

We might indeed re-conceptualize civil society as a civil society of quasi-objects, or 'car-drivers' and 'car-passengers'. It is not a civil society of separate human subjects who can be conceived of as autonomous from these all-conquering machines. Such a hybrid of the car-driver is in normal circumstances unremarkable as it reproduces the socio-technical order (Michael, 1998). There is a careful, civilized control of the car machine deploying considerable technical and interactive skills. But in situations of what in the UK is known as 'road rage' another set of scripts are drawn upon, those of aggression, competition and speed. But these scripts of the other are always components of automobility that is polysemic, encouraging us to be careful, considerate and civilized (the Volvo syndrome) *and* to enjoy speed, danger and excitement (the Top Gear syndrome [a BBC car programme]). There is multiple scription and hence different elements of the hybrid car-driver (Michael, 1998: 133).

Specifically in the case of road rage: '. . . one actually needs to be more skilful, to push both body and machine into quantitatively greater alignment, than in the case where one is a responsible civilized driver . . . In order to exercise "loss of social control", one needs to practise greater technological control' (Michael, 1998: 133). Michael describes this as 'hyperhybridization' with the human being more or less immersed within the technology and vice versa. According to motoring organizations, however, such a virulent hybrid should be purified by changing not the human-machine hybrid but the pathological 'road-raging' human (analogous to the presumed pathology of the 'drunk driver': Hawkins, 1986: 70–1). What is not proposed by such organizations is that the hybrid should itself be transformed, such as by the fitting of long sharp spikes sticking out from the centre of every steering wheel pointing to the heart of each driver. Such a transformed hybrid would be unlikely to 'rage' or to be alcohol-impaired (Adams, 1995: 155)!

Different inhabitings

I have so far talked rather generally about how we inhabit the car, with little acknowledgement of the enormous differences involved across different societies and across different periods. We can begin by noting that women appear to inhabit cars somewhat distinctly. In the inter-war period automobility was generally organized around a cosiness of family life both in Europe and the US. The automobilization of family life not only brought the newest and most expensive car models first to male 'heads of families', while women had to settle for second-hand models or smaller cars, but also led to the uneven gendering of time-space. While working, men became enmeshed in the stresses of daily commuter traffic into and out of urban centres, suburban 'housewives' had to juggle family time around multiple, often conflicting, schedules of mobility epitomized by 'the school run' and mom-as-chauffeur. Once family life is centred within the moving car, social responsibilities tend to push women, who now drive in very significant numbers, towards 'safer' cars and 'family' models while men often indulge in individualistic fantasies of fast sports car or the impractical 'classic car'. Cars were originally designed to suit the average male body and have only recently been designed to be adjustable to drivers of various heights and reaches. The distribution of company cars has also benefited men more than women, due to continuing horizontal and vertical segregation in the job market, which

keeps most women out of positions with access to such 'perks'. Actuarial statistics, however, show that male drivers are more likely to externalize risks onto
others through a much greater tendency to speeding and hence to maiming and
killing others (Meadows and Stradling, 2000).

I will now go on to suggest rather more generally that there have been three
characteristic modes of dwelling within the car, from 'inhabiting-the-road', to
'inhabiting-the-car', to 'inhabiting the intelligent car'. I sketch some moments
in these transitions drawing on British and American examples.

First, then, inhabiting the road. At the beginning of the last century cars were
seen as speed machines. There was a preoccupation with the breaking of speed
records, especially as these were recorded by increasingly precise watches. Life
appeared to be accelerating as humans and machines combined in new and intricate 'machinic complexes', following the development of railway. The car was
constituted as a speed machine to propel humans ever-faster (in fact rather rich
and male humans). Male motorists described their experience of speed in mys-
tical terms, as though this were an experience which expressed the inner forces
of nature. The author Filson Young wrote of the sensuous experience of riding
in a racing car: 'It is, I think, a combination of intense speed with the sensation
of smallness, the lightness, the responsiveness of the thing that carries you, with
the rushing of the atmosphere upon your body and the earth upon your vision'
(quoted in Liniado, 1996: 7).

In Edwardian and inter-war England, a related way of inhabiting the road
developed. This was based around the concept of the 'open road' and the slow
meandering motor tour. Motor touring was thought of as 'a voyage through the
life and history of the land'. There was an increasing emphasis upon slower
means of finding such pleasures. To tour, to stop, to drive slowly, to take the
longer route, to emphasize process rather than destination, all became part of
the performed art of motor touring as ownership of cars became more widespread (and more inhabited by families). Filson Young wrote of how 'the road
sets us free . . . it allows us to follow our own choice as to how fast and how far
we shall go, to tarry where and when we will' (quoted in Liniado, 1996: 10).
Such a novel spatial practice was facilitated by organizational innovations partially taken over from cycling clubs. These 'paved' the way for the inter-war
transformation of the motor car, from alien threat to a 'natural' part of the rural
scene. Light notes how 'the futurist symbol of speed and erotic dynamism – the
motor car – [was turned] into the Morris Minor' in the inter-war years (1991:
214). In that period motoring had become an apparently 'natural' yet hugely
fateful way of inhabiting the countryside. This began to change especially with
the inter- and post-war period of massive suburban housing predicated upon
low density family housing with a sizeable garden, many domestic production
goods for the 'wife' to use, and a car to enable the 'husband' to travel quite long
distances to get to work. It has resulted in 'auto sprawl syndrome' in which cars
make urban suburbanization/sprawl possible and in so doing force those living
in such areas dependent upon the use of cars (O'Connell, 1998).

In the US car ownership became 'democratized'; even the dispossessed of the Great Depression travelled by car (Graves-Brown, 1997: 68; Wilson, 1992: ch. 1). Movement itself became a measure of hope; the road itself seemed to offer new possibilities, of work, adventure, romance. *The Grapes of Wrath* tells the story of hope and opportunity travelling along perhaps the most famous of roads, Route 66 (Eyerman and Löfgren, 1995: 57). In the US the massive pro-gramme of road building beginning in 1952 was seen as having an important democratizing role. Indeed American culture is inconceivable without the culture of the car and its sounds (such as Kerouac's *On the Road* or the films *Easy Rider, Rolling Stone, Alice Doesn't Live Here Anymore, Bonnie and Clyde, Vanishing Point, Badlands, Thelma and Louise, Paris Texas* and so on: Eyerman and Löfgren, 1995).

Thus up to the Second World War automobility involved 'inhabiting the road'. The car-driver is part of the environment through which the car travels and the technologies of insulation do not exist or have not been repaired. The car-driver dwells-on-the-road and is not insulated from much of its sensuous-ness, whether the driver is breaking speed records or slowly meandering the open road.

In the second stage the car-driver in the west dwells-*within*-the-car, one effect of which has been to provide much greater safety for the car-driver, since risks have been externalized onto those outside. Those who dwell within the car are able not only to prevent the smells and sounds of the road outside from enter-ing the car but also to produce an environment in which a certain sociability can occur. Car-drivers control the social mix in their car just like homeowners control those visiting their home. The car has become a 'home-from-home', a place to perform business, romance, family, friendship, crime, fantasy and so on, a home that according to Pearce transforms actual 'home' as one may be con-stantly on the move to and from, especially, the home of one's childhood (1999).

Unlike 'public' transport, the car facilitates a domestic mode of dwelling. The car-driver is surrounded by control systems that allow a simulation of the domestic environment, a home-from-home moving flexibly and riskily through strange and dangerous environments. As one respondent to Bull expressed it: 'You and your car are one thing and that's it and that's your space. Outside it's different. You're in your time-capsule, it's like your living room, your mobile living room' (2004). The car is a sanctuary, a zone of protection, however slender, between oneself and that dangerous world of other cars, and between the places of departure and arrival.

Central to this zone is the soundscape of the car, as new technologies of the radio, the cassette player and the CD player have increasingly ensured that this mobile home is filled with sound (Pearce, 1999). Almost better than 'home' itself the car enables a purer immersion in those sounds, as the voices of the radio and the sound of music is there, in the car, travelling right with one as some of the most dangerous places on earth are negotiated (see Bull, 2004, on research-ing the soundscapes of the car). Stockfeld describes the car as 'the most ubiquitous concert hall and the "bathroom" of our time' as sounds are privatized out of the context in which they are produced (quoted in Bull, 2004; see Urry, 2000: ch. 4 on the senses). Music and voices in the car fill the space and substitute for other forms of sociality and life. Indeed in a sense inhabiting the car becomes inhabiting a place of sound and of technologies connecting people to a world beyond. As Heidegger said about the radio in 1919: 'I live in a dull, drab colliery village . . . a bus ride from third-rate entertainments and a considerable journey from any educational, musical or social advantages of a first-class sort. In such an atmosphere life becomes rusty and apathetic. Into this monotony comes a good radio set and my little world is transformed' (quoted in Scannell, 1996: 161). The car radio analogously connects the 'home' of the car to the world beyond.

Third, at the beginning of this century, there is a new shift occurring towards 'inhabiting the intelligent car'. As information has been digitized and released from location, cars, roads, and buildings have been rewired to send and receive digital information – for example in the building of 'Intelligent Transport Systems' (ITS). Information is now inhabiting the car in very significant ways. Until now this information has been mainly for traffic control or car and road safety, for example through computer-assisted operation control systems, dynamic route guidance, repairs, and traffic information systems.

More significant than this, however, is the possible development of transformed vehicles, smaller, lighter, smarter, information-rich, communication-enhanced vehicles better integrated into the public transport systems and public spaces. Telecommuting will not be *the* key to transforming urban life because people like and need to be physically mobile, to see the world, to meet others and to be bodily proximate, and to engage in 'locomotion' (see Boden and Molotch, 1994, on the compulsion to proximity). Current developments such as the huge popularity of mobile telephones instead suggest that many people want to engage in communication simultaneously with locomotion – to walk and talk or to drive and jive. Mobile ICTs are also increasingly central to work-practices and information gathering in contexts of unavoidable time-space distanciation and fragmentation. The introduction of flexitime would smooth out and redistribute rush-hour peaks if communication could occur in transit. It is already possible to check voicemail from a mobile phone, but e-mail is now found in the car or train, electronic memos will be sent, and mobile banking and electronic shopping are commonplace in what Graham terms 'cybercities' (2004).

Car manufacturers have already begun production of various micro-cars, such as the Mercedes Smart Car, the Honda Insight made mostly of aluminium and powered by both an electric motor and a small petrol engine, and BMW's motor cycle/car hybrid the C1. Such micro-cars, in the next decades, will probably be powered by the hydrogen fuel cell and made of carbon-based fibres derived from nanotechnology which can be 100 times stronger than steel at one-sixth of the weight (US Department of Transportation, 1999; and see Hawken *et al.*, 1999, on other moves to replace the 'steel-and-petroleum' car). The key to integrating such 'post-steel-and-petroleum' cars into a mixed transportation system will lie in a multifunction 'smart-card' that will transfer information from home, to car, to bus, to train, to workplace, to web site, to shop-till, to bank (a system already under development possibly through the use of 'iris-recognition technology'). Cars could then be partially deprivatized by making them available for public hire through using such a smart-card to pay for their use, as well as to pay fares on buses, trains, or more flexibly-routed collective mini-vans. Smart cards for welfare recipients, students, families with young children, and the elderly could be subsidized. But all of these vehicles would have to become *more than* technologies of movement – they would also have to be hybridized with the rapidly converging technologies of the mobile telephone, the personal entertainment system and the laptop computer (see Urry, 2004, for more detail on all this).

Such micro-cars and all other forms of transport would be personalized with one's own communication links (e-mail addresses, phone numbers, world wide web addresses, etc) and entertainment applications (digitally stored music in its memory, programmed radio stations, etc), but only when these are initiated by inserting the smart-card. Thus any public vehicle could instantly become even more of a home away from home: a link to the reflexive narratives of the private self in motion through public time-space scapes. Streetscapes could thus be transformed through a more mixed flow of slow-moving semi-public micro-cars (often for one rather than four persons and not built of steel), bike lanes, pedestrians and improved mass transport.

Inhabiting smart-cars would allow people to travel lighter, if not weightlessly, and could restore some civility to public spaces destroyed by current traffic flows and the spatial patterns of segregation and fragmentation generated by automobility. Could such smart-cars be the best way to lure twentieth-century speed-obsessed car-drivers to give up their dependence on 'steel-and-petroleum' cars, a system unsustainable on most measures and really a very old-fashioned Fordist technology? Urban planning that recognizes the need for a radical transformation of transport could use existing legislation and regulation in new ways, to build 'integrated' and 'intermodal' public transport systems.

Rather than trying to stifle mobility, which has been the strategy until now, societies will draw on and harness the power of the democratic urge to be mobile, hybridized and inhabiting the iron cage of motorized modernity. Overcoming the awesome constraints of existing automobility could make us recognize and harness its peculiar auto-freedom as we may increasingly come to inhabit the intelligent car.

Conclusion

In this chapter I have described the car as something that is inhabited, resulting in part from its simultaneously flexible *and* coercive form. I described the form taken by such a way of *inhabiting*, dwelling within, a mobile, semi-privatized and hugely dangerous auto-mobile capsule. The car is not simply a means of covering distances between A and B. I then outlined three principal ways in which the car is inhabited or dwelt within. At the end I have engaged in some futurology as to how the 'car' may come to be dwelt within very differently in the coming century, a shift that would have almost untold consequences for human life much more generally.

References

Adams, J. (1995) *Risk*. London: UCL Press.

Adorno, T. (1972) 'Fetish character in music and regressive listening' in A. Arato and E. Gebhardt (eds) *The Essential Frankfurt School Reader*. New York: Continuum.

Augé, M. (1995) *Non-Places*. London: Verso.

Bachmair, B. (1991) 'From the motor-car to television: Cultural-historical arguments on the meaning of mobility for communication' *Media, Culture and Society*, 13: 521–33.

Ballard, J. G. (1995) *Crash*. London: Vintage.

Bauman, Z. (1987) *Legislators and Interpreters*. Cambridge: Polity.

Boden, D. and H. Molotch (1994) 'The compulsion to proximity' in R. Friedland and D. Boden (eds) *Now/Here. Time, Space and Modernity*. Berkeley: University of California Press.

Bull, M. (2004) 'Soundscapes of the car: A critical study of automobile habitation' *Theory, Culture and Society*, 21: 243–59.

Clifford, J. (1997) *Routes*. Cambridge, MA: Harvard University Press.

Eyerman, R. and O. Löfgren (1995) 'Romancing the road: Road movies and images of mobility' *Theory, Culture and Society*, 12: 53–79.

Flink, J. (1988) *The Automobile Age*. Cambridge, MA: MIT Press.

Featherstone, M., N. Thrift and J. Urry (eds) (2004) 'Automobilities' Special Issue of *Theory, Culture and Society*. 21.

Freund, P. and G. Martin (1993) *The Ecology of the Automobile*. Montreal: Black Rose Books.

Giddens, A. (1991) *Modernity and Self-Identity*. Cambridge: Polity.

Graham, S. (ed.) (2004) *The Cybercities Reader*. London: Routledge.

Graves-Brown, P. (1997) 'From highway to superhighway: The sustainability, symbolism and situated practices of car culture' *Social Analysis*, 41: 64–75.

Haraway, D. (1991) *Simians, Cyborgs, and Women: The Reinvention of Nature*. London: Free Association Books.

Hawken, P., A. Lovins and L.H. Lovins (1999) *Natural Capitalism*. London: Earthscan.

Hawkins, R. (1986) 'A road not taken: Sociology and the neglect of the automobile 1' *California Sociologist*, 9: 61–79.

Ihde, D. (1974) 'The experience of technology: Human-machine relations' *Cultural Hermeneutics*, 2: 267–79.

Kunstler, J. (1994) *The Geography of Nowhere: The Rise and Decline of America's Man-Made Landscape*. New York: Touchstone Books.

Light, A. (1991) *Forever England: Femininity, Literature and Conservatism Between the Wars*. London: Routledge.

Liniado, M. (1996) *Car Culture and Countryside Change*. MSc Dissertation. Geography Department, University of Bristol.

Lynch, M. (1993) *Scientific Practice and Ordinary Action*. Cambridge: Cambridge University Press.

Lynd, R. and H. Lynd (1937) *Middletown in Transition*. New York: Harvest.

Marsh, P. and P. Collett (1986) *Driving Passion*. London: Jonathan Cape.

Meadows, M. and S. Stradling (2000) 'Are women better drivers than men? Tools for measuring driver behaviour' in J. Hartley and A. Branthwaite (eds) *The Applied Psychologist*. Milton Keynes: Open University Press.

Michael, M. (1998) 'Co(a)gency and the car: Attributing agency in the case of the "road rage"' in B. Brenna, J. Law and I. Moser (eds) *Machines, Agency and Desire*. Oslo: TMV Skriftserie.

Miller, D. (ed.) (2000) *Car Culture*. Oxford: Berg.

Morris, M. (1988) 'At Henry Parkes Motel' *Cultural Studies*, 2: 1–47.

Morse, M. (1998) *Virtualities: Television, Media Art and Cyberculture*. Indiana: Indiana University Press.

O'Connell, S. (1998) *The Car in British Society*. Manchester: Manchester University Press.

Pearce, L. (1999) 'Driving North/Driving South: Reflections upon the Spatial/Temporal Co-ordinates of "Home"', Mimeo. Lancaster University.

Pinkney, T. (1991) *Raymond Williams*. Bridgend: Seren Books.

Sassen, S. (1996) 'The spatial organization of information industries: Implications for the role of the state' in J.H. Mittelman (ed.) *Globalization: Critical Reflections*. Boulder CO: Lynne Rienner.

Scannell, P. (1996) *Radio, Television and Modern Life*. Oxford: Blackwell.

Sheller, M. (2004) 'Automotive emotions: Feeling the car' *Theory, Culture and Society*, 21: 221–42.

Sheller, M. and J. Urry (2000) 'The city and the car' *International Journal of Urban and Regional Research*, 24: 737–57.

Shove, E. (1998) *Consuming Automobility*. SceneSusTech Discussion Paper. Dept of Sociology, Trinity College, Dublin.

Simmel, G. (ed.) (1997) *Simmel on Culture*. London: Sage.

Thrift, N. (1996) *Spatial Formations*. London: Sage.

Urry, J. (2000) *Sociology Beyond Societies*. London: Routledge.

Urry, J. (2004) 'The "system" of automobility' *Theory, Culture and Society*, 21: 25–40.

US Department of Transportation (1999) 'Effective Global Transportation in the Twenty First Century: A Vision Document', 'One Dot' Working Group on Enabling Research, US Department of Transportation, http://www.volpe.dot.gov/infosrc/strtplns/dot/glbtrn21, accessed 6 April 2005.

Virilio, P. (1997) *The Open Sky*. London: Verso.

Whitelegg, J. (1997) *Critical Mass*. London: Pluto.

Williams, R. (1988) *Border Country*. London: Hogarth Press.

Wilson, A. (1992) *Culture of Nature*. Oxford: Blackwell.

Driving the social

Joanna Latimer and Rolland Munro

All our invention and progress seem to result in endowing material forces with intellectual life, and stultifying human life into a material force. (Karl Marx, *The People's
Paper*)

Prologue

*David leans back, glances into the side mirror, and tightens his grip on the wheel
as he pumps the floor. There is a slight hesitation before the car responds and, in
the flick of a wrist, leaps out into the space created by a break in the flow of oncoming traffic. For a moment the inside car and he are parallel, then the big engine
pulls quickly away and he can dive in front, just ahead of the on-coming car with
its flashing lights and frightened faces.* Just making it. *David settles down, thinking:* Better car, better driver. *Looking for the next space, he prepares to take on
the next car in front. It's a Volvo.* No problem. *While he waits, his thoughts turn
to the morning meeting.*

*Later that morning June considers her options. She made her bid early, a logical
summary of the project, well prepared and fully articulated to company priorities.
Not a weakness or flaw in it. Yet all the subsequent discussion has been on David's
suggestion. As if that was the only option. She doesn't know how he has overtaken
her. No detail, no priorities, just a flat request, made late in the meeting.* Just as
she had thought her own bid was home and dry. *Her case, all her careful reasoning and evidence, well received at the time, seems to be tailing away and she
doesn't know how to get back in front.* Road hog, *she thinks. But then she remembers advice given to her about driving: don't engage. Don't excite road rage. Stay
out. Don't make it personal. So she waits, thinking: she'll live to fight another day.*

Introduction

In this chapter we talk about driving. We explore ways in which the experience
of driving comes to 'inhabit' other forms of relation, including thought and
conversation. In pressing these possibilities, we are happy to acknowledge the

credence the thesis of automobility carries – even going well beyond the extant limits of its monstrous scope. Yet, in also juxtaposing a contrasting thesis of automotility, our aim is to set other relations alongside those of the car system. Other 'totalizing' possibilities exist and so we consider how people shift perspective; and even perhaps navigate contemporary life as a process of 'forgetting' as much as of reasoning.

Ahead of this focus on driving, we engage with current debates on automobility. Specifically, we ask how the cultural dominance imputed to the 'car system' is supposed to work. How, exactly, might the car system engross the social body? And how might all this operate at the level of affect? Could conversation – as the embodiment of many conceptions of the social – be giving way to a stultifying of 'human life into a material force'? And is this what is meant by the idea of automobility – a driving of society away from decorums governing the freedoms of speech into a celebration of the 'freedoms of speed'?

What this chapter offers is a cultural analysis that sidesteps these current stories of 'dominance' by exploring the existential and social implications of automobility. This is to juxtapose the phenomenon of *motility* (Munro, 1996a; 2000) alongside the current fix on mobility that underpins the automobility thesis. To adopt phrases like Urry's (1999) 'conquering hybrid of automobility' is not yet fully to accept automobility's 'totalizing' narrative. Certainly there is a need to explain how the car, on occasion, can appear all pervasive and all controlling. But there are other times, other occasions, in which different technologies come into play and the car is far from people's thoughts.

A first aim is to explicate driving as a process of *engrossment*. We acknowledge the many commentators who point to what they see as an increasing colonization of the life world by the car. But we think such views, even unwittingly, tend to re-circulate the kind of 'atomising' theses, in which the social is seen as abandoned, with people supposedly turning inward to become their own projects (eg, Giddens, 1991). Part of our concern with the thesis of automobility is precisely this implicit individuation of society; an individuation that is visualized as growing apace, to the exclusion of other possible ways of being and relating.

As yet, though, justifications for attributing to the car its coercive properties have stopped short of theorizing the car as a self-constructing system.[1] Accounts to date rely heavily instead on suppositions that treat the car *as* culture, as if this is the missing structural property governing the conduct of individuals. It is hard, however, to see how the gurus of automobility can have it both ways. Either they accept the thesis of individuation and thus accept, consequently, that there is no 'culture' in which domination can be reproduced, or at least nothing like the kind of holistic system envisaged by Durkheim. Or they should recognize that individuation (and its counterpart, globalization) is not all that it seems, and work harder to trace the relations making up the social body.

Taking a more grounded approach to culture in what follows, we offer a reading of automobility that takes care of the engrossment of *affect* as much as it pays attention to material devices and technologies. This is to say that we indicate first how driving becomes embodied as a cultural system, gaining material 'extension', and then, once animated through its 'elicitation' of relations, gains its powers of extrusion. Much of the dominance attributed to the car, we suggest, can be teased out by a more careful depiction of the 'powers' of the car in these terms. What forms of extension does the car afford? And what kinds of relations are elicited, precisely, by the car in general, or by driving in particular?

The concern is to suggest how 'attachment' to cars, at the same time as positioning us within extreme and unexpected relations, also comes to stand in the place of, and even as a relief from, face-to-face encounters. Here, thinking of Simmel's analysis of the city, we allude to how 'incorporation' in the car system – especially in the form of driving – involves extrusion of other kinds of relations, other kinds of affect. This discussion leads on to questions in which we raise the 'transport' of affect. The questions we raise ask not how driving replaces other forms of transport, such as the horse or the train. The pressing issue is how driving intermittently effaces, and interpenetrates, other cultural systems, such as those built around conversation, the home, the mobile phone and the computer.

Our argument is that cultural systems involve twin processes of incorporation and extrusion for their engrossing effects. After a preliminary discussion of the literature on the 'cultures' of the car in Section I, we then draw on anthropological notions of *extension* (Strathern, 1991) in Section II. Here the ways in which the car system engrosses the social body can be made visible by paying attention to affect as well as to more generally distributed effects. Further discussion in Section III sketches ways in which processes of 'incorporation' peculiar to the car entail processes of *extrusion*.

Section I

Visions of automobility

Automobility indexes a contested world in which the car appears, variously, as social and anti-social; the destroyer of the planet is also an essential enabler of family life, while the right to drive turns intermittently into the instant murder weapon. Consequently, 'conspiracies' between the motor manufacturers and the oil companies are being matched increasingly by the 'red tape' of policy-making bodies that seek to regulate car use, and by lobbies that voice its negative impact socially, as well as environmentally.

More recent critique develops this political image of society one stage further, suggesting that the love affair with the car is turning into a technological dystopia of global dimensions. Critiques here draw, implicitly or explicitly, upon Heidegger's idea of machinery unfolding a 'specific character of domination' and a 'specific kind of discipline' over humans (see Zimmerman, 1990). Urry, in particular, suggests that the disciplining and domination through technology is 'most dramatically seen in the system of production, consumption, circulation, location and sociality engendered by the "motor car"' (1999: 1).

As noted in the introduction to this volme, Urry traces the specific character of this domination to a unique combination of six components: 1) the car as the quintessential *manufactured object*; 2) the car as the major item of *individual consumption*; 3) as an extraordinarily powerful *machinic complex* of technical and social inter-linkages with other industries, such as petrol-refining, road-building, motels and advertising; 4) the predominant global form of 'quasi-private' *mobility* that subordinates other 'public' mobilities like walking, cycling, rail travel etc; 5) the dominant *culture* that organizes and legitimates socialities; 6) the single most important cause of *environmental resource-use* resulting from the sheer range of scale of material, space and power involved (1999: 2; see also Shove, 1998).

Sociology, Urry urges, has barely noticed these components of automobility, despite the car being, at least in what Urry sees as its middle phase, the main protagonist in an upheaval of communities. The immense and systematic, if unintended, consequences which this 'complex hybrid' of automobility exercises across the globe include the intensification of divisions between work and home, neighbourhood and shops, and domestic and leisure sites, to say nothing of the splitting up of families. All this requires the type of movement in which people have to 'orchestrate in complex and heterogeneous ways their mobilities and socialities across very significant distances' (1999: 2).

As Urry (this volume) adds, automobility is a Frankenstein-created monster that extends the individual into realms of freedom and flexibility, whereby inhabiting the car can be viewed positively, but also as highly constraining. Automobility may well bring freedoms of a sort, but it also coerces people into an intense flexibility, forcing them to 'juggle tiny fragments of time so as to deal with the temporal and spatial constraints that it itself generates'. This 'instantaneous' time has to be managed in ways that help produce the kind of sociality in which choice becomes ever more pressing and the kind of reflexive self imagined by Beck (2000) and Giddens (1991), seems ever more necessary.

All in all, Urry's image of the car as the 'conquering hybrid of automobility' focuses on the kind of domination and discipline that is perhaps unparalleled in the annals of history. His analysis throws up a powerful vision of the car as a latter day Leviathan. Having become almost a state-in-itself, automobility stretches its six fingers – production, possession, pipelines, projection, pressure and power – to tighten its global grasp on humankind.

Yet the basis to this vision of automobility is not entirely new. Society has long been imagined in terms of vast structures: capitalism as envisioned by Marx, the 'iron cage' of bureaucracy as explicated by Weber, and the 'organic solidarity' of culture in Durkheim. Each of these entails 'wholes' that are always greater than the sum of its parts, the workers who grind the mills of exploitation, or the 'cultural dopes' who instate the collective conscience. Ahead of any further analysis, therefore, we turn next to consider different ways in which we could imagine ourselves being so enrolled.

'Cultures' of the car

The debates on automobility suggest a cultural dominance of the car that goes well beyond its collective status as a key artefact over which distinction is manufactured and consumed (cf. Bourdieu, 1986). Drawing on the Frankfurt School, Gartman (2004) argues that the culture of mass consumption legitimates class differences, not so much by displaying differences in a symbolic hierarchy, as Bourdieu holds, but by hiding these:

> For Theodor Adorno in particular, consumer commodities like the automobile obscure the class relations of their production behind reified facades of mass individuality, giving consumers different quantities of the same illusions to compensate for the denials of mass production. (Gartman, 2004: 170)

For example, ever since Alfred Sloan ran General Motors, the car industry has been learning how to drip out design features in ways that not only create a simulation of the same but also make a simulacrum of difference.

Urry's vision of the car as a latter day Leviathan, however, stretches well beyond the conventions of an analysis of class; nor, for that matter, will it be contained within Weber's (1946) considerations of status and parties. The conflict and struggles over the car have outgrown these old divisions; even exploding past the duality of Berger and Luckmann's (1970) social constructionism of mutually linking objective and subjective worlds. The 'politics' of automobility, in Habermas's (1987) terms, would seem to involve nothing less than an analysis of the conflict between the *system* and the *lifeworld*, an aporia in which the system itself becomes the 'environment'.

Yet any reintroduction of systems theory to sociology raises key theoretical issues. To be sure it is not so difficult to reify the intricate inter-weavings and combinations of Urry's six components into the kind of purposive system beloved of functional analysis (even when this purposiveness has turned inward into the car system becoming an end in itself). In ways reminiscent of earlier analyses of television, where viewers were pictured as 'working *for* capital' – locked into watching advertisements to extract the full value of their investment – so, too, the car system seems to constrain freedoms and dictate the very choices it appears to offer.

Indeed, within debates on automobility, the car system is perceived to have turned itself into the ultimate consumer. As Elizabeth Shove (1998) argues, 'it is the car, not the urban community, which dominates discussion in planning meetings and which is the real focus of attention' (1998: 9). For her, cars 'consume' the very populations they serve:

> . . . they eat up time, they steer people towards different sorts of lives, they structure everyday routines, and they dominate the management of time and space.

If bought as a 'convenience' good, the car soon introduces its own difficulties: new problems of congestion are created, traffic jams eat up travel time. As Shove herself describes them, cars are 'Frankenstein-like devices that structure and constrain their "users", and "live" in a sort of symbiotic – but perhaps unequal – relation to their makers' (1998: 9).

We have some sympathy with this analysis, which at least has the merit of reversing the ideology of car ownership reflecting consumer choice. Yet we fail to see exactly how a Frankenstein-like device turns into the Leviathan? We have no doubt that some people do get enrolled, as Shove (1998) indicates, in speaking for the car in the public sphere, in committees and on other decision-making bodies. But how is this enrolment forced? How is it that people end up speaking on behalf of the car system? The more or less implicit answer here would seem to be 'culture'.

An intrusion of *system* concepts into an analysis of culture would seem to rely too heavily on Mary Douglas's analysis of consumption; and, in particular, her Durkheimian move to induce the presence of culture (the whole) from patterns of expenditure (its particulars). But it is one thing to acknowledge, with Douglas, that any purchase, or use, of a good is to make a 'display' of culture (see Douglas and Isherwood, 1980), in ways reminiscent of Durkheim's analysis over suicide. It is quite another matter to suggest that one object of consumption, almost single-handedly, is highjacking the *mores* of Western ritual and tradition into becoming, in its own terms, *the* culture.

What has yet to be explained by the proponents of the automobility thesis is why it should be the car rather than, say, the house or, indeed, the computer, that has become the Leviathan. And to date, explanations for this putative dominance of the car as system are rather piecemeal. For all the citing of matters such as the rising returns to scale, radical monopolization of space, co-evolution of automobility and surburbanization, the actual *systems* properties are largely left black-boxed.

The car as 'system'

The kind of system we are faced with in discussions of automobility is not to be conflated, we would argue, with the merely systematic. To take the totalizing effects of the 'car system' seriously is not just to be asked to consider the contingently agglutinative effects of commerce, policy and planning. Yes, sociologically, the 'car system', like any other institution, is subject to a process of sedimentation over time, but the propositions of the automobility thesis surely raise issues of a different order? Most properly these issues can be adduced with reference to other self-constructing systems noticed by earlier sociologists, notably money (cf. Parsons, 1963; Simmel, 1978).

As a system of proper sociological interest, money is unlike many pseudo-systems designed and built to help run administrative and business organizations. What makes money different is not simply the sheer scale with which it inhabits social life, but the extent to which – as a system – it profoundly affects and alters the social. The point is not, as Parsons would have it, just that 'money in the economy' is a good analogy for 'power in the polity'. The crux of the matter, we suggest, is that money, once up and operating, exerts an extrusive force. First and foremost, money drives out certain forms of exchange, especially barter. In our terms, it is their processes of *extrusion* that define self-constructing systems and differentiate them from loosely coupled arrangements that are merely systematic.

As explicated in Munro (1986; 1997), it is this self-construction of forms of extrusion that define systems *as* systems. Specifically, money can buy goods, on the one hand, and goods can buy money, on the other, but it is no longer the case that goods can buy goods. Practices of barter become subject to an implacable process of extrusion in which their very conditions of possibility cease. It should be noted that no fiat or law is specifically necessary to outlaw barter; it is simply that practices enabling barter are driven out[2] as a consequence of the existence and use of money. This is a defining moment. From this moment on there is not only an inevitable differentiation, a separation in which the economy appears to become autonomous and disjunct from the polity, it is also the point at which the polity itself will become for ever more colonized by the economy.

Evidence, even in the extant literature, is not hard to find that suggests processes of extrusion are at work in respect of cars. For example, Urry (2003: 26, drawing on Freund and Martin, 1993: 120–121) discusses a variety of ways in which automobility appears to coerce changes in daily habits:

> Dwelling at speed, car-drivers lose the ability to perceive local detail, to talk to strangers, to learn of local ways of life, to stop and sense each different place. And as cars have increasingly overwhelmed almost all environments, so everyone is coerced to experience such environments through the protective screen and to abandon streets and squares to these omnipotent metallic iron cages. (2003: 26)

Large areas of neighbourhoods are also seen as being made unsafe and 'non-navigable' (Kunstler, 1994) for those without cars, such as children and older people.

All this, though, leaves the more totalizing effects of the car system unexplicated. Such examples are offered largely as illustrative of 'dominance'; their authors do not go on to theorize these aspects as evidence, say, of a self-constructing system, such as has been explicated by Luhmann (1995; see also Mingers, 2002). To date, the car system's capacity to affect people seems to have been attributed to a notion of a car 'culture'. But this does not explain some of the key issues. Where there is room to express one's belonging variously, why would someone 'belong' to the car culture? Or at least engage with cars sufficiently in ways that would entail them as working *for* that culture, as Beynon (1975) notably depicted in the case of Ford?

These issues may not have arisen previously because the missing structural properties, as discussed earlier, have been attributed to the car as *the* 'culture'. Although there are good reasons for regarding the car (and all its associated parts) as *a* culture, few grounds have yet been offered for thinking in the more holistic terms made familiar by Durkheim. What is missing from the automobility thesis is an argument that does not just rely on associating the car with a particular form of culture; one that merely includes, as if in passing, practices of exclusion. Our contention is that automobility can only be understood *as* 'the car system' if its capacity to affect people *and* incorporate them can be made explicit. A more full analysis, we argue next, would indicate how the car becomes embodied, gaining material 'extension', and then, once animated, gains its power through 'elicitation'.

Section II

The prosthetics of extension

How do cars, to coin a phrase, come to 'drive' the social? What is needed to help answer this question is an approach that allows us to begin to understand how an object like the car becomes a system by virtue of its engrossment of the social body. As suggested earlier, we can begin to make a system visible through meticulous attention to the specific effects through which the car is distributed, produced, recreated and consumed. This involves closer consideration of cars as materials of extension.

In a major reworking of anthropological thought, Strathern (1995), drawing on Fortes, suggests relations are 'bodied forth' through materials. For her, relations are *elicited* from moment to moment; relations are never permanent or fixed, but are always having to be made and remade. Thus relations among persons do not depend on some intrinsic or imagined essence to be found *within* the body, such as the blood links in traditional depictions of kinship, but on the many ways whereby people 'figure' themselves by incorporating the materials of cultural events and occasions.

In this context of relations being bodied forth, Strathern (1991) outlined what can be termed a theory of *extension* (Latimer, 1997; 1999; 2001; 2004; Lury, 1998; Munro, 1996b; 1999). Beginning with the conventional notion of prosthetics, such as an artificial limb, Strathern points out that extension involves attachment, but in a double sense. First, attachment has to be understood in terms of affiliation, and, only second, as material additions. Incorporation of materials thus involves a 'doubling' of parts, rather than the merely representative move of letting one part stand for another, the signifier for the signified.[3] Different relations are made present and brought into circulation less by people attaching themselves directly to each other (whatever this could mean) and more by virtue of the displays created by persons attaching (or detaching) themselves to material devices.

Yet the process of attaching (and detaching) ourselves to some specific materials (and therefore not to other materials) does more than make 'visible' identities already available to self and others. The relations brought into view are *motile*, the 'worlds' they create depending in turn on how, and when, different materials are attached, or detached (Latimer, 1997; 1999; 2001; 2004; Munro, 1996b; 1999; Palli, 2004). At one moment, for example, people might 'figure' themselves as family, the parent, say, reading the school report of the child, the next moment they may reappear as friends, clinking glasses to celebrate appearing together in a school debate.

Extension, strictly understood, is a never-ending process of incorporation whereby people 'figure' and 'refigure' themselves across the spectrum of relations. While this notion of relations of course overlaps with the Western focus on relationships, we add quickly that it should not be conflated with the more reductive idea of social dyads, typically formed by one individual joining up strategically with another. Ahead of relations, there are no prior 'persons', or 'individuals'. As much as the cutting of any other figure, becoming visible *as* a person, or *as* an individual, involves rituals of extension.

It is important to understand here the very different ontology involved in these ideas of extension. The notion that materials are 'symbols of significance' is well rehearsed in the anthropological literature. These kinds of materials include:

> ... words for the most part but also gestures, drawings, musical sounds, mechanical devices like clocks, or natural objects like jewels – anything in fact that is disengaged from its mere actuality and used to impose meaning upon experience. (Geertz, 1993: 45)

In this way, reading significance off materials, as Douglas and Isherwood (1980), among others, have explicated, is all part of expressing identity and making displays of belonging.

Within extension, however, the argument is quite different from the more simplistic notion of artefacts 'expressing' identity and the like (see also Munro, 2005). The suggestion is that any incorporation of materials is literally an *in-car-nation,* an incarnation that actually changes the bodies involved, and thereby the relations being created. It is by incorporating the materials of culture (faces, masks, gestures, sounds, goods, and any other stuff that happens to be lying around) that people, in Strathern's analysis, are literally altering the forms, and therefore the relations, that are being made manifest. Thus, through extension, the social body as materialized in specific relations, is given either presence or absence.

Refining automobility

In his explication of car cultures, Urry (this volume) uses the image of inhabiting the car. He describes the kind of 'extension' we experience daily in our use of cars:

> The driver's body is itself fragmented and disciplined to the machine, with eyes, ears, hands, and feet, all trained to respond instantly and consistently, while desires even to stretch, to change position, to doze or to look around being suppressed. (Urry, this volume, ch. 2.)

As Urry immediately adds, 'the car becomes an extension of the driver's body, creating new subjectivities around the extraordinarily disciplined "driving body" (Hawkins, 1986; Morse, 1998)'.

Drivers, or passengers, certainly engage with the prosthetics of the car, in terms of its playing a part in the physical transportation of our bodies. The importance of Urry's analysis is his focus inwards on the almost autoerotic relation the car takes on as *self*:

> There is a sexualization of the car itself as an extension of the driver's desires and fantasies. The car takes part in the ego-formation of the driver as competent, powerful, and masterful (as advertisers have shamelessly deployed). (This volume, ch. 2.)

As he says, 'the car can be thought of as an extension of the senses so that the car-driver can feel its very contours, shape and relationship to that beyond its metal skin' (this volume: ch. 2).

Yet such matters may only be the first aspect in a doubling of the car's effects upon relations. Urry's vision of the car clearly identifies an enhancement of the range and powers of any human body that inhabits the car, but only from a limited perspective. Specifically, when extension works to transmute parts of people into a fusion with the instruments – and turns other parts into the 'psyche' of the car – we are no longer simply in the mode of representation, displaying the car merely as *our* attachment, an object of belonging.

The list of effects provided by Dery (this volume: ch. 13), for example, are focused *inwards*, to provide new accounts of the self and the individuated subjectivity which driving excites. Indeed, the professional driver Lyn St James describes herself as 'becoming one with the car' and being strapped in so tightly that you 'end up wearing it'. As she remarks, this is 'when she is in her most powerful form' (Lieber, 1993). This specific kind of enhancement, however, is entirely contingent. There is nothing in these descriptions which conveys any totalizing experience comparable, say, to the 'rush' described by Vittelone (2003). Sitting in a parked car, even in the gloss and polish of the showroom, does not quite do the trick.

Lost in the maze of extension the car affords, the kind of attachment Urry imagines brings into presence only the car's enhancement of individuality – choice, freedom, flexibility, mobility, speed, the lot! But we still need to go further than this to understand fully the engrossment of the car system. As already indicated, we can understand how incorporation by the car elicits our engagement with other materials *beyond* the car, such as the strips of tarmac along which we can drive, and thereby positions us in other, sometimes extreme, often unexpected relations; an encounter, say, with a frightened rabbit or the violence of an incipient road-rager. It is the engagement with other similarly 'enhanced bodies' that electrifies. Presumably what Lyn St James actually feeds on is the impulsion created by racing others round the track. So, too, the 'boy racers', piggy-backing on an endless clutch of other drivers, while negotiating never-ending sets of roundabouts.

This kind of extension of course goes well beyond Urry's descriptions of our feeling that the car's metal becomes a second skin, or a prosthesis whereby the instruments and controls have conjoined with the hands, feet, eye and brain. What is different between Urry's analysis and our own, are the various kinds of relations we see being elicited through extension with the car. We would argue that it is only driving along the road, at certain speeds, or in certain traffic conditions, that there is the kind of *totalizing* engagement envisioned by Durkheim (1915).[4] To see past these immediate matters is to look for a 'social body' that extends well beyond the shell of the individual car. Brilliant as Urry's analysis is, we are pressing for a much wider understanding of the relations that extension with cars elicits.

Incorporation and elicitation

Through processes of extension we do not just make our attachments visible. Strathern's discussion of extension suggests how the attachment of cultural materials incorporates people within the very relations that are being created. Materials are implicated in the constitution of relations not simply because they are 'expressive', in the limited terms of the conventional wisdom; merely conveying a message cybernetically from one person to the other, while bodies and worlds remain the same. What matters are what relations *carry*; and that this transporting of the social body usually involves changing worlds.

More specifically, Strathern points to the place of materials in the *ordering of relations*. Here it is important to allow the idea of relations to 'double' for the 'conceptual relations that link data' (and which discursive practices constitute, mobilize and circulate), as well as the 'lived relations people have with one another' (Strathern, 2003: 4). Thus, insofar as they help make our relations, both conceptual and lived, materials also help *position* people within the relations being made manifest.[5]

Strathern's (1991: 63–65) specific example of Wantoat evokes a ritual occasion in which dancers manifest themselves as waving trees. The performers literally magnify themselves by wearing barkcloth and attaching large bamboo extensions to their bodies, often 18 or 20 metres tall. What is important in Strathern's analysis of the response of these villagers to the dance (originally studied by Schmitz, 1963) is an elicitation of the spirits of their forbears, the ancestors who are understood to inhabit the trees.

Strathern emphasizes how this doubling of parts, of men dancing attached to these giant poles, enables the villagers to be moved, back and forth, between different relations. One moment they are an audience enjoying a vision of trees swaying and dancing in the wind, the next moment they are enjoined with the spirits of their ancestors. This 'transportation' is made all the more possible by the retelling of the myth of creation in which the first people are 'figured' as emerging from the blood of a god being poured into stalks of bamboo.[6]

Bodies in extension with cars are similarly productive of the social, because people in extension with cars make present the very relations that *car*-ry the social.[7] Cars, particularly the modern automobile, might seem a long way from the kind of extension figured through bamboo poles. Yet if the principles by which extension works, incorporation and elicitation, are surely not so different, it is the relations created that can be expected to have their very different affects. For example, witnessing cars travel, taking part in their speed and their mobility, 'transports' us into framing society (and ourselves) as technologically advanced, and, specifically, as developing at a pace, a progress gaining in rapidity with each instance witnessed.[8]

So, too, the relations elicited through our 'attachment' to cars might also be explained through a 'doubling' of parts. The attachments that are made manifest – between, for example, mind, flesh, metal and tarmac – coalesce in ways that have coercive powers. That is, the combined effects of these attachments (always changing, always attaching and detaching from and to persons) institute different kinds of relations because they make visible very specific versions of the social, such as those relations that privilege motels, petrol stations and oil refineries, rather than those composed around inns, stables and pastures. And make the BMW the family car at the weekend, while passing it off as a masculine 'trophy' when outside the pub or the office during the week.

Yes, as Urry examines in careful detail, we inhabit cars. But it is how cars come to *embody* us, which is even more important, not merely the status or lifestyle they have come to represent. What Urry, among others, leaves out is the extent to which driving, momentarily and provisionally, lets us dwell in the future. We experience freedom, speed, flexibility and mobility only when we enter into this larger embodiment of automobility, when we both strap ourselves in *and* drive in ways that change the 'social body'.

With Strathern (and the Wantoat), we can also imagine how materials of extension, such as the car, help to create relations that enjoin us *outwards* to others, dead or alive, animate or inanimate. It is for the car's intimations of immortality, not just the enrolment of our physical parts, that we take the thesis of automobility seriously. Whereas Strathern's analysis of Wantoat transports its participants, via the spirits of the trees, back into 'the past' to become one with their ancestors – and in this way give intimations of immortality – so it is our extension with the car that enjoins us to modernity and enables us to feel part of the future, one moment, and perhaps feel the flush of shame (Probyn, 2005) the next.

Section III

Engrossment and obviation

In our view, the car can be best considered as a 'cultural system of enhancement'. To understand the 'powers' of the car is to appreciate how a car 'culture', at least on occasions, and in very special circumstances, becomes transformed into a car system. Today we can no longer assume, as did Mary Douglas and Emile Durkheim, that a culture itself acts like a system (if indeed we ever could). Only where there is sufficient evidence of extrusion, such as those cases Douglas (1975) evidences in her discussion of 'matter out of place', can we assume that there is sufficient 'body' being created to carry culture.

So what is the social body that is being made manifest in extension with the car? One answer to this, as Urry makes clear, is to visualize the kind of machinic hybrid to which Michael (1998 drawing on Serres) calls attention. Yet, all too soon what Urry calls 'inhabiting the car' decomposes the hybrid back into its constituent parts:

> The machinic hybridization of the car-driver extends into the deepest reaches of the psyche. A kind of libidinal economy has developed round the car, in which subjectivities get invested in the car as an enormously powerful and mobile object. (This volume: 26)

On the one hand, there is the 'purified' machine (cf. Latour, 1993); the car is denied any share of agency that Michael gives hybrids. On the other, there is self, reduced to psyche.

Unfortunately either vision, whether of hybrids or of psyches, inevitably atomizes the social. It is to suggest, in some fundamental way, that automobility is asocial, even anti-social. Certainly, understood as a cultural system of enhancement, extension with the car elicits and excites those relations that body forth the 'individual', as *the* key figure in contemporary culture. The 'individual', being itself a prized cultural object, is made visible in extension with the car, at the self same moment in which the social body is effaced. Such shifts in extension make for motility: presence is, at critical moments, magnified *or* diminished (Munro, 1996b; Strathern, 1991). So that in cutting the figure of the individual, extension with the car seems to magnify individuation, as it simultaneously cuts from our view the social body which our extension with cars helps (re)produce.

The social body that 'carries' relations is effaced by the car system. The enhancement effects of the cultural system radiate the contemporary image of the individual, coerced into subjectivity:

> Consumer culture springs from the perpetual emanations of desire held to radiate from each individual person. This wellspring is like the bottomless pit of need that Euro-Americans are also supposed to suffer, such as the celebrated biological need for women to have children – a '*drive* to reproduce'. (Strathern, 1997: 304, our italics)

In this iconic meeting of Western desire and need, it is the individual who is seen to express the essential self: '[a] rhetoric of accumulation is thus bound to the voluntarism of individual effort'. As Strathern immediately adds, the constant necessity for the individual to implement his or her subjectivity has its own 'coercive force'.

The car affords regular opportunities to satisfy this constant necessity for the individual to implement his or her subjectivity. More than this, the car, above all other forms, epitomizes the kind of extension within which what is figured *is* individualism, as the radiation of desire and need. While at one level the car appears both to produce a self and to be itself consumed by that self, the inwards effect on 'subjectivities' personifies the notion of subjectivity as itself being a display of culture: a display through which people are made visible *as* persons. But these are only one aspect of the relations elicited by driving.

In this way, the kind of relations that we discussed earlier as carrying auto-mobility are *obviated*. Wagner (1986: xi) suggests obviation is manifested in a 'series of substitutive metaphors that constitute the plot of a myth (or the form of a ritual), in a dialectical movement that closes when it returns to its beginning point' (cf. Weiner, 1988). In a recursive and processual magnification, individuals in extension with the car set out to 'do' individual; that is, they busy themselves doing 'person-subject'. The complex social relations elicited through driving are thus backgrounded by the effect of people being magnified in ways that make visible their personhood as individual-subjects. It is this magnification of the individual *as* subject (figured by the iconic meeting of need and desire) which occludes the extent to which the broader relations of driving succour the spiralling engrossment of the car system.

Total figuration can be grasped, according to Strathern (1991: 79) by an obviational analysis that 'replicates for the observer the temporal and spatial sequences by which persons move themselves from one position to another through their constant perception and reperception of relations' (cf. Weiner, 1988: 9). At the same time as the 'figure' of the individual is made visible through extension with the car, other relations are diminished and indeed effaced. It is the relations that are obviated which have to 'car-ry' the culture to effect the process of *engrossment*. In a set of substitutive moves, in which one trope is replaced by another, the broader relations that are elicited through forms of automobility such as driving, motoring or cruising, are effaced by the trope of individualism-subjectivity, with all its implications of social atomism.

The social as driving

Arguably, among other struggles, the idea of the car as *the* modernist icon of freedom of movement (Crist, 1996) is supplementing, rather than simply supplanting the democratic ideal of freedom of speech. Notional 'powers' of the car are manifold, but include their ability to: 1) enlist spokespersons to lobby for cheaper petrol and even more road building; 2) excite people into diverse behaviours like those of boy racers or road ragers; 3) close off large areas of the land and city to all who are not properly equipped.

Given our earlier discussion of the money system, and its extrusion of barter, the social body of the car can be made more visible by attending to all that the car system extrudes. Put simply, what we want to bring into view is what it is, in the drive to drive, that gets driven out.

In the prologue we have evoked an image of David in which we have mirrored his style of driving in his style of argumentation. He's the kind of guy that comes 'right up your arse' on the local A-road, flashing his lights, and thrusting his way forward regardless of others' safety or sensibilities. Similarly, in discussion, he is totally focused on where *he* is going, leaving no space for discussion with others, and no room for manoeuvre. His appraisal sheet for promotion would no doubt be written up under the flattering acronym that Nicholas Cage, as Little Junior (the son of the King of organized car crime in

Barbet Schroeder's 1995 film *The Kiss of Death*), applies to himself – 'B.A.D. – Balls; Attitude; Direction.'

Where some lead, others will follow. Those who benefit from the shameless possibilities offered by driving, and, by analogy, styles of argument, are not only bent on saving their own time and energy. Others too get behind people they see as having the drive and will to exploit an incipient opening, and so avoid all the delays, queues and gridlock of the common places of social convention.

Through driving, one of the things people may be escaping are the restrictions of the everyday world of conversation and account giving. What we are pointing to here is how driving can elicit kinds of behaviour that step outside the widely accepted rituals and customs of social interaction. In this way driving extrudes the kinds of attachments, such as turn-taking, that have supported the organization of dialogics developed intermittently from the classical period onwards. Specifically, we are suggesting that, through driving, we are incorporated in a car system, and that what gets extruded by the car system are the very kinds of relations afforded by other systems, such as the modes of argument built around the notion of classical logic.

More generally, what gets driven out is the kind of social relations implied by the sociological tradition (cf. Shilling, 2002), especially that which stressed intersubjectivity (Schutz, 1970). The following passage from the opening sequence of Milan Kundera's novel *Slowness* nicely captures this shift in mores:

> I check in the rear-view mirror: still the same car unable to pass me because of the oncoming traffic. Beside the driver sits a woman. Why doesn't the man tell her something funny? Why doesn't he put his hand upon her knee? Instead, he's cursing the driver ahead of him for not going fast enough, and it doesn't occur to the woman, either, to touch the driver with her hand; mentally she's at the wheel with him, and she's cursing me too. (Kundera, 1996: 1)

Today, might it be the car, not conversation, which (re)produces normalizing behaviour in the name of progressing individual liberty? Viewed in such ways, we argue, driving appears far from asocial.

Overtaking ourselves

We now turn to discuss views that imagine the car system as colonizing the lifeworld. Here we are being asked to entertain the idea that the car system is eliminating other ways of being in the world afforded by other cultural systems of enhancement. We need not of course, with Habermas, suggest that there ever was, or could be, a pure life-world that stands outside of, or is unadulterated by systems. In line with our ideas of extension, we would rather argue that persons are *always* being incorporated by systems, but go on to recognize that different systems elicit different ways of being in the world, while extruding other kinds of relations.[9]

Following Levi-Strauss' opposition between societies that are anthropoemic and those that are anthropophagic, Bauman (2001: 24) clarifies the 'emic' and the 'phagic' as a contrast between societies based on ingestion and assimilation, and those based on vomiting and annihilation. Adapting and modifying these oppositions, we have argued that the affect of any system can be made visible through attending to the dual processes of incorporation and extrusion. Indeed, going beyond Levi-Strauss and Bauman, we would assert that any system exhibits, to a great or less extent, *both* of these powers. Specifically, we have suggested that automobility is to be 'seen' as a cultural system of enhancement through its engrossment.

This engrossment, as we have argued, consists of a feeding on combinations of parts in ways that become ever more demanding and ever more selective. It is for this reason that we have pointed to a growing intensification in the metaphor of driving, on the one hand, and an escalation of its powers of extrusion on the other. It is through the intermittent incorporation of specific combinations of parts – adeptness of limbs and flexibility of cognitive capacities – that certain relations can be understood as being elicited, often momentarily, and partially ingested.

This incitement to drive has further repercussions and incorporating effects. Ever-increasing amounts of territory (landscapes, towns, as well as raw materials) are called in to be converted into roads. The landscape itself becomes quarried and ingested: valleys and vegetation become the scenic background to roads and long-distance transportation. As with Heidegger's example of the bridge, the landscape becomes 'tied into the network of long-distance traffic, paced and calculated to maximum yield' (Heidegger, 1993a: 354). In all this, we press that there is more going on than the 'practices of exclusion' hitherto noted by other commentators. While certain forms of land use are ingested and assimilated, others are expectorated and annihilated: such as children playing in the street, cyclists on major highways, or older people crossing the road, to say nothing of the litter of animal carcasses that decorate the tarmac. Additionally, certain uses of the car can also be viewed as driven out. In particular, forms of car use we have denoted as driving have replaced 'motoring' and 'cruising' as ways of enjoying the countryside. Yes, the production of cars and the building of roads have led to opportunities for people to explore the wilderness but, equally, such spaces have become fewer and far between because their very accessibility through the car undoes them.

We have, in passing, also considered a different kind of extrusion, one elicited by the specifics of the relations exhibited by an extension with cars (and driving in particular). There is a possibility that the car system, in many ways, is in competition with, although hardly mutually exclusive to, other systems, especially those incorporating materials of extension, such as houses, computers and mobile phones. For example, extension through houses affords us possibilities of 'dwelling' (Heidegger, 1993b) which are not open to, say, nomadic or refugee groups. Similarly, computers offer ways of passing on knowledge along networks, unmarked by social identity (ethnicity, class, age and gender) (Poster, 1990). In turn, mobile phones permit children to enjoy private and independent social lives in conditions of close propinquity.

Here we are drawing attention to a 'motility', wherein different enhancement effects can be 'punctualized' momentarily (Munro, 2004) as we switch, to and fro, among these major systems. In contrast to Urry's thesis, which stresses only the mobility in automobility, we want to broaden the debates to allow for the extent that we are able to switch 'worlds', and not just piecemeal attachments. As we argued earlier, it is only driving along the road, at certain speeds, or in certain traffic conditions, that there appears to be the kind of *totalizing* engagement envisioned by Durkheim.

In making this analysis of automobility, we have also wondered how much this kind of extension with cars has its counterpart in the concept of *auto-motility*. Shifts in extension surely allow for sudden and dramatic switches between relations, conceptual and lived, and these should hardly be thought of as being entirely within 'our' control. For example, one minute we may embody the car to magnify ourselves as a material force; and the next detach ourselves to perform, as Marx anticipates, a metaphysics of intellectual life. Thus shifts in extension also transmute the world.

In intruding the concept of automotility we are emphasizing that not all movement in time/space is fulfilled by references to mobilities, however enhanced these may become. Movement in time/space concerns shifting worlds, in ways that lift us out of one social body and into another. One minute the car is taking us from A to B, the next minute the car has become a 'mobile bedroom'. As we turn off the engine and answer the phone, we can also be shifting universes. Even within the confines of his car, we have depicted David as moving to and fro between modes of transport and modes of argument. But we want to suggest that each of these other systems may be interpenetrated by the car system (and vice versa), through our notions and practices of driving. David is, within the limits of our vignette, driving in both systems – the car system and argument in discussion. June, if more subtly, is likewise affected.

In our view, processes of colonization are not conducted between systems and the life-world, *vide* Habermas, but are transacted among systems through processes of extension, incorporation and elicitation. Indeed, the sheer amount of cinematic and video footage devoted to the car in film and television illustrates this. If not driving ourselves we can always be busy watching others do it. What we are drawing attention to here is more than a kind of leakage that might take place between systems. For example, homes are not seen as just for dwelling. Like cars, houses too can be thought of as being *driven*. In extension with houses, people are being incorporated into another system of enhancement: they are constantly being called to steer their homes towards modernity and improve the house's chance of upward mobility; and, through 'overtaking' their neighbours, so drive their own position up the social and economic scale.

Conclusions

In this chapter we have argued first for an approach to automobility that returns us to a way of understanding the car as a cultural system of enhancement, rather than just accept in total Urry's 'conquering hybrid of automobility'. For example, Rajan (this volume) argues that freedom is a compulsory constraint, to be exercised along designated modes. He then goes on to claim that auto-mobility is its major expression. We agree. But we are also pressing these issues of 'system' and 'culture'. In addition to eliciting a particular form of psyche in which cognition plays the supreme role of balancing different streams of 'feed-back', we are suggesting that the car system is also eliciting as well as extruding other relations of exchange.

Our approach thus returns analytical attention to the issue of relations more generally. Far from society being atomized by the car, we have emphasized how aspects of the car system, such as driving, constitute and *incorporate* persons. Much attention has been drawn in recent writing to the individuating effects of the car, best exemplified by the auto-erotic effect of being wrapped in the metal-lic shell of the car propelled at speed through time and space. In contrast we have suggested that there is a need to understand how it is that the car also comes to be 'driving the social'. This is not to suggest that neat descriptions of the social body can be offered directly. Rather, following Durkheim in his analy-sis of suicide and Douglas in her analysis of practices of exclusion, we stress that it is only possible to impute the presence of larger systems, Strathern's 'total figuration', by working backwards from an analysis of their effects.

Driving, as a form of incorporation, elicits particular kinds of relations and ways of being in the world. We go on therefore to propose tentatively a growing attachment to the experience of driving and a parallel detachment between the rules of formal logic and ordinary conversation. More, then, is at a stake than an epistemic shift, one taking place by virtue of a system of distinctions, in which specific tropes such as 'overtaking', 'changing gear', and 'cutting in' per-meate and instantiate our cultural values. The nub of the shift is the embodied experience of movement with the car and commensurate association of discus-sion and logic being 'gridlocked' by a democracy organized around turn-taking and opinion. Our contention is that current transformations in the nature of argument go to the heart of changes in our 'extension', the being-in-the world of persons by virtue of the social and material construction of their relations. Being static, stationary, or even just being 'slow', are increasingly more difficult ways of being-in-the-world to defend.

Going further, we have argued the case for the concept of motility to be added to that of mobility. The fix on mobility – and its hyperextension into automo-bility – masks much else that is going on apart from its individuating effects. It is at this point that we speculate that the car has become the contemporary carrier of the social, much as conversation could once have been said to define the social (eg, Harré, 1983). We aren't, however, suggesting a conversation era has been replaced by a car era. Rather, the kind of substitution we are pointing to attends more to the kind of *momentary* enjoyment, or shame and embar-rassment, that takes place as people 'switch' between the different kinds of rela-tions each affords. Specifically, extension with the car can be considered to be seductive and engrossing, partly *because* it provides relief from other kinds of sociality.

In drawing attention to the car as system, therefore, we are certainly opposing all too glib references to the car as culture. We are neither in the business of suggesting that automobility has triumphed over more traditional systems of bed, board and cult, nor are we claiming that the car system has become predominant over say house-systems, which can also on occasion offer temporary relief from other demands of sociality (to say nothing of the virtues of the computer-system or the mobile phone system, each of which is engrossing through their own peculiar processes of ingestion and extrusion). What we want to propose, in contrast, is both the *partiality* of any one cultural system of enhancement and its *complicity* with many of the other systems that flood our lives today.

Contemporary life might better be represented, in a more full analysis, by a constant movement in and out of very different relations and very contrasting occasions. Our analysis, limited as it is, thus not only questions the individualising thrust of the automobility debate, but points, instead, to the potential for automotility – the reframing that is constantly, if intermittently, taking place as we transport ourselves, or are transported, between systems. This idea of systems being *automotile* raises profound issues we cannot follow up here. For example, it is not to be thought that we are always, as individuals, exercising our supposed 'freedom' to switch between systems. Rather, further research should take the possibility more seriously that it is our engrossment with these systems – the car, the house, the computer, and the mobile phone – that, more often than not, may be 'switching' us.

Notes

1 The thesis of automobility is suggestive of a contemporary apparition of technological determinism. Implicit and unstated is the theory of autopoiesis (Maturana and Varela, 1980); the idea of a self-constructing system is one that has moved long past either the control by, or the understanding of, its cellular constituents.

2 This is not to make claims that practices of barter disappear altogether. Specific conditions such as hyperinflation can encourage barter, although other forms of pseudo-money, such as cigarettes, tend also to be used. Perhaps, more importantly, the Internet facilitates attempts to barter, although even here money is typically implicit as a unit of account and a unit of value. Certain trading associations, known as LETS (Local Exchange and Trading Systems) or LAMS (Local Alternative Money Schemes), have also sprung up in recent years among ecologically minded groups.

3 Dramaturgically, in order to 'play' their part and figure their relations anew, people must also become 'their parts', this time understood in terms of their co-option of lines, gestures, props and costumes. However, as becomes clear below, Strathern (1991) is throwing her net much wider than thinking of relations purely in terms of people.

4 With Durkheim, Collins (1994: 211) argues religion may be produced by rituals; that is, by certain configurations of social interaction in the real world. Yet to press this insight is also to be clear that the kind of relations that 'carry' driving can go well beyond the more glib form of identities established between gods and cars from, say, ritual car washing and polishing on Sundays.

5 The potency of discursive practices can never be disassociated from the specificities of the materials through which they make relations visible. On the contrary, 'we can only encounter effects when they are effected, that is already realized' (Strathern, 2003: 5).

6 In passing Strathern helps us to understand how the phenomenon of the 'big man' can be created and reproduced without the need to theorize hierarchy.

7 The body that carries a group, like the Norton Street Gang (Whyte, 1955), or acts as a vehicle for the Bund (Hetherington, 1994), is not, for example, of the same order as the kind of agglutative propinquity assimilated with a team of individuals, each supposedly busy with their functional task.

8 The reverse is also the case. Where people demonize the car as destructive to the planet, it appears as the very devil; and car drivers as the worshippers.

9 As is clear from the text, we have sympathy with those who take a view of society being 'driven' by the car writ large, an ironic inversion of the individuated freedoms celebrated in popular car mythology. Yet we would disagree with views that go on to suggest that the world is a place in which humans have entirely lost control. By way of summing up, therefore, we want to draw our material together in a way that attempts to overtake the limited discussion we have already achieved.

References

Bauman, Z. (2001) 'Uses and disuses of urban space' in B. Czarniawska and R. Solli (eds) *Organizing Metropolitan Space and Discourse*. Malmo: Liber.
Beck, U. (2000) *The Brave New World of Work*. Cambridge: Polity.
Berger, P. and T. Luckmann (1970) *The Social Construction of Reality*. Harmondsworth: Penguin.
Beynon, H. (1975) *Working for Ford*. Milton Keynes: Open University Press.
Bourdieu, P. (1986) *Distinction*. London: Routledge.
Collins, R. (1994) *Four Sociological Traditions*. Oxford: Oxford University Press.
Crist, P. (1996) Selected Excerpts from the Norwegian Institute of Transport Economics/OECD Literature Review on Individual Travel Behaviour. OECD.
Douglas, M. (1975) *Implicit Meanings*. London: Routledge and Kegan Paul.
Douglas, M. and B. Isherwood (1980) *The World of Goods: Towards an Anthropology of Consumption*. Harmondsworth: Penguin.
Durkheim, E. (1915) *The Elementary Forms of the Religious Life*. London: Allen & Unwin.
Freund, P. and G. Martin (1993) *The Ecology of the Automobile*. Montreal: Black Rose Books.
Gartman, D. (2004) 'Three ages of the automobile: The cultural logics of the car' *Theory, Culture and Society*, 21(4/5): 169–195.
Geertz, C. (1993) *The Interpretation of Cultures: Selected Essays*. London: Fontana Press.
Giddens, A. (1991) *Modernity and Self-identity*. Cambridge: Polity Press.
Habermas, J. (1987) *Theory of Communicative Action, Volume Two: System and Lifeworld*. Cambridge: Polity Press.
Harré, R. (1983) *Personal Being: A Theory for the Individual*. Oxford: Basil Blackwell.
Hawkins, R. (1986) 'A road not taken: Sociology and the neglect of automobile' *California Sociologist*, 9: 61–79.
Heidegger, M. (1993) 'Building, dwelling, thinking' in *Basic Writings*, ed. D.F. Krell. London: Routledge.
Hetherington, K. (1994) 'The contemporary significance of Schmalenbach's concept of the Bund' *The Sociological Review*, 42(1): 1–25.
Kundera, M. (1996) *Slowness*, trans. L. Asher. London: Faber and Faber.
Kunstler, J. (1994) *The Geography of Nowhere: The Rise and Decline of America's Manmade Landscape*. New York: Touchstone Books.
Latimer, J. (1997) 'Older people in hospital: The labour of division, affirmation and the stop' in K. Hetherington and R. Munro (eds) *Ideas of Difference: Social Spaces and the Labour of Division*. Oxford: Blackwell.
Latimer, J. (1999) 'The dark at the bottom of the stair: Participation and performance of older people in hospital' *Medical Anthropology Quarterly*, 13(2): 186–213.

Latimer, J. (2001) 'All-consuming passions: materials and subjectivity in the age of enhancement' in N. Lee and R. Munro (eds) *The Consumption of Mass*. Oxford: Blackwell.

Latimer, J. (2004) 'Commanding materials: (Re)legitimating authority in the context of multi-disciplinary work' *Sociology*, 38(4): 757–775.

Latour, B. (1993) *We Have Never Been Modern*. Hemel Hempstead: Harvester Wheatsheaf.

Lieber, J. (1993) 'A road less taken' *Sports Illustrated*, May 3rd (quoted by Dery, this volume).

Luhmann, N. (1995) *Social Systems*. Stanford: Stanford University Press.

Lury, C. (1998) *Prosthetic Culture: Photography, Memory and Identity*. London: Routledge.

Maturana, H. and F. Varela (1980) *Autopoiesis and Cognition: The Realization of the Living*. Dordrecht: Reidel.

Michael, M. (1998) 'Co(a)gency and the car: Attributing agency in the case of the "road rage"' in B. Brenna, J. Law and I. Moser (eds) *Machines, Agency, and Desire*. Oslo: TMV Skriftserie.

Mingers, J. (2002) 'Can social systems be autopoietic? Assessing Luhmann's social theory' *The Sociological Review*, 50(2): 278–299.

Morse, M. (1998) *Virtualities: Television, media art and cyberculture*. Indiana: Indiana University Press.

Munro, R. (1986) *Knowledge Systems*. PhD Thesis: University of Edinburgh.

Munro, R. (1996a) 'Alignments and identity-work: The study of accounts and accountability' in R. Munro and J. Mouritsen (eds) *Accountability: Power, Ethos and the Technologies of Managing*. London: Thomson International Business Press

Munro, R. (1996b) 'The consumption view of self: Extension, exchange and identity' in S. Edgell, K. Hetherington and A. Warde (eds) *Consumption Matters*. Oxford: Blackwell.

Munro, R. (1997) 'Belonging on the move' *The Sociological Review*, 46(2): 208–243.

Munro, R. (1999) 'The Cultural Performance of Control' *Organization Studies*, 20(4): 619–640.

Munro, R. (2000) 'Motility and mobility: Identity, reversibility and stability' Paper presented at the conference on Inside/Outside at ZIF, Beidelfeld.

Munro, R. (2004) 'Punctualising identity: Time and the demanding relation' *Sociology*, 38(2): 293–311.

Munro, R. (2005) 'Partial Organization: Marilyn Strathern and the elicitation of relations' in C. Jones and R. Munro (eds) *Contemporary Organization Theory*. Oxford: Blackwell, 245–266.

Parsons, T. (1963) 'On the concept of political power' *Proceedings of the American Philosophical Society*, 107: 232–262.

Poster, M. (1990) *The Mode of Information: Post-structuralism and Social Contexts*. Cambridge: Polity Press.

Schmitz, C.A. (1963) *Wantoat: Art and Religion of the Northeast New Guinea Papuans*. The Hague: Mouton and Co.

Schutz, A. (1970) *On Phenomenology and Social Relations*, H. Wagner (ed.). Chicago: University of Chicago Press.

Shove, E. (1998) *Consuming Automobility*. SceneSusTech Discussion Paper. Dept of Sociology, Trinity College, Dublin.

Shilling, C. (2002) 'The two traditions in the sociology of emotions' in J. Barbalet (ed.) *Emotions and Sociology*. Oxford: Blackwell.

Simmel, G. (1978) *Philosophy of Money*, trans. T. Bottomore and D. Frisby. London: Routledge and Kegan Paul.

Strathern, M. (1991) *Partial Connections*. Maryland: Rowman and Littlefield.

Strathern, M. (1995) *The Relation*. Cambridge: Prickley Pear Press.

Strathern, M. (1997) 'Partners and consumers: Making relations visible' in A.D. Schrift (ed.) *The Logic of the Gift*. London: Routledge.

Strathern, M. (2003) 'Abstraction and decontextualisation: an anthropological comment or: e for ethnography' http://virtualsociety.sbs.ox.ac.uk/GRpapers/strathern.htm.

Urry, J. (1999) 'Automobility, car culture and weightless travel' http://www.comp.lancs.ac.uk/sociology/soc008ju.html.

Vittelone, N. (2003) 'The rush: Needle fixation or technical materialization' *Journal for Cultural Research*, 7(2): 165–178.

Wagner, R. (1986) *Symbols That Stand for Themselves*. Chicago: University of Chicago Press.

Weber, M. (1946) *From Max Weber: Essays In Sociology*, ed. and trans. H.H. Gerth and C. Wright-Mills. Oxford: Oxford University Press.

Weiner, J.F. (1988) *The Heart of the Pearlshell: the Mythological Dimension of Foi Sociality*. Los Angeles: University of California Press.

Whyte, W.F. (1955) *Street Corner Society, 2nd Edition*. Chicago: University of Chicago Press.

Zimmerman, M.E. (1990) *Heidegger's Confrontation with Modernity*. Bloomington: Indiana University Press.

Part Two
Governing Automobility

Transport: disciplining the body that travels

Jennifer Bonham

Introduction

Over the past century, the place of the automobile in the city has been challenged on a number of grounds, most notably those of citizens' rights, public safety, social justice and urban aesthetics. The most recent challenge to the automobile centred on the environmental impacts of different 'modal choices', in particular, the differential environmental effects of bus, bicycle, or automobile travel. This debate quickly reached a stalemate. While environmentalists drew on a variety of statistics to support the case for improvements in public transport services and cycling facilities, advocates of the automobile used other statistics to demonstrate that, given the right roads, traffic flows, speed limits, engines and fuels, cars could be environmentally-friendly 'green machines'. More than a decade on, the use of automobiles in Australian cities, indeed in many cities, continues unabated. The persistent increase in automobile usage is often explained by reference to technological progress, increases in personal wealth and the considered choices of free individuals (eg, Adams, 1980; Donovan, 1996). Alternatively, it has been explained in terms of the power of particular fractions of capital and the shaping of individual choices by capitalist interests and liberal ideologies of self-interest (eg, Franks, 1986; Hodge, 1990). The former explanation operates to naturalize contemporary practices of mobility while the latter tends to position motorists as victims of automotive companies and their technologies (Bonham, 2002: 19–24).

This chapter locates the proliferation of automobile usage within a broader study of how urban populations have been incited to think about and conduct their journeys. The approach I have taken draws on the insights of Michel Foucault's genealogical studies (Foucault, 1977; 1978) as it examines the micro techniques by which bodies have been disciplined to the use of 'public' space and the practice of travel. Discipline, to paraphrase Foucault, '. . . centres on the body as a machine, optimizing its capabilities, increasing its usefulness and docility, integrating it into systems of efficient and economic controls' (Foucault, 1978: 139). The body of the traveller – motorist, pedestrian, child – is not a 'natural' body but a body worked upon through relations of power and knowledge to conduct the journey in particular ways. It is argued in this chapter that disciplining the travelling body has been essential to the government of urban mobility.

Bodies have been disciplined to and subsequently governed through two interrelated ways of thinking about mobility. First, changes in travel technologies have been linked, both positively and negatively to freedom, as individuals are able physically to remove themselves from their daily routines, everyday responsibilities and immediate social networks (Kern, 1982: 111–4; Creswell, 1997). The second way of thinking about travel is that of *transport*: movement from one point to another in order to participate in the activities at the 'trip destination' (Schumer, 1955; Hensher, 1976; Allan *et al.*, 1996). This innovation, more significant than the train, tram or automobile, has made it possible to objectify travel practices and create knowledge about the efficient completion of the journey. The production of transport knowledge has involved separating out, classifying, and ordering travel practices in relation to their efficiency. This ordering of travel establishes a hierarchy which not only values some travel practices (rapid, direct, uninterrupted) and some travellers (fast, orderly, single-purpose) over others but also enables their prioritization in public space. All trips, not just those to sites of production, consumption, and exchange, can be made economically. The journey to a friend's house, the beach, or the doctor (so called 'social' journeys) can be made with greater or lesser economy. As transport experts (from engineers and transport modellers to sociologists, environmentalists, and feminists) deploy the logic of the economical journey they are fundamentally implicated in the ordering of urban travel and the consequent prioritization of some travellers – specifically motorists – over others.

The conceptualization of urban travel as transport has rendered urban movement calculable while at the same time ameliorating the dangers of too much freedom to move. Travel has been made manageable as it has been anchored between an origin and destination. 'Freedom of movement' has been re-conceptualized through traffic and transport discourses into 'freedom to access destinations'. Thinking about urban travel in terms of transport has made it possible to govern the movement of urban populations, to maximize choice and to secure the economical operation of the urban environment. The motor vehicle is centred in transport discourse as maximizing travel choice while the motorist's field of action can be structured toward the efficient conduct of the journey.

This chapter examines the proliferation of automobile usage in the Australian city of Adelaide but it does not begin with the automobile. Rather, it locates the motor car within a broader historical investigation of the objectification of the spaces, bodies, and conduct of urban travel. The discussion is especially concerned with that period through the late nineteenth and early twentieth century when efficient movement was popularized as the principle by which to guide the arrangement of street-space and the ordering of urban traffic. The first part of the chapter focuses upon the re-ordering of street space through the nineteenth century and considers the effects of this in facilitating automobile usage in the twentieth century. The discussion then turns to examine the way in which the travelling body has been disciplined to the efficient conduct of the journey. As the ordering of movement (spaces and bodies) was entrenched and mobility was rationalized as 'transport', a new field of inquiry emerged – urban transport. This new field provided further techniques to guide the conduct of the population. The concluding section of the chapter reflects on the dissonance between the subjects brought into effect within transport discourses and the multiple ways in which mobility and the motor car might be understood.

Spaces of travel

Numerous writers have commented on the shift in the pre-dominant use of street spaces through the nineteenth and twentieth centuries (eg, Jacobs, 1961; Gutman, 1978; De Jong, 1986; Rabinow, 1989; Sennett, 1994; Brown-May, 1995; Fyfe, 1998). Like Paris, London, Amsterdam and Melbourne, the streets of Adelaide have undergone significant changes (Bonham, 2000). Andrew Brown-May argues that while changes witnessed in Melbourne have been attributed to the automobile they are related to broader processes of the spatialization of social relations that characterize modernism (Brown-May, 1995: 3). Richard Sennett locates the spatialization of social relations within the specialization of activities that occurs through the development of the capitalist city (Sennett, 1994: 263–5). I certainly agree that the use of automobiles must be located within these broader processes of change. I would suggest, however, that these changes are more fragile and open to reversal than either Sennett or Brown-May allow.

Throughout the eighteenth and nineteenth centuries the division and regulation of street spaces in Amsterdam, Paris and London were debated in relation to the health, safety, morality, and economic well-being of the population (De Jong, 1986; Rabinow, 1989; Sennett, 1994). These debates were brought into the Australian colonies of Melbourne and Adelaide as they were founded in the early 1800s (Brown-May, 1995; Bonham, 2000). The discussions carried on in Adelaide's newspapers, parliament, and local council focused upon the conditions of and activities upon the streets rather than the conduct of traffic. Residents' complaints about poorly formed roads and government intervention into street spaces were usually related to public health and safety. Health risks included the refuse from slaughterhouses and fishmongers, animal excrement, human spit and stagnant water. Threats to safety included being gored, bitten, or kicked by animals, tripping or running into advertising signs, falling into open cellars and getting stuck in the mud (eg, *Adelaide Independent*, 1841; *Register*, 1855; Adelaide City Council Archives, 1849–50; Blacket, 1911: 160–1). The division of streets into footpath and carriageway, once explained in terms of a natural hierarchy of humans and beasts (Palladio, 1964), was rationalized in Adelaide on a case-by-case basis and it was discussed in terms of health and safety rather than speed of passage (Adelaide City Council Archives, 1852; Worsnop, 1878: 121).

59

Street spaces were also scrutinized in relation to the morality of the population. This concern with 'public behaviour' – prostitution, gambling, sleeping, sunning and socializing in public spaces (Adelaide City Council, 1863; South Australia Parliament, 1904: 255–6) – may be understood as the imposition of middle class values on the broader population. Anson Rabinbach's (1992) work, however, suggests that problems such as idleness and wasting time cannot be understood as a straightforward attempt to institute a work ethic. Rather, the emergence of scientific discourses on energy, including its use and wastage, may have shaped or at least informed those discussions about laziness and wasting time that circulated in parliament and the popular press from the late nineteenth century. These concerns over the morality of the population led to practices such as removing seating and placing spikes in window ledges to keep the population moving.

I have discussed the division of street space in relation to health, safety and morality in considerable detail elsewhere (Bonham, 2000; 2002). The important point to be made in the present context is that the practices rationalized through these discourses served to alter both the physical appearance of the street and the conduct of the population upon the streets. Journeys could be conducted without obstruction or impediment. Further, as non-travel activities were moved out of the streets it became possible to observe the journey. The changes rationalized by reference to health, safety and morality facilitated circulation of the urban inhabitants but they did not order that movement.

Perhaps the most significant change in the use of street space was in terms of the economic role of the street (Rabinow, 1989; Sennett, 1994). Adelaide's streets were a site for a range of economic activities, including scavenging, breaking in horses, trading goods and services, betting, and providing access to business premises (South Australia Parliament, 1883: 15, 1904: 255; Adelaide City Council, 1913: 27; Morton, 1996: 210). These activities were directly and indirectly challenged as some urban residents complained about the time taken to travel within certain parts of the city. The debates over cutting roads through the city's public squares, in particular Victoria Square located in the centre of the city grid, demonstrates a shift in thinking about the economic role of the street (Bonham, 2000: 55–7). The cutting through of Victoria Square was put to Parliament in the 1850s, 1870s, and 1880s and was debated on points of health, safety, and the economical role of the street. Those business owners whose premises lined the square complained that physical and visual access to their premises would be blocked if a road was put through the middle of the Square (South Australia Parliament, 1883: 15). Others argued that a road through the middle of the Square would secure quicker access to the businesses in the southern portion of the city (South Australia Parliament, 1883: 10). The cutting through of the Square was defeated in the 1850s and 1870s but the proposal finally gained assent in the 1880s. These debates indicate a slippage between the street as a place for conducting (or accessing) economic activities and the street as a site for facilitating the economical conduct of movement between activities.

Two decades after these debates urbanists such as Raymond Unwin claimed:

> Roads are primarily highways for traffic. They serve also a secondary purpose in affording sites for buildings. They should be considered in relation to both these functions, and in the order of their relative importance. For the roads in a town to satisfy properly their primary function of highways, they must be so designed as to provide generally for easy access from any point in the town to any other. But they should provide, in addition, special facilities for the ebb and flow of particular tides of traffic, such as that from the outskirts to the centre and back again which daily takes place in most large cities, or that across the town from a residential district to a quarter occupied by works, factories, or other places of employment, or to important railway stations, harbours, and other centres of industry. (Unwin, 1909: 235)

As Unwin and his contemporaries situated the street within the metropolis, they ignored the economic activities which might be located upon the street, focusing instead upon the economical movement of goods and people along it. In the early 1900s, motor lobby groups such as the Automobile Association deployed the conceptualization of the point-to-point journey claiming that 'The ideal [road] system appears to be one by which traffic would be conducted by the shortest and most inexpensive route to its destination' (Automobile Association, 1913: 68). Streets and street users were increasingly brought under scrutiny for their potential to facilitate or impede movement.

Various processes were already underway in British, North American and Australian cities whereby street users, street spaces, and streets, were classified according to the speed and order of travel. From the first decade of the 1900s, the Adelaide City Council began to scrutinize and classify all the phenomena to be found upon the streets according to whether it moved, how it moved (by human, animal, mechanical action), and its role in moving other objects (humans or goods). Objects which remained stationery (boxes, barrels, signs) constituted an obstruction and were eventually excluded from the street (Adelaide City Council, 1906: 2). The multiplicity of phenomena which did move (traffic) were brought into broad classifications such as foot passengers, animals, carts, carriages, and motors (Adelaide City Council, 1906: 2). How the object moved implied how quickly it moved and this came to be used in designating the space upon the street in which it might travel.

The Automobile Association drew on the work of French urbanist Eugene Henard to describe how the internal spaces of the street should be arranged to ensure the efficient conduct of the journey (Automobile Association, 1914: 134). Slow and disorderly travellers were now confined to the footpaths (foot passengers, hawkers), slightly faster but potentially disruptive traffic (wagon drivers, turning vehicles) was allocated the left lane while the centre of the street was reserved for fast and orderly travellers – preferably motor cars. As the internal spaces of the streets were being re-arranged, South Australia's first town planner, Charles Reade, drew up plans for suburbs in which he sorted the streets into a hierarchy according to the speed and order of the travel practices anticipated upon them (South Australia Parliament, 1919: 38, 47). These various processes of differentiation and classification informed a growing concern with efficient movement and provided practical strategies for securing such movement.

Although numerous changes to urban street space acted to facilitate the circulation of the urban population, the conceptualization of travel as a point-to-point journey was a key innovation in urban circulation. Thinking travel as *transport* provided a rationale for the ordering of urban movement and the street spaces in which that movement took place. It was through this ordering that a hierarchy of urban travel was established and those travellers who were the fastest (specifically motor car operators) were positioned and prioritized as the most efficient. Many urban residents, however, resisted the re-ordering of street spaces and the priority given to the speedy traveller.

Struggles over street space

At the same moment that urbanists were reflecting upon how best to achieve the efficient movement of the urban population, debate was underway amongst the urban population on the place of the speedy traveller. The introduction of motors, like trains and bicycles before them, was neither simple nor straightforward. Contrary to claims by authors such as Donovan (1996: 201) people expressed a mixture of opinions about the motor car and differed in their reasons for embracing, rejecting, or remaining cautious about the new technology (Manning, 1991; Bonham, 2002). Automobiles were advertised to men and women in South Australia as objects of leisure, pleasure, sport, and hobby interest. Newspapers quickly established weekly Motoring Sections where motorists and would-be motorists were informed about an array of issues from how to deal with particular mechanical problems to what they should pack in the motoring picnic hamper. Above all, the automobile was identified as a source of freedom, enabling people to step beyond the day-to-day. Although motor vehicle advertisements were targeted at the wealthy, other classes could participate in the new technology in a number of ways: by reading the motoring section of the newspaper; attending the races and speed trials held on country roads; purchasing second-hand motor cars or, the next best thing, motor cycles; and if all these failed, young lads might 'acquire' a motor for the day and go joy-riding.

The popularization of automobiles in the newspapers and magazines, through references to freedom, contrasts markedly with the arguments put by politicians to support, or protest, the use of vehicles in the city streets. In parliament, the motor car was almost exclusively endorsed for its economic role. Motors, it was argued, would *facilitate* economic activity – processes of production, consumption, and exchange. They were also a *source* of economic activity – especially in manufacture and servicing – but most importantly they *facilitated the economical conduct of journeys* and consequently the economical operation of the city.

The interests of the upper classes and the interests of capitalists were certainly served as people were allowed to use their new cars on the streets. Further, politicians and the population more generally were cognisant of these interests being served. For some commentators, however, the motor was not, or not only, a plaything for the wealthy:

> The motor was useful to the business and professional man, because it was a quick means of transit, and if the pace of motors was limited by law, what was the advantage of the motor? (South Australia Parliament, 1904: 946)

For others, inhibiting the new technology would undermine the very reason for its existence:

> From perusing the newspapers I see that it is suggested that the speed of motor-cars be limited to a uniform rate of 12 miles an hour, not only in the principal streets, but in all the streets of Adelaide. I am afraid if such a course is adopted other corporations will follow suit in and about Adelaide, and the consequence will be the motor-cars will be made practically useless. (South Australia Parliament, 1904: 862)

In South Australia, the place of the automobile was argued for on the basis of its role in facilitating the efficient conduct of economic activities and the efficient movement of the population. The motor car operator had the potential to be the most efficient traveller and on these grounds motorists could make a strong claim for priority over the use of street space.

The use of motors in the public streets also provoked opposition. Motorists were not challenged in terms of their rights as individuals to travel by whatever means they chose. Rather, many people expressed concern (either in writing or through acts of resistance) about *how* these new travellers might conduct their journeys and the nature of their relation to other street users. Taking the second point first, motorists were often challenged on their right to claim public space from those who already occupied it. Foot passengers, wagon drivers, horse riders, tram passengers, children at play, and adults in conversation asserted their claim on public space by refusing to cede ground to, or change their behaviour for, fast travellers.

The Commissioner for Public Works commented to Parliament that:

> . . . he had been much impressed, on country roads particularly, with the fact that people would not take notice of the warning given by drivers. They appeared to say, 'I have the right to the road, and you can blow as much as you like'. Those people deserved a little bump sometimes. (South Australia Parliament, 1908: 691)

In a letter to the Police Department, members of the Automobile Association complained that:

> At the corner of Commercial Road and Charra Street Unley, any day and almost any hour is to be found a collection of small children playing in the middle of the road. A lot of dirty, impudent children of tender years who take a delight in forcing motorists to jamb on both brakes to avoid running over them. (State Records Office, 1924: 2144)

As late as 1936, the Select Committee appointed to investigate the Road Traffic Act also complained that:

Pedestrians in daylight wander about the streets and 'jay-walk' and cross at any and every part of the street; they 'dare' motorists to run them down, by dawdling across in front of them and ignoring warning signals. (South Australia Parliament, 1936: 17)

Recalcitrant citizens asserted their rights to occupy public space both on the streets and through the courts (Adelaide City Council, 1911: 57, 1912: 41, 1913: 27; South Australia Parliament, 1930: 18; Manning, 1991: 46–50).

The claims pedestrians made on public space could be readily ignored when rationalizing travel in terms of the efficient conduct of the journey. Those who did not move quickly or who used street space for activities other than travel were themselves guilty of wasteful and inefficient conduct. The rights of such citizens could be ignored in the interests of those who used their time economically. Nonetheless, the efficiency of the speedy traveller was annulled if it meant the injury or death of other travellers. The ensuing debates over motor vehicle usage quickly closed around the issue of safety. The space of travel, the performance of the journey and the body of the traveller were all scrutinized in relation to safety.

The body that travels

The rising rate of deaths and injuries was taken up as an issue by both opponents and proponents of the new motoring technologies. If motors were to be used on the public streets, the problem of safety had to be addressed. This section examines the mechanisms through which knowledge was produced about crashes and travelling bodies as well as the techniques deployed to discipline those who travelled. The disciplining of the body – which continues through to the present day – has been fundamental in enabling the government of travel through self-regulation and the desire for freedom (see also Packer, 2003).

Throughout the early decades of the 1900s, travellers, travel practices, and conduct upon the street more generally were scrutinized for their potential to cause accidents. Following Foucault, the data accumulated in the day-to-day reporting procedures of agencies both within and beyond the State – the police, the coroner, hospitals, insurance companies, passenger and freight companies – provided a basis for a new sub-field of knowledge on road accidents (eg, South Australia Parliament, 1916, 1921, 1926, 1930, 1931, 1936). These agencies recorded information on the age and gender of those involved in the crash as well as where each crash occurred: in which localities; on which streets; the precise point on the street – at intersections, on foot-crossings, near the kerb or the centre of the streets. They also obtained data on the conditions and circumstances under which crashes occurred: the actions of those immediately prior to the crash; the weather conditions – cloudy, rainy, sunny; the time of the day – dawn, dusk, night; the condition of the road and so forth. This information could be aggregated to calculate frequencies and determine patterns of distribution in where and when crashes occurred, the characteristics of those involved, and the attributes of those at fault (South Australia Parliament, 1930: 23–4, 1931: 26, 1936: Tables 1-16; State Records Office, 1927, 1932). This information was taken up and deployed by engineers as they designed roads conducive to speedy, but safe, journeys (Cardew, 1922: 14–6).

Through the analysis of crash records, travel practices were separated out, sorted, and classified according to their potential to lead to accidents. Driving through or stopping at intersections, passing stationary trams, backing out from the kerb, weaving back and forth across the road, walking behind stationary vehicles, driving in the rain, standing on or walking along the road, stepping off the kerb, signalling one's intentions to other travellers, looking along the street before stepping off the kerb could all be ranked as more or less hazardous practices (State Records Office, 1927, 1932). As the body of knowledge grew about the actions and behaviours that led to or averted accidents, so a range of programs and strategies were devised to guide the traveller in the performance of the journey. Through the first decades of the twentieth century, street spaces and travel practices were simultaneously ordered and intervened upon to secure the safe conduct of travel. The safety measures that could be introduced were delimited by the imperative to travel economically. The desire for economical travel was (and continues today as) a largely unstated assumption of the discourse on safety. Interventions related to safety reinforced and entrenched practices related to speed. Those travellers who resisted the ordering of the speedy street could be positioned as irrational because they simultaneously resisted the order of safety.

Not only were the actions, interactions, and conditions surrounding the accident examined but road crashes led researchers deeper into the body of the traveller. Knowledges produced in the fields of Psychometrics, Industrial Psychology, and Medicine were readily deployed in the study of motor crashes. Researchers in these areas either used machines to investigate human actions and capacities (eg, reflexes, eyesight, and hearing) or examined the interactions of human beings with machines (Rabinbach, 1992; Crary, 1999). Industrial psychologists analysed the employee records of freight and passenger companies to determine the crash rates of individual employees and the personal characteristics of those involved in crashes (Miles and Vincent, 1934: 245–57). Transport workers were subjected to examinations to determine the characteristics, capacities and competencies necessary to motoring. Researchers set about measuring, recording, and comparing phenomena such as muscular movements, neuromuscular co-ordination, intelligence, temperament, and attention span (eg, Little, 1934: 730–1; Miles and Vincent, 1934: 245–57; Myers, 1935: 740–2; Selling, 1937: 93–5; *Medical Journal of Australia*, 1937: 635–6). These researchers also identified factors that could optimize or undermine the performance of the motoring body – fatigue, alcohol, narcotics and so forth (*Education Gazette*, 1931: 187–8). This knowledge provided a basis for interventions that would develop the body's capacities and optimize efficiency of movements. Speedy travellers required speedy responses.

Research into the capacities of the travelling body revealed 'norms' as well as the limits of the normal body (eg, *Education Gazette*, 1931: 187–8; Miles and Vincent, 1934). The norms created through these studies were used in setting limits upon how different bodies could travel. Only those who fell within the bounds of the 'normal' could assume the position of the motorist – the most efficient traveller. The identification and disqualification of certain people from operating a motor vehicle made it possible, over time, to position non-drivers as 'abnormal'.

Drivers' licences, introduced into South Australia in the early 1900s, mark the first time in the state's history that private travellers were required to obtain permission to travel by their preferred means of mobility. The driver's licence established a record for each motorist whereby a history of these travellers – their traffic violations, crashes and penalties – could be created. As knowledge about motorists was produced it informed the grounds upon which people could qualify for or be disqualified from motoring. Morality, defined in terms of age and criminal record, was the first criteria to be used in distinguishing those who should from those who should not operate a motor car. By 1921, other regulations previously applied to 'public vehicle' operators such as cab drivers and motormen, were being applied to the motor car user. Applicants with specific conditions, such as blindness, were disqualified from acquiring a driver's licence while the Registrar of Motor Vehicles was empowered to test anyone with an infirmity deemed to make them dangerous on the roads (South Australia Parliament, 1918; South Australia, 1921). The motorist was not conferred with a driver's licence on the basis of a natural right of citizenship nor was the decision to drive based simply on the ability to purchase a car. A person's right to drive a motor, and thereby assume the position of the motorist, was established and monitored through studies of the efficient and safe conduct of the travelling body.

The rule of law was informed by scientifically established norms but legislation was only one of many mechanisms used in securing the safe conduct of the journey. As Merriman (in this volume) points out in the British context, the production of knowledge and the implementation of programmes which targeted the traveller were not confined to agencies of the State. Representatives of the Automobile Association of South Australia not only lobbied parliamentarians and State administrators on behalf of their members, but also drew on the work of experts (psychologists, medical professionals, and urbanists) to guide their members in the safe conduct of travel. The Association published tips on safe driving practices in its Newsletters, it circulated guides on driving signals and good driver behaviour to new motor car owners, and initiated or assisted in road safety campaigns.

Although the motorist was (potentially) the most efficient traveller, some people would never attain this position nor the priority on the streets that went with it. Nonetheless all travellers could be guided toward the efficient conduct of the journey. The body of the pedestrian, like that of the motorist, was brought under scrutiny as it interacted with machinery. The motoring body was invariably studied as an adult body but investigations of the pedestrian often targeted the body of the child. Where the adult pedestrian was studied, s/he was infantilized within the classifications of accident causes which began to circulate in the 1920s–30s. Motorists at fault in accidents were found to be guilty of *negligence, failure, improper* actions, *inattention* (*Education Gazette*, 1931: 188). The adult pedestrian, similar to the child, was guilty of *confusion, carelessness*, or not meeting the physical or intellectual norm. Pedestrians, like children, were constructed as refusing or being unable to accept and assume responsibility for their own safety.

The susceptibility of children to accidents had been identified in studies of industrial accidents and once again this research provided a point of entry into the study of the traveller. Herbert Stack found that worry, tiredness, thirst for adventure, rebelliousness, and lack of intelligence were likely to diminish the child's capacities, such as reflexes and concentration, that were necessary to travel (Stack, 1931: 284). Glück's 1935 research identified developmental characteristics, including lack of dexterity and undeveloped ability to deal with fear, as increasing children's susceptibility to travel related accidents (Glück cited in *Psychological Abstracts*, 1935: 4855). Any attempts that children made to disrupt or resist the motorist were silenced through medical and psychological discourses. Knowing the body of the travelling child made it possible to elaborate strategies, programmes, and techniques to intervene in the conduct of the child's journey.

One such programme, the *Look Both Ways Club*, was initiated in Canada and established in Adelaide in 1930 (*Advertiser*, 1930a: 16). The Club effectively operated at two different levels. Like other safety organizations, it had an executive committee which comprised representatives from government agencies such as the Education and Police Departments as well as representatives from non-government agencies such as the Returned Soldiers League, Retail Motors Association, School Parents and Citizen's Associations (*Advertiser*, 1930a: 16). The role of the committee was to direct and publicize the activities of the club. It also provided a site through which participating organizations problematized travel conduct, broadened the circulation of discourses on such conduct, and multiplied techniques for intervening in the journey. Further, the committee operated as a forum in which the interests of its constituent organizations were knitted together and advanced through the concern for children's safety. The *Look Both Ways Club* differed from other safety organizations in that it sought primary school children as members and, to this end, branches were established in schools. These branches were usually initiated and administered by teachers but occasionally they were instigated and run by the children themselves. Within its first six months of operation, the club claimed a membership of 50,000 South Australians (*Advertiser*, 1930b: 16).

The *Look Both Ways Club* targeted children in the quest to make particular walking practices widespread amongst the population. Specifically, it sought to '... cultivate the habit of looking to the right then looking to the left before leaving the safe haven of the footpath' (Dollman, 1930: 14). The presence of

67

vehicles on the road signalled to the child that their safety lay in waiting on the kerb; the absence of traffic gave the child their signal that it was safe to continue the journey. On leaving the kerb, the child was instructed to travel directly across the road, that is at a right angle, rather than walking diagonally along the road (Dollman, 1930: 14). The child should walk briskly in anticipation of the sudden appearance of a vehicle. These small sequences of actions instilled as '. . . semi-automatic habits' in childhood would, it was expected, persist into adulthood (*Medical Journal of Australia*, 1937: 636.). The minute practices, 'look to the left – look to the right' and 'stop – look – listen' (initiated by the police department), to be performed at the kerbside prior to crossing the road were drilled into every child, in the classroom, at the school gate, and in the home.

The activities of the *Look Both Ways Club* supported and expanded the Education Department's classroom-based road safety campaigns (*Education Gazette*, 1930: 93). Schools were supplied with 'road safety' posters through the late 1920s–30s. These posters had been created in conjunction with the Automobile Association and teachers were directed to display these posters and use them as the basis of lessons in 'civics' and 'morals' (*Education Gazette*, 1929: 102, 1930: 77). Each poster depicted the road 'faults' of children and served as examples of inappropriate behaviours. Children were taught the principle of safety first and then provided with the opportunity to reflect upon journeys, their own and others', bearing this principle in mind. The safety posters distributed to schools, the road safety assignments set by teachers, and the travel stories children were incited to tell in the classroom all required children to assume the subjectivity of the traveller and the subject position of the pedestrian. These techniques also required children to reflect upon how they might conduct their journey to ensure their own safety. But in case children failed to regulate their behaviour, teachers and parents monitored the conduct of children at the school gate, ensuring the actions rehearsed in the classroom were practised on the way to and from school. Further, when the child reached home the 'Kerbside Song', learnt in school, might also be playing on the radio to reinforce the sequence of steps they may or may not have practiced on their way home.

Safety programmes such as the *Look Both Ways Club* primarily targeted children but they were conducted through a range of sites such as the school, the radio, newspapers, Scouts and Guides associations, and children's clubs (eg, the Twinklers), thereby reaching beyond the child into the family. Parents, siblings, and any other family member prepared to honour the pledge and abide by safety first principles were encouraged to join the *Look Both Ways Club*. The knowledge of childhood accidents and the conditions which increased accident risk were addressed to parents, but particularly mothers, through newspaper articles and women's magazines. A mother might place her own life at risk through carelessness, lack of attention, or resisting the emergent street order, but she was an irresponsible parent if she placed her child at risk. The family not only provided a site through which children were disciplined in their travel, but also parents were disciplined to this order through their responsibilities to their children.

The spatial ordering drilled into the population, but especially children, through road safety campaigns coalesced with the spatialising effects of discourses on Town Planning, Engineering and Psychology. At the same time that town planners were allocating play spaces for children in their new town plans and engineers were designing roads to accommodate fast, heavy traffic, psychologists such as Herbert Stack argued the appropriate places for children to have adventures were the schoolyard, playground and park (Stack, 1931: 285–6). Those rebellious and adventurous children who disrupted the new street order could sate their thirst for danger on the expeditions to national parks and camping grounds organized by the Boy Scouts (Stack, 1931: 285). The spatial ordering explicit in town plans was reinforced through the activities of organizations that extended well beyond the State.

The capacities of the travelling body, like the spaces of the street, were brought under scrutiny to secure the efficient conduct of the journey, efficiency being measured in terms of both speed and loss of life. The production of knowledge about safety and the programmes implemented to ensure safe travel were underpinned by a concern for rapid movement. The concern for safety placed limits around how the journey could be conducted – the efficient journey was fast and (preferably) accident free. There were also limits to safety, however. Certain actions (forbidding fast travel) ran counter to the logic of the economical journey and a certain number of deaths and injuries could be tolerated in view of the economies to be gained from rapid travel.

The disciplining of the travelling body has been examined in detail elsewhere (Bonham, 2002), the main point to be made in this chapter is the historical specificity of that body. The normalizing discourses which have brought the efficient (or economical) traveller into effect have been so utterly effective because they have been produced, circulated, and elaborated by a multiplicity of experts working across a number of disciplines and agencies. The knowledges brought into effect by these experts not only coalesced with each other but also normalized the efficient traveller. This normalization was made complete when, in 1949, George Zipf announced that an underlying principle of all human behaviour was the desire to minimize human effort (Zipf, 1949: v). This naturalization of the 'efficient body', which underpins present day transport research, placed the modern body outside of the political domain and therefore beyond question. As the body was disciplined to move efficiently, knowledge began to proliferate on the journey and on how to secure its economic conduct.

One hundred years of micro-investigations and interventions into the spaces, bodies, mechanisms, and conduct of travel are difficult to unravel. I would argue, however, that breaking motoring into its constituent parts is an important task for three reasons. First, because it disrupts the fusion – or the illusion of unity (car, body, space, conduct) – that transport experts (road and vehicle designers, road safety experts, transport planners and modellers) work in earnest to create. Second, each of these constituent parts is linked into broader socio-spatial relations that are marginalized or excluded as researchers – once again – prioritize the motorist and motoring as a site of investigation. Finally, it seems it is in these constituent parts that the apparent dominance of the motoring experience can be fractured and destabilized.

Dissonant travellers: a conclusion

The first part of this chapter focused upon the objectification of, and interventions into, the spaces and uses of the street from the late nineteenth to the early twentieth centuries. It was argued that these interventions reinforced each other to produce the street not just as a site of movement but as a site of efficient movement. The logic of the economic journey provided the basis for designating street space for a new order of mobility. The second part of the chapter focused upon the objectification of the travelling body and the human capacities necessary to fast, orderly movement. As these capacities were identified, norms were established and individual travellers could be positioned in relation to these norms. Those bodies that fell outside of the norm were excluded from particular travel practices such as driving. Nonetheless, all travellers were targeted to conduct themselves efficiently both at the micro level of their own bodies and in reference to the journeys made by others. The ordering of street uses and street spaces within discourses on urban planning and engineering coalesced with the ordering of travelling bodies within discourses on psychology and medicine to value the efficient body and secure the economical operation of the city.

It was through the first half of the twentieth century that the street was entrenched as a site of economical travel and travellers disciplined to this ordering of movement. As this order was established, it became meaningful to produce knowledge about journeys and innovations in the travel survey made this practicable. The origin-destination survey enabled transport planners to identify the precise points in the urban environment between which people moved – the point-to-point journey, or 'trip', was no longer an abstraction. These surveys, in turn, enabled the elaboration of the journey in terms of the timing and duration of journeys, the routes along which people travelled and the mode of travel. Norms could then be established in relation to each of these 'trip criteria' (origin, destination, duration, route). Transport planners used these criteria to determine which modes of travel maximized choice and they intervened in the urban environment to secure the conditions necessary for these travellers (Bonham, 2002). The new field of transport enabled the elaboration of a range of mechanisms (safety programmes, regulatory devices such as traffic lights, street and vehicle designs) to structure the field of action of the 'free' urban traveller toward the efficient conduct of the journey. The ordering of urban movement established in the first part of the twentieth century was (and still is) fundamental to the field of urban transport and the present-day conduct of travel.

The focus of transport experts on efficient movement fails to take into account the many other motivations and meanings that people attach to their travel. The travelling subject constituted within transport (and many other expert) discourses is not necessarily taken up by the being that travels in any straightforward way. The simple observation that many people are prepared to sit in automobiles when train, tram or bicycle journeys might be more efficient indicates a certain dissonance between the subject of transport and the body that travels. The fact that in cities such as Adelaide (where travel by motor car is often more efficient than other means of travel) people continue to resist the use of an automobile also indicates the poverty of the transport story. Certainly, transport behaviouralists have examined a range of factors which might influence the modal choices people make; however, transport experts continue to comprehend these factors within the framework of the efficient journey.

Confining the study of urban travel to a story about transport has silenced a multiplicity of travel stories which spill out and are beyond the origin and destinations of each trip. Travel stories might be told in many different ways. They might emphasize the experiences of journeys, the social interactions (pleasant and unpleasant) which take place through (and outside) the journey, or the way in which racialized and gendered identities are worked upon and elaborated through the journey. Here I am thinking of the stories that teenagers might tell about their journeys on the school bus, the interactions of children and parents in the family car (Blakely, 1986). I am also thinking about the way in which travel experiences are gendered by middle-aged male security experts as these latter claim the right to speak on behalf of women about safety in public spaces. If travel stories could be told in more complex and diverse ways than transport experts allow then the present day ordering and prioritization of certain travellers (specifically motorists) would be called into question. Perhaps this might ease the ongoing proliferation of automobiles.

Acknowledgements

Thanks to Caryl Bosman, Donna Ferretti and Peter Tisato for their detailed and thoughtful comments on earlier drafts of this paper. Thanks also to two anonymous reviewers for their helpful comments. I hope my revisions have done some justice to their thoughtful suggestions.

References

Adams, J. (1981) *Transport Planning: Vision and Practice.* London: Routledge & Kegan Paul Ltd.
Adelaide City Council Archives (1849–50) *Reports of Inspectors of Nuisances – 1849–1850*, ECR/0038 BD2:01.
Adelaide City Council Archives (1852) *Reports of the Committee of Streets, Sewers and Bridges – 1852*, ECR/0030 BD2B:01.
Adelaide City Council (1906) *By-Laws*. Adelaide: Adelaide City Council.

Adelaide City Council (1911) *Annual Report*. Adelaide: Adelaide City Council.

Adelaide City Council (1912) *Annual Report*. Adelaide: Adelaide City Council.

Adelaide City Council (1913) *Annual Report*. Adelaide: Adelaide City Council.

Adelaide Independent (1841) 5 August 1841: 4.

Advertiser (1930a) 21 January 1930: 16.

Advertiser (1930b) 9 April 1930: 16.

Allan, A., M.A.P. Taylor and G. D'este (1996) *Adelaide 21: Access and Movement*. Adelaide: Adelaide 21 Steering Committee.

Automobile Association (1913) *South Australian Motor*, 1(3).

Automobile Association (1914) *South Australian Motor*, 2(5).

Barry, A., T. Osborne and N. Rose (eds) (1996) *Foucault and Political Reason: Liberalism, neo-Liberalism and Rationalities of Government*. London: UCL Press.

Blacket, J. (1911) *History of South Australia: A Romantic and Successful Experiment in Colonisation*. Adelaide: Hussey & Gillingham Ltd.

Blakely, M. (1986) 'On the road again, and again and again' *Ms,* April: 14 and 62.

Bonham, J. (2000) 'Safety and speed: Ordering the street of transport' in C. Garnaut and S. Hamnett (eds.) *Fifth Urban History/Planning History Conference*. Adelaide: University of South Australia.

Bonham, J. (2002) *The Conduct of Travel: Beginning a Genealogy of the Travelling Subject*. Unpublished PhD Thesis. University of Adelaide.

Brown-May, A. (1995) *Highways of Civilisation and Common Sense: Street Regulation and the Transformation of Social Space in Nineteenth and Early Twentieth Century Melbourne*. Urban Research Program Working Paper No. 49, Australian National University, Canberra.

Cardew, H. (1922) 'Roads and road making in England' *The Australasian Engineer*, 19(69): 14–16.

Crary, J. (1999) *Suspensions of Perception*. Cambridge, MA: MIT Press.

De Jong, R. (1986) 'The recapture of the street' in E. de Boer (ed.) *Transport Sociology: Social Aspects of Transport Planning*. Britain: Pergamon Press.

Dean, M. and B. Hindess (eds) (1998) *Governing Australia: Studies in Contemporary Rationalities of Government*. Cambridge: Cambridge University Press.

Dollman, W. (1930) '"Look Both Ways", Safety's Watchword' *Advertiser*, 3 March: 14.

Donovan, P. (1996) 'Motor cars and freeways: measure of a South Australian Love Affair' in B. O'Niel, J. Raftery and K. Round (eds) *Playford's South Australia: Essays on the history of South Australia 1933–1968*. Adelaide: Association of Professional Historians.

Education Gazette (1929) 15 March 1929: 102.

Education Gazette (1930) 15 February 1930: 77 and 93.

Education Gazette (1931) 15 June 1931: 187–8.

Ferretti, D. and J. Bonham (2001) 'Travel blending: Whither regulation' *Australian Geographical Studies,* 39(3): 302–12.

Foucault, M. (1977) *Discipline and Punish: The Birth of the Prison*. London: Penguin.

Foucault, M. (1978) *The History of Sexuality Vol. 1*. London: Penguin.

Franks, H. (1986) 'Mass transport and class struggle' in E. de Boer (ed.) *Transport Sociology: Social Aspects of Transport Planning*. Britain: Pergamon Press.

Fyfe, N. (ed.) (1998) *Images of the Street: Planning, Identity and Control in Public Space*. London: Routledge.

Gordon, C. (1991) 'Governmental rationality: An introduction' in G. Burchell, C. Gordon and P. Miller (eds) *The Foucault Effect: Studies in Governmentality*. Chicago: University of Chicago Press.

Gutman, R. (1978) 'The street generation' in S. Anderson (ed.) *On Streets*. Cambridge, MA: MIT Press.

Hensher, D. (ed.) (1974) *Urban Travel Choice and Demand Modelling*. Canberra: Australian Road Research Board.

Hodge, D. (1990) 'Geography and the political economy of urban transportation' *Urban Geography,* 11(1): 87–100.

Jacobs, J. (1961) *The Death and Life of Great American Cities*. Harmondsworth: Penguin Books.

Kern, S. (1983) *The Culture of Time and Space 1880–1920.* Cambridge, MA: Harvard University Press.

Little, G. (1934) 'Letter' *British Medical Journal,* 21 April 1934: 730–31.

Manning, I. (1991) *The Open Street.* Sydney: Transit Australia Publishing.

Medical Journal of Australia (1937) 24 April 1937: 636.

Miles, G. and Vincent, D. (1934) 'The Institute's tests for motor drivers' *The Human Factor,* VIII(7–8): 245–57.

Morton, P. (1996) *After Light: A History of the City of Adelaide and its Council 1878–1928.* Kent Town: Wakefield Press.

Myers, C. (1935) 'The psychological approach to the problem of road accidents', *Nature,* 9 November 1935: 740–42.

Packer, J. (2003) 'Disciplining mobility: Governing and safety' in J. Bratich, J. Packer and C. McCarthy (eds) *Foucault, Cultural Studies, and Governmentality.* Albany: State University of New York Press.

Palladio, A. (1964) *The Four Books of Architecture* (reprint of English Edition 1737). London: Dover Publications.

Psychological Abstracts (1935) Entry 4855, 1935: 9.

Rabinbach, A. (1992) *The Human Motor: Energy, Fatigue, and the Origins of Modernity.* Berkley: University of California Press.

Rabinow, P. (1989) *French Modern: Norms and Forms of the Social Environment.* Cambridge, MA: MIT Press.

Register (1855) 28 June 1855: 3.

Rooney, A. (1998) 'Transport systems and cities viewed as self organizing systems' in *Proceedings of the 22nd Australasian Transport Research Forum.* Sydney: Transport Data Centre – NSW Department of Transport.

Rose, N. (1990) *Governing the Soul: The Shaping of the Private Self.* London: Routledge.

Rutherford, P. (1999) 'The entry of life into history' in E. Darier (ed.) *Discourses of the Environment.* Oxford: Blackwell.

Schumer, L.A. (1955) *The Elements of Transport.* London: Butterworth & Co.

Selling, L. (1937) 'The physician and the traffic problem' in *Journal of the American Medical Association,* 108(2): 93–95.

Sennett, R. (1994) *Flesh and Stone: The Body and the City in Western Civilization.* London: Faber and Faber.

South Australia Parliament (1883) *Select Committee of the Legislative Council: Report on the Victoria-Square Thoroughfare Bill,* Parl Paper 159, South Australia, Adelaide.

South Australia Parliament (1904) *Debates,* 17th Parliament, 3rd Session, South Australia, Adelaide.

South Australia Parliament (1908) *Debates,* 19th Parliament, 3rd Session, South Australia, Adelaide.

South Australia Parliament (1916) *Satistical Register of South Australia, 1915–16: Part VII, Religious, Educational and Charitable Institutions,* Parl Paper 3, 1916, Table 47, South Australia, Adelaide.

South Australia Parliament (1918) *Select Committee of the House of Assembly: Report on the Motor Vehicles Bill 1918,* Parl Paper 77, South Australia, Adelaide.

South Australia Parliament (1919) *Government Town Planner: Report on Planning and Development of Towns and Cities in South Australia,* Parl Paper 63, South Australia, Adelaide.

South Australia Parliament (1921) *Satistical Register of South Australia, 1920–21: Part VII, Religious, Educational and Charitable Institutions,* Parl Paper 3, 1921, Table 33, South Australia, Adelaide.

South Australia Parliament (1926) *Satistical Register of South Australia, 1925–26: Part VII, Religious, Educational and Charitable Institutions,* Parl Paper 3, 1926, Table 29, South Australia, Adelaide.

South Australia Parliament (1930) *Commissioner of Police, Report for the Year Ended 30th June-1930,* Parliamentary Paper 53, South Australia, Adelaide.

South Australia Parliament (1931) *Commissioner of Police, Report for the Year Ended 30th June-1931,* Parliamentary Paper 53, South Australia, Adelaide.

South Australia Parliament (1936) *Honorary Committee Appointed to Report upon The Road Traffic Act 1934, Report and Recommendations*, Parl Paper 20, South Australia, Adelaide.

South Australia (1921) 'Motor Vehicles Act, 1921' *Acts of the Parliament of South Australia*, No 1480, South Australia, Adelaide.

State Records Office (1924) South Australia GRG Series 2, *Police Dept. of South Australia, Correspondence.*

State Records Office (1927) South Australia GRG Series 2, *Police Dept. of South Australia, Correspondence.*

State Records Office (1932) South Australia GRG Series 44, *Coroner, Statistics.*

Stack, H. (1931) 'The mental causes of child accidents' *Mental Hygiene,* 15: 283–9.

Unwin, R. (1909) *Town Planning in Practice.* London: T. Fisher Unwin.

Worsnop, T. (1878) *Worsnop's History of the City of Adelaide.* Adelaide: J. Williams.

Zipf, G. (1949) *Human Behaviour and the Principle of the Least Effort: An Introduction to Human Ecology.* Cambridge, MA: Addison-Wesley Press.

'Mirror, Signal, Manoeuvre': assembling and governing the motorway driver in late 1950s Britain

Peter Merriman

Introduction

In recent years social scientists have paid increasing attention to the complex relations between drivers and cars, drawing upon the writings of Bruno Latour, John Law, Donna Haraway and others to trace the materialities and practices associated with such hybrid or cyborg figures as 'human-car co(a)gents' (Michael, 2000: 73), the 'car-driver' (Sheller and Urry, 2000: 752; Lupton, 1999), and 'cason' (a conflation of car-person) (Michael, 2000: 93; cf. Katz, 1999; Urry, 2000; Böhm *et al.*, this volume).[1] As the accounts of these different writers suggest, while the normalized *and* individualized figure of the driver, and the mass-produced yet invariably customised vehicle, may appear to lie at the centre of these mobile assemblages, it is futile to attempt to understand the movements, politics, semiotics, emotions and ontological formations associated with driving by attempting (endlessly) to separate or purify these hybrid assemblages into constituent parts. In this chapter I argue that while academics can usefully examine the complex processes of hybridization, purification and distribution that are performed in acts of writing, talking about and doing driving, these associations, assemblages and social relations must be seen to extend far beyond the confines of the car (cf. Böhm *et al.*, this volume; Urry, 2000, 2003). As Sheller and Urry (2000: 447) have shown, the diverse 'scapes' associated with car travel – including motorways, flyovers and service areas – are intricately related to the 'machinic hybridization of the car driver', as are the heterogeneous networks which Urry terms the 'global fluid' of automobility (Urry, 2003: 69). Social scientists have paid particular attention to the regularized practices, movements and spaces associated with driving, but in this chapter I examine how the emergence of a new type of driving environment in Britain – with the construction and opening of the M1 motorway in the late 1950s – led a range of cultural commentators and experts to attempt to predict, measure, problematize and effect changes on the movements of drivers and vehicles. New spaces, architectures, technologies, techniques of regulation, and patterns of roadside planting and landscaping were conceived and placed around the movements of drivers and vehicles, becoming inhabited by drivers and incorporated into the spaces of the driving-subject in new ways.

Drawing upon the writings of Michel Foucault and Nikolas Rose, different architectures, knowledges, instruments and legal frameworks may be seen to function as 'technologies of government' which translate political rationalities and shape the performances and movements of drivers, vehicles, and the spaces of the road (Miller and Rose, 1990: 8; Barry, 2001). While Foucault's writings on discipline and confinement have been seen to provide a somewhat disabling account of the control and domination of 'docile bodies' (Foucault, 1991a; McNay, 1994), Foucault's later writings on government trace a more open and productive account of the diverse forces, relations, and techniques entailed in governing *both* others and oneself (Foucault, 1988, 1991b; Rose, 1996, 1999; cf. Bonham, this volume). Disciplinary techniques and practices form just one dimension of programmes of government, while practices of self-government are recognized as being crucial to the workings of governmental regimes. In this chapter I examine how a number of devices were devised and distributed by experts in order to serve as 'technologies of government' (Miller and Rose, 1990: 8), and how certain things were encountered and appropriated as 'technologies of the self', which as Foucault states:

> permit individuals to effect by their own means or with the help of others a certain number of operations on their own bodies and souls, thoughts, conduct, and way of being, so as to transform themselves in order to attain a certain state of happiness, purity, wisdom, perfection, or immortality. (Foucault, 1988: 18)[2]

In the case of motorway driving, one can examine the practices, spaces and devices through which drivers relate to themselves and their vehicles in particular ways, while politicians, police officers, Road Research Laboratory scientists and a host of other experts become engaged in ongoing, partial, and contingent attempts to assemble and govern driving-subjects through and in relation to their bodies, vehicles, and other spaces, texts and thoughts – as travellers, consumers, criminals, statistics and participants in scientific experiments.

In the first section of the chapter I examine the debates which emerged in the late 1950s and 1960s about the conduct of drivers and the movements of vehicles on Britain's newly opened M1 motorway (see also Merriman, 2003, 2005, forthcoming). Experts focused their attention on the performances of both driver *and* vehicle, distributing and localizing agency, competence, blame, trust, autonomy and mobility across their spaces and forms (Latour, 1992; Michael, 2000; Böhm *et al.*, this volume). I then examine how a broad range of things – from performance enhancing tyres and clutches, to codes of conduct and wing mirrors – became enfolded into the spaces of the motorway vehicle driver. In the following section I focus my attention on the movements of two figures – the Automobile Association (AA) patrolman and British grand prix racing driver – who were seen to have the necessary expertise to advise the inexperienced motorway driver. I examine how they proceeded to purify, divide and localize the different movements, bodies and materials involved in motorway driving: blaming drivers, vehicles or poor weather for causing disruptions, accidents or breakdowns. In section three I examine how the spaces of the motorway itself were designed around the movements of motorway travellers, who were partially assembled as drivers, consumers, statistics and criminals. I focus on the attempts of the government's Road Research Laboratory to identify the role played by the motorway in serious accidents, and examine how the motorway traveller was constructed as a consumer in relation to the spaces of motorway service areas. In the final section I conclude by arguing that a relational approach to driving can provide an invaluable insight into the continual processes of hybridization and purification that occur in the performance of driving (Latour, 1993). I suggest that while academics have tended to see the driver's inhabitation of their vehicle and the spaces of the road as giving rise to *detached* experiences of 'placelessness' (Relph, 1976) in ubiquitous 'non-places' (Augé, 1995), these are quite specific feelings which arise from momentary associations and *attachments* that are integral to the ongoing, performative constructions of places.

Motorway driving in late 1950s Britain

In 1958 and early 1959 – before the opening of the M1 in November 1959 – journalists, politicians, police and motoring organizations began to express concern about the potential of drivers and vehicles to cope with the speeds and stresses of motorway driving. A number of questions emerged at the heart of discussions. Would Britain's drivers, many of whom had little or no experience of driving on multi-lane dual carriageway roads, know which lane to drive in, stay in one lane, or check their mirrors when overtaking? Would they or their vehicles be able to cope with the high speeds that were possible and legal with the absence of a speed limit? Would they understand the new signs or be able to negotiate flyover junctions safely?

In an article published in *Punch* just days before the opening of the motorway, the satirist H. F. Ellis predicted scenes of chaos caused by a number of caricatured vehicle drivers. While it was expected that 'the young and ardent' would drive their sports cars and motor-cycles at speeds of over 90 mph, his attention focused on those who had neither the skill, experience nor vehicles to attain such speeds (Ellis, 1959: 362). It was the lorry drivers 'released from the constraints of A5', the 'old fool in a worn-out soap box', and the 'normally rational people in unbalanced saloons' who Ellis expected to exceed their mental and physical abilities; becoming corrupted, poisoned and paralysed as their mobile hybridized bodies failed to cope with the new speeds and spatialities of the motorway (Ellis, 1959: 363). In such accounts, the age, status, styles and conditions of drivers become inseparable from those of their vehicle, and it was felt that the capabilities and performances of drivers and vehicles must be complementary and appropriate to the speeds attempted and spaces traversed. This assumption, of a 'distribution of competences' (Latour, 1992: 233) or abilities across the spaces and bodies of the vehicle, driver, and road, was implicit in the government's motorway regulations, which were devised prior to the opening of the Preston Bypass Motorway in December 1958 (see *Parliamentary Debates*, 1958). The motorway regulations limited access to vehicles that were: of an accepted type, size and weight; centred on an inanimate source of power; fast; and were controlled by a qualified human operator. Motorways are spaces from which cyclists, mopeds, animals, unauthorised oversized loads, agricultural vehicles, pedestrians, learner drivers and invalid carriages were, and are, excluded (see MOTCA and COI, 1958, 1959).

Drivers were informed of the motorway regulations through prominent notice boards on slip roads. These immobile public signs presented the statutory rules to drivers entering these spaces, but the Ministry of Transport and Civil Aviation and Central Office of Information also issued a much smaller and mobile (non-statutory) advisory code in time for the opening of the Preston Bypass (*The Times*, 1958). The Motorway Code was designed to reside in, and enfold the networks of social and political responsibility associated with driving in public into, the privatized spaces of the home and car, to enable the education, prompting, and guidance of motorists (MOTCA and COI, 1958; Merriman, 2005). It was drafted as a code of good conduct, a quasi-moral contract that would serve as a 'technology of government': a tool to be bought, read, learned and translated by motorists into a series of practical embodied techniques by which they could relate to themselves, their vehicle and other drivers, and move swiftly and safely through the (public) spaces of the motorway (Rose, 1996; also Foucault, 1988, 1991). Drivers would learn and embody the tenets of the Motorway Code through practices of reading, reflection *and* driving, while publication of the Code was backed up with supplementary campaigns. Sections of the Code were displayed on posters attached to the back of a fleet of Bedford lorries which used the motorway (*The Autocar*, 1959), while public information films – addressing issues such as lane discipline, turning, and 'the correct use of hard shoulders' – were shown on television (*The Times*, 1959a: 14). The Code was expected to aid drivers to adapt their ways of moving and being; becoming incorporated into the heterogeneous networks and spatialities associated with the performances of vehicle drivers. As a Northampton *Chronicle and Echo* reporter stated in November 1958, the motorway driver would 'only become a being apart while he is actually on the motorways. When he leaves them he will automatically be transformed into an "ordinary" motorist . . .' (*Chronicle and Echo*, 1958). The transformation was expected to be immanent, with the subjectivities and very being of motorway drivers being performed through specific vehicles, materials and spaces, and the Motorway Code providing advice on how to cope in these new landscapes: on how to join and leave the motorway, driving at night, overtaking, 'lane discipline', and where to stop in an emergency (MOTCA and COI, 1958, 1959).

The Motorway Code was just one of a series of technological and political devices that was distributed with the intention of governing the performances, desires and experiences of drivers-in-vehicles; subtly changing the relations between the bodies of drivers, vehicles, and the spaces through which they travel (Merriman, 2005). The Code was expected to serve as a medium- and long-term tool for educating drivers, while for short-term results sections were reprinted in guides to the opening of the M1 in local and national newspapers, the motoring press (eg, *The Autocar* and *The Motor*), and leaflets issued by the Automobile Association and Royal Automobile Club. The AA's 'Guide to the Motorway' contained a map of the M1's location, guides to the new signs, a reprinted Motorway Code, details of the Association's motorway service, and advice on 'your car on the motorway' (AA, 1959). This latter section was deemed to be particularly important, and the RAC, motoring magazines, newspapers and a range of manufacturing companies also emphasized the importance of maintaining and modifying one's vehicle. While John Urry (2000: 63) has argued that vehicles insulate drivers 'from the environment', reducing 'the sights, sounds, tastes, temperatures and smells of the city and countryside' to 'the two-dimensional view through the car windscreen', many of the vehicles which traversed the M1 in 1959 would have been fairly noisy, cold and draughty – producing very different embodied experiences of driving. Motoring correspondents stressed the need for more powerful headlights and radios, overdrive gears, wing mirrors, better insulation, and they predicted the launch of a specially designed 'motorway cruiser' (*The Motor*, 1959: 135). The emphasis here was on controlling the sensory experiences and enhancing the capabilities of the hybridized vehicle driver; engineering the intricate relations between drivers, passengers, vehicles, and the spaces of the motorway.

Manufacturing companies took the opportunity to associate their automotive products with high performance driving and the spectacle of the new M1; attempting to persuade owners to incorporate new technologies into their vehicles. In *The Times*, on the opening day of the motorway, India Tyres urged Britain's drivers to purchase their high performance tyres 'For that motorway outlook' (*The Times*, 1959b: 5; see Figure 1). The advert suggested that driving required a balance between the capabilities of driver and machine, and that while the masculine driver-consumer would be able to raise *his* performance, 'India Super' and 'India Super Multigrip' would be required to 'make the most of your car's power' and to match these skills (*The Times*, 1959b: 5). Durability, capability, and competence become distributed throughout this mobile consuming assemblage, whose driver is seen to perform his masculinity through his body, automotive body-work, and the spaces of the road.[3] In a similar advert, Automotive Products Associated Limited suggested that motorway drivers would 'need more than skill behind the wheel' (*The Times*, 1959c: 9; see Figure 2). Drivers must ensure that the capabilities and performance of their vehicle match their skills and expertise, while high speed driving is seen to increase the importance of networks of trust and faith weaving together drivers, vehicles, respected companies, numerous organizations, engineers, and the government (see Hawkins, 1986; Giddens, 1990; Lynch, 1993; Latour, 1992). As Automotive Products Associated Limited stated: because 'you need complete *faith* in your

Figure 1: *India Tyres advertisement, 1959. Reproduced by permission of Goodyear Dunlop UK.*

Figure 2: *Automotive Products Associated Limited advertisement, 1959. Reproduced by permission of Automotive Products Group Limited.*

vehicle' you 'can put your *trust* in LOCKHEED disc and drum brakes . . . , *rely* on a BORG & BECK clutch . . . , [and] be *sure* of steering accuracy with THOMPSON Tie Rods and Ball Joints' (*The Times*, 1959c: 9, emphasis mine).

While the ideal situation was one where driver and machine had complementary abilities and competences, the remarks of commentators suggest that there was frequently perceived to be an asymmetry between the performances of drivers and vehicles on the motorway. When Minister of Transport Ernest Marples opened the M1, he expressed shock at the speed and general conduct of the first drivers on the motorway and the poor maintenance of the vehicles that passed him (Mennem, 1959). As civil servants had predicted, and Marples bitterly complained, many drivers displayed poor lane discipline and 'showed a blithe disregard of common-sense overtaking rules' (quoted in *Daily Telegraph*, 1959: 1). Marples argued that drivers must learn and abide by the motorway regulations, while *The Times*'s (1959f) motoring correspondent argued that direction indicator lights and wing mirrors should be made compulsory fittings for vehicles using the motorway. In the accounts of a range of different commentators it is implied that mirrors and indicator lights, as well as written advice and codes, will become inseparable from the performance of new spatialities, ways of being, and subjectivities associated with the motorway (cf. Lynch, 1993). Spaces and movements behind and alongside one's vehicle gained a new importance, and were performed through the texts of commentators, the openings of mirrors, and the glances of drivers. As the BBC producer David Martin stated in a *Radio Times* article about his television documentary on M1, 'driving techniques must be altered. The motorist will have to realize that what is coming behind him is of more importance than what is in front of him' (Martin, 1959). Motoring correspondent John Eason Gibson made similar observations when writing on 'The pros and cons of M1' for *Country Life* in 1959:

> the motorway calls for a completely different type of skill. Because one's vision both forwards and to the rear through the mirror is greatly extended on the motorway, one can easily be faced with the task of judging the relative speeds of four cars in front and the same number visible in the mirror. This is far from being as easy as it might at first appear. (Eason Gibson, 1959: 1089)

Expert commentators believed that motorway driving necessitated an adjusted and heightened sense of speed and spatial awareness, new bodily capabilities, and differing strategies for dwelling in the spaces of the car and traversing the landscapes of the motorway, while a diverse range of technologies or 'things' were seen to be inseparable from the networks of skill, competence, trust, sensing, and dwelling that ensured the safe and efficient movement of vehicles and drivers (Urry, 2000).

Expertise and government

While the conduct and movements of motorway drivers surfaced in numerous debates, a diverse range of individuals and organizations were seen to have the necessary expertise to predict, measure and control the movements, conduct and experiences of vehicle drivers who used the M1. The relations these experts established and maintained with motorway drivers and vehicles were clearly quite diverse, but in this section and the next I examine the different ways in which a number of experts assembled and disassembled the figure of the motorway driver.[4]

One organization which attempted to sculpt a distinct position for itself in relation to motorway drivers and vehicles was the Automobile Association. The AA were vying with the RAC for press coverage of their services on the newly opened M1, which were designed to ensure that both drivers and vehicles performed in an orderly manner. A key task the Association bestowed on its team of elite motorway patrolmen was to record both unusual *and* everyday occurrences during the first few months of operation. The AA perceived their role as being to study, as well as effect and facilitate changes to, the performance of drivers *and* vehicles: studying the behaviour of motorists and vehicles; educating motorists about good driving and vehicle maintenance; and spotting and repairing vehicles that had broken down. The AA's 'Guide to the Motorway' operated as a more enabling and informative 'technology of government' than the Ministry of Transport's more proscriptive Motorway Code, but while these different educative and preventive technologies were designed to modify the embodied practices and movements of vehicle drivers – preventing poor conduct and facilitating good practice – many of the other activities of the AA were intended to visualize, register, and cope with the aftermath of errors or breakdowns in the performance of drivers and vehicles.

The first patrol to register a problem was often the AA's 'hovering eye': a de Havilland Rapide spotter aircraft that would radio the position of stationary vehicles to the 'Super Mobile Office' near Newport Pagnell (*Daily Express*, 1959: 5). As it was, and is, illegal to stop without due cause, immobility was automatically registered as problematic, a threat to order, and an AA patrolman would be despatched in a car or van to resolve the issue. When he reached the stranded vehicle, the AA patrolmen would attempt to identify and localize the failings of this mobile assemblage – attributing causes and blame to such purified things as drivers, vehicles, and tyres – but as sociologists have argued, such attributions and localizations often prove to be too simplistic (Latour, 1992; Michael, 2000; Lupton, 1999; Katz, 1999). To journalists, politicians and the AA, punctures, overheating, and cars running out of petrol and oil provided evidence of poor driving or lack of maintenance by the public; but such failures can be seen to emerge as a result of the complex relations and 'tight coupling' weaving together drivers, manufacturers, mechanics, vehicles and policy makers across diverse spaces and times (Perrow, 1999: 8). When a tyre bursts at high speed, the driver, a vehicle component, the vehicle's manufacturer, a mechanic, the weather, or highway engineers might all be blamed in different ways for this failing (Hawkins, 1986). In the case of serious incidents the police and judiciary often proceed to purify these assemblages and attribute blame, but in a country such as Britain even the laws relating to accidents and death on the roads acknowledge the tightly coupled relations, associations and processes of hybridization weaving together drivers, vehicles and the spaces of the road. Thus while killers convicted of murder or manslaughter may be blamed in isolation from their knives and guns, those who are convicted of causing death by dangerous driving are forever associated with their instruments of death. The injunction 'you should have driven your vehicle with care' supersedes 'thou shalt not kill'.

While AA patrolmen, police and the judiciary sought to govern the movements of drivers and vehicles in distinct ways, a series of other experts were constructed as experienced, skilful and exemplary role models for the average motorist. At the formal dinner at the Savoy Hotel marking the opening of the M1, the former Minister of Transport and Civil Aviation Harold Watkinson expressed hope that drivers would seek to improve their skills and take the Institute of Advanced Motorists' test, 'a passport to safe driving on motor roads' (Watkinson, 1959). But the ultimate figure who was seen to be both physically and mentally equipped to cope with the speeds and driving conditions on M1 was the British grand prix racing driver.[5] Who better, then, to cast an expert opinion on the performance of the M1? On 8 November 1959, Ferrari's 27-year-old racing driver Tony Brooks wrote a critical review of the M1 for *The Observer* newspaper, comparing the performance of the motorway and its drivers and vehicles with that of the latest motor roads in America and Europe (Brooks, 1959). Brooks was constructed by the newspaper's editors as the ideal figure to write about the motorway; an expert driver with a high performance car and superb reactions (which had been scientifically verified on a British School of Motoring reaction test machine). He and his Aston Martin set off from Marble Arch, and the frustrations and exertions of the slow journey through North London are suggested by his tally of over 100 gear changes and remarks on the endless use of brake and accelerator pedals. The labour of driving leads Brooks to highlight, divide out and localize specific actions in the car and events on the road, but when he reaches the motorway the car, its controls, other vehicles, other drivers and the spaces of the road are soon gathered and placed into his descriptions of a collective performance, which emerges from the complex relations and encounters weaving together and through these spaces and things:

> At first everything was wrong: an L-driver teetering along uncertainly in the middle of the road, a van broadside on and reversing on a feed-off, many cars sitting complacently astride the lanes. But then we all seemed to settle down . . .
> The three smooth-surfaced lanes, good standard of driving by every-one (lorry drivers in particular), the good conditions and the effortless cruising of the Aston Martin were hurrying us along. (Brooks, 1959: 5)

Brooks' description of his drive up the motorway highlights the complex associations weaving together the endlessly purified figures of the driver, vehicle and motorway in the hybrid networks and performances associated with motorway driving (Latour, 1993). Different materials, texts and atmospheres become incorporated into the spaces of the driving-subject, from signs, trees, and service areas, to the rain, light conditions and dazzle which troubled Brooks on his return journey to London, and the fog and ice which he feared may turn the motorway into a death-trap (Brooks, 1959). These presences may be all-too-familiar to many drivers, but they are often absent from the accounts of sociologists, and in the next section I focus more specifically on these broader spaces of the road as they are performed through and arranged around the figure of the motorway vehicle driver.

Spaces of the motorway

The engineers, landscape architects and government committees that were involved in designing different aspects of the M1 arranged (or 'placed') their designs and constructions around the expected movements and capabilities of drivers and vehicles, while the spaces of the motorway became incorporated into the subjectivities of auto-mobilized assemblages in distinct yet partial ways. Government committees and civil servants established numerous design standards, while the government's Advisory Committee on the Landscape Treatment of Trunk Roads ensured that the motorway's designers, Sir Owen Williams and Partners, planted trees and shrubs that were appropriate for a high speed motorway (Merriman, 2003, 2006, forthcoming).[6] The debates around this latter issue proved particularly lengthy.

Different species of plants were woven into socio-natural-technical networks with designers, engineers, tarmac, motorway drivers and a whole host of other things in distinct ways (Latour, 1993). While Sir Owen Williams and Partners had included colourful species of vegetation in their original planting schedules, the Landscape Advisory Committee criticized their plans for the inclusion of 'exotic' species that were too complicated, fussy, colourful and detailed to be experienced by drivers in the desired manner. The Committee suggested that detailed plants of a semi-urban character would distract the attention of motorway drivers and result in accidents. One Committee member, Sir Eric Savill, stated: 'a fast motorway is not a place for the encouragement of interest in flowering shrubs. "Eyes on the road" should be the motto!' (Letter 6/2/58, The National Archives, Kew PRO MT 121/78).[7] It was argued that the design and planting of the motorway should enliven drivers – keeping them awake, guiding their attention, screening certain views, but not distracting their attention for long periods. Vegetation emerges as a key element in governing the experiences and movements of vehicle drivers, and different shapes, silhouettes, textures, colours, and arrangements of plants were predicted to have either beneficial or detrimental physical and psychological effects on motorway drivers (Colvin, 1959; Crowe, 1960).[8]

The construction of this new and largely experimental motorway was of great interest to scientists at the government's Road Research Laboratory. Engineers investigated the merits of the different materials and construction techniques used to build the motorway, as well as examining the movements of

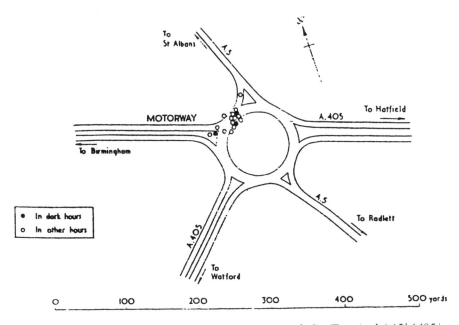

Figure 3: *'Approximate position of accidents at Park St. Terminal (A5/A405) in twelve months ending Oct. 31, 1960'. Line drawing in* Traffic, Engineering and Control, *Volume 3, July 1961, p. 179. Reproduced by permission of The Hemming Group.*

the motorway itself – detecting problems just days after the opening, including the deterioration of large sections of grassed hard shoulder (*The Times*, 1959e; see TNA PRO DSIR 12/152). The Road Research Laboratory set up three automatic traffic counters to register and quantify the presence of drivers, and they soon became concerned with the irregular movements of drivers and vehicles involved in accidents and breakdowns – whose presence, absence and trajectories generated ideas, conversations, and texts relating to the effectiveness (or otherwise) of experimental crash barriers, fog warning signs, anti-dazzle fences, speed limits, and propaganda distributed at different times. The figure of the motorway vehicle driver was frequently reduced to a statistic and then quantified or mapped. In one investigation, the occurrence of a series of accidents, and their location on a map of a motorway junction (Figure 3), was seen to highlight the need for a 'reduce speed now' sign that may govern or affect the relationship drivers had with them-selves, their vehicle, and the spaces of the motorway – aiming to prevent similar accidents by impressing on vehicle drivers the need to slow *their* speed from that point on (Adams, 1961).

In other cases Road Research Laboratory scientists attempted to investigate more specific events and the movements of individual vehicle drivers – attempting to attribute or distribute causes and blame and assess the role played by a driver, vehicle, or the spaces of the motorway in a single, serious accident. This was the case with the Laboratory's investigation into the cause of a crash on the evening of 3 June 1960, in which Mrs Valerie Hopkins – the driver of a car containing her husband and two children – was killed. At the inquest into Valerie's death, her husband had suggested that their car overturned after she swerved to avoid what they thought was 'a furniture lorry with no lights' parked under a bridge, but the police hadn't managed to trace the mystery vehicle (*Daily Express*, 1960: 13). Mr Hopkins expressed some doubt as to whether it had actually existed, and this was confirmed by the evidence of a lorry driver who witnessed the incident and attested to the existence of a shadowy 'phantom menace' which he and his colleagues frequently observed under the bridges (*Daily Express*, 1960: 13). With the absence or disappearance of the lorry, journalists and other commentators began to attribute blame to Sir Owen Williams' bridges, whose unguarded supports and plinths on the central reservation had already been implicated in a number of fatal accidents (Adams, 1961; Smith, 1961; Baker, 1961). Politicians picked up the story and asked the Minister of Transport whether alterations would need to be made to the bridges (*Parliamentary Debates*, 1960), and the Road Research Laboratory were instructed to investigate the cause of the shadows and the safety of the bridges. Laboratory scientist V. J. Jehu (1960) prepared a report on the 'Phantoms on the M1 motorway', in which he attempted to account for the Hopkins' irregular movements and experiences, and identify the causes and apportion blame. While the press described the presence of mysterious shadows, which appeared to disturb the orderly spaces of the motorway, Jehu set out to explain away these disordering ghostly presences by providing a scientific explanation of the visual effects drivers had experienced. Jehu's investigations were inconclusive, but he did argue that the bridges (and hence the engineers) were not to blame and that if the headlights of the Hopkins' Ford Popular had been at full beam then the edge of the road would have been clearly visible, and the illusion unlikely (Jehu, 1960).

While one may trace a broad range of spaces, forces and practices of resistance through which the hybridized motorway driver emerged, acted and moved, this figure was not simply assembled as a *driver*. As civil servants, advertisers and numerous companies recognized, drivers, vehicles and passengers required rest and refuelling; stopping at specially designed service areas to go to the toilet, 'refuel' with petrol, oil, water, tea or sandwiches, and rest their bodies and vehicles. These were spaces where numerous experts and campaigners sought to govern the consumptive practices of drivers, passengers and vehicles. The Ministry of Transport scrutinized the prices, facilities, and range of petrols available. Operators devised specific services for different types of consumer, while motorists themselves experienced, dwelled in, and moved through these spaces in distinct ways (Merriman, 2001). While many food critics, cultural commentators and members of the public soon expressed a dislike of the food and surroundings associated with service areas, these sites became integral to the social lives and identities of a whole 'generation of teenagers who did not know there was anything special about being young but forsook the coffee bars of Soho to spend Saturday night "doing a ton" on this long straight road' (Greaves, 1985: 8). Newport Pagnell service area emerged as an exciting 'place of pilgrimage for teenagers hoping for instant glamour' (Greaves, 1985: 8), with Cona coffee, fresh ice cream, and plastic vinyl seats, as well as motorbikes, cars and other teenagers, becoming bound into the subjectivities and identities of teenagers-on-a-night-out. But while coffee, ice cream and petrol seemed like harmless substances for vehicles and drivers to consume in regularized or accepted ways, alcohol emerged as a fluid whose presence and circulations, it was argued, could disrupt the orderly movements of vehicles and drivers. When Motorway Services Limited applied to magistrates for a license to serve drinks in the restaurant at Newport Pagnell service area, the proposals were challenged and defeated by a broad array of public bodies, organizations and concerned individuals, includ-ing: the police, two local breweries, the local congregational church, the Tem-perance Council of the Christian Churches, the Methodist Circuit, the Baptist Union, the National British Women's Total Abstinence Union, lorry drivers, and over 2000 local petitioners (*The Times*, 1960). These protests served as one of a number of attempts by a range of experts and authoritative figures to govern the conduct, experiences, consumption practices, and movements of the motor-way vehicle driver in the spaces of the motorway. Vehicle drivers *should* consume high-performance accessories, petrol and the Motorway Code, but *not* alcohol, picnics on verges, or the spectacle of 'exotic' roadside vegetation.

Conclusions

> Practices of government rely on an array of more or less formalized and more or less specialized technical devices from car seat-belts and driving codes to dietary regimes . . . [T]o analyse the conduct of political and economic life without considering the importance of material and immaterial devices and artefacts is simply to miss half the picture. (Barry, 2001: 5–10)

In this chapter I have explored how a range of technological devices – from high performance tyres to articles on good driving – were deployed or distributed by experts in an attempt to assemble and govern the movements and subjectivities of the motorway vehicle driver; a figure whose performances, capabilities, desires, movements and very being cannot be explained or understood by attempting to separate it into particular components. While academics have explored the more durable or familiar practices and relations of the hyphenated car-driver, I have argued that many other 'things' became bound into the con-tingent and momentary orderings and spacings of the driving subject. Legisla-tive codes, roadside trees, wing mirrors, cups of tea, and fog served as important elements in the relational performance of motorway driving, enabling politi-cians, car manufacturers, 'the weather' and drivers to influence or shape the movements of vehicle drivers. Experts and others frequently attempt to under-stand the performances and movements of the motorway driver by purifying, localizing and identifying asymmetries in the different movements and elements which make up the tightly coupled vehicle driver (Latour, 1993; Perrow, 1999). Blame is distributed and shifted, fixed or localized, by different authorities, but during the often mundane and everyday movements and practices of motorway driving, the driver, vehicle and spaces of the road became woven together in contingent, momentary and repetitive ways which are overlooked by experts. The spaces of the vehicle and road are inhabited and embodied by the motorway driver in particular ways, becoming incorporated into their subjectivities and very being. During these moments of apparent calm and order drivers may not reflect upon their actions as they simply drive, giving rise to a sense of detachment, apathy, forgetting, and experiences which academics have associated with 'placelessness' (Relph, 1976) or 'non-places' (Augé, 1995). As I have suggested elsewhere, these experiences of detachment, solitariness, boredom or dislocation – which are often associated with roads, shopping centres or airports – are not limited to these so-called non-places (Merriman, 2004). These experiences are bound up with the dynamic, performative construction or 'placing' of even the most familiar and seemingly located places. Until, of course, something goes wrong, unexpected orderings occur, or the driver or passenger reflects on their movements and being (Latour, 1993; Dant, 2004). A child spills something on the backseat. A driver gets caught in a tailback. A crash occurs. In these instances the constituent elements in these assemblages – the soiled seat, blocked road or offending vehicle, driver or child – may be purified, divided, blamed, or constructed as an 'other' place or abject body.

Acknowledgements

I would like to thank the editors and anonymous referees of the present collection for their guidance. Participants at the Automobility Conference in Keele, Alternative Mobility Futures Conference in Lancaster, and the ESRC Mobile Network Seminar in Bristol provided invaluable comments, as did seminar audiences in geography departments at the universities of Bristol, Hull and Reading.

Notes

1 Tim Dant prefers the term assemblage for his descriptions of the 'driver-car', suggesting that 'hybrid' and 'cyborg' imply permanent associations and mixings of things and that 'human subjectivity is in no sense constituted by getting into a car; it is a temporary assemblage within which the human remains complete in his or her self' (Dant, 2004: 62). Dant appears to operate with a rather narrow conception of hybrids and cyborgs, and a somewhat essentialist construction of subjectivity that overlooks the multiple, partial and ongoing shaping of human subjectivity in relation to a variety of things in different spaces and times.

2 In his writings and interviews Foucault uses a number of phrases somewhat interchangeably, including technologies of the self, techniques of the self, and practices of the self (see Foucault, 1988; McNay, 1994). More recently, sociologists such as Nikolas Rose have introduced terms such as 'technologies of government' (Miller and Rose, 1990: 8) and 'technologies of subjectification'

(Rose, 1996: 186). In this chapter I limit myself to a discussion of 'technologies of government' and their translation through 'technologies of the self'.

3 While discussions of motorway driving in the late 1950s tend to construct the motorway driver as a masculine figure, I have not encountered any articles from the period which addressed issues of gender and motorway driving *per se*, or suggested any differences in the performances of men and women on the motorway.

4 Of course, experts are themselves hybrid figures who are assembled as individuals with the necessary capabilities, tools, vehicles, uniforms, and bodies to govern others; while the effects of power and authority associated with such individuals emerged from their 'work' within broader political, cultural, scientific, and legal networks.

5 In the late 1950s Stirling Moss had become a household name and the successes of British racing drivers were widely praised, but at the opening of M1 Marples argued that even expert drivers must drive with care on the new motorway: 'There must be skill and judgement and discipline. Skill alone is not enough at high speed' (quoted in *The Guardian*, 1959). To illustrate the point, Marples referred to the tragic death of Britain's first ever motor-racing world champion, Mike Hawthorn, who crashed his Jaguar on the Guildford Bypass in January 1959, just three months after winning the 1958 Drivers' World Championship with Ferrari (*The Times*, 1959d).

6 The Advisory Committee on the Landscape Treatment of Trunk Roads formed in April 1956, and were commonly referred to as the Landscape Advisory Committee (see Merriman, 2001, 2006, forthcoming).

7 Hereafter, I refer to files in The National Archives (formerly the Public Record Office), Kew, using the prefix TNA PRO followed by the file reference.

8 Civil servants also considered the provision of anti-dazzle planting on the central reservation, which the Landscape Advisory Committee felt was preferable to metal screens. In the early 1960s experiments were conducted using hessian screens which were placed along a six mile stretch of the M1 to simulate different planting patterns (see Advisory Committee on the Landscape Treatment of Trunk Roads, 'Anti-dazzle planting on motorways', LT/243, TNA PRO MT 121/150).

References

AA [Automobile Association] (1959) 'Guide to the motorway' Motorways File, Automobile Association Archives, Basingstoke.
Adams, W. F. (1961) 'Safety aspects of motorway design' *Traffic Engineering and Control*, 3: 178–181.
Augé, M. (1995) *Non-Places*. London: Verso.
The Autocar (1959) 'A series of posters . . .' *The Autocar*, 111, 20 November: 671.
Baker, J. F. A. (1961) 'Discussion on the London-Birmingham motorway' *Proceedings of the Institution of Civil Engineers*, 19(May–August): 105–111.
Barry, A. (2001) *Political Machines*. London: Athlone.
Brooks, T. (1959) 'The hazards of M1' *The Observer*, 8 November: 5.
Chronicle and Echo (1958) 'Motorway code' *Chronicle and Echo*, 26 November.
Colvin, B. (1959) 'The London-Birmingham motorway: a new look at the English landscape' *The Geographical Magazine*, 32: 239–246.
Crowe, S. (1960) *The Landscape of Roads*. London: The Architectural Press.
Daily Express (1959) 'The hovering eye above the M1' *Daily Express*, 20 October: 5.
Daily Express (1960) 'The phantom of the M1' *Daily Express*, 21 June: 13.
Daily Telegraph (1959) '100 breakdowns on first motorway day – Mr. Marples "frightened" by early user' *Daily Telegraph*, 3 November: 1.
Dant, T. (2004) 'The driver-car' *Theory, Culture, and Society*, 21(4–5): 61–79.
Eason Gibson, J. (1959) 'The pros and cons of M1' *Country Life*, 3 December: 1089.
Ellis, H. F. (1959) 'M1 for murder' *Punch*, 28 October: 362–363.

Foucault, M. (1988) 'Technologies of the self' in L. H. Martin, H. Gutman and P. H. Hutton (eds) *Technologies of the Self: A Seminar with Michel Foucault.* London: Tavistock.

Foucault, M. (1991a) *Discipline and Punish.* Harmondsworth: Penguin.

Foucault, M. (1991b) 'Governmentality' in G. Burchell, C. Gordon and P. Miller (eds) *The Foucault Effect: Studies in Governmentality.* London: Harvester Wheatsheaf.

Giddens, A. (1990) *The Consequences of Modernity.* Cambridge: Polity Press.

Greaves, S. (1985) 'Motorway nights with the stars' *The Times,* 14 August: 8.

The Guardian (1959) 'Mr Marples appalled by motorway speeds' *The Guardian,* 3 November.

Hawkins, R. (1986) 'A road not taken: sociology and the neglect of the automobile' *California Sociologist,* 8: 61–79.

Jehu, V. J. (1960) 'Phantoms on the M1 motorway' (DSIR/RRL Research note no. RN/3860/VJJ, October 1960, BRL263), The National Archives, Kew, PRO DSIR 12/200.

Katz, J. (1999) *How Emotions Work.* London: The University of Chicago Press.

Latour, B. (1992) 'Where are the missing masses? The sociology of a few mundane artefacts' in W. E. Bijker and J. Law (eds) *Shaping Technology, Building Society: Studies in Sociotechnical Change.* London: MIT Press.

Latour, B. (1993) *We Have Never Been Modern.* Hemel Hempstead: Harvester Wheatsheaf.

Lupton, D. (1999) 'Monsters in metal cocoons: "road rage" and cyborg bodies' *Body and Society,* 5: 57–72.

Lynch, M. (1993) *Scientific Practice and Ordinary Action.* Cambridge: Cambridge University Press.

McNay, L. (1994) *Foucault: A Critical Introduction.* New York: Continuum.

Martin, D. (1959) 'Britain's first motorway' *Radio Times,* 23 October.

Mennem, P. (1959) 'Motorway 1 opens – and Mr. Marples says: "I was appalled"' *Daily Mirror,* 3 November: 5.

Merriman, P. (2001) *M1: A Cultural Geography of an English Motorway, 1946–1965.* Unpublished Ph.D. thesis. University of Nottingham.

Merriman, P. (2003) '"A power for good or evil": Geographies of the M1 in late-fifties Britain' in D. Gilbert, D. Matless and B. Short (eds) *Geographies of British Modernity.* Oxford: Blackwell.

Merriman, P. (2004) 'Driving places: Marc Augé, non-places and the geographies of England's M1 motorway' *Theory, Culture, and Society,* 21(4–5): 145–167.

Merriman, P. (2005) 'Materiality, subjectification, and government: the geographies of Britain's Motorway Code' *Environment and Planning D: Society and Space,* 23: 235–250.

Merriman, P. (2006) '"A new look at the English landscape": Landscape architecture, movement and the aesthetics of motorways in early post-war Britain' *Cultural Geographies,* 13: 78–105.

Merriman, P. (forthcoming) *Driving Spaces.* Oxford: Blackwell Publishing.

Michael, M. (2000) *Reconnecting Culture, Technology and Nature.* London: Routledge.

Miller, P. and Rose, N. (1990) 'Governing economic life' *Economy and Society,* 19: 1–31.

Ministry of Transport and Civil Aviation and the Central Office of Information [MOTCA and COI] (1958) *The Motorway Code.* London: HMSO.

Ministry of Transport and Civil Aviation and the Central Office of Information [MOTCA and COI] (1959) *The Highway Code Including Motorway Rules.* London: HMSO.

The Motor (1959) 'Topical technics: an engineering notebook by J.L.' *The Motor,* 116(9 September): 135.

Parliamentary Debates, House of Commons (1958) 'Motorways (traffic regulations)' *Parliamentary Debates, House of Commons,* 592, 23 July, oral answers: 402–405.

Parliamentary Debates, House of Commons (1960) 'M.1 (bridges)' *Parliamentary Debates, House of Commons,* 626, 6 July, written answers: 39.

Perrow, C. (1999) *Normal Accidents: Living With High-Risk Technologies.* Princeton, NJ: Princeton University Press.

Relph, E. (1976) *Place and Placelessness.* London: Pion.

Rose, N. (1996) *Inventing Our Selves.* Cambridge: Cambridge University Press.

Rose, N. (1999) *Powers of Freedom.* Cambridge: Cambridge University Press.

Sheller, M. and J. Urry (2000) 'The City and the Car' *International Journal of Urban and Regional Research,* 24: 727–757.

Smith, J. G. (1961) 'Discussion on the London-Birmingham motorway' *Proceedings of the Institution of Civil Engineers*, 19(May–August): 77–78.

The Times (1958) 'Motorway code guidance' *The Times*, 26 November: 13.

The Times (1959a) 'Industrial films' *The Times*, 14 December: 14.

The Times (1959b) 'India Tyres advert' *The Times*, 3 November: 5.

The Times (1959c) 'Automotive Products Associated Limited advert' *The Times*, 2 November: 9.

The Times (1959d) 'Mr. M. Hawthorn killed' *The Times*, 23 January: 10.

The Times (1959e) 'Motorway "hard shoulder" slips' *The Times*, 4 November: 9.

The Times (1959f) 'Overtaking technique the key for drivers' *The Times*, 10 November: 4.

The Times (1960) 'Magistrates reject plea for drinks at M1 restaurant' *The Times*, 11 February: 6.

Urry, J. (2000) *Sociology Beyond Societies*. London: Routledge.

Urry, J. (2003) *Global Complexity*. Cambridge: Polity.

Watkinson, H. (1959) 'Printed version of speech given at the Savoy Hotel by Mr Harold Watkinson, Minister of Defence and Former Minister of Transport, 2 November 1959' unpublished document 330A, Motorways File, Automobile Association Archives, Basingstoke.

Quantifying automobility: speed, 'Zero Tolerance' and democracy

Per-Anders Forstorp

Vision Zero is conceived from the ethical base that it can never be acceptable that people are killed or seriously injured when moving within the road transport system. It centres on an explicit goal, and develops into a highly pragmatic and sci-entifically-based strategy which challenges the traditional approach to road safety. (Vision Zero[1])

The aim of analysing 'automobility' is to look beyond the car itself as an eco-nomic and technological object, towards the basic socio-cultural notions of time, space, and desire which make automotive culture and automobile subjects possible. The notions of time, space, and desire condition automobilities and its subjects and are as important for mobility as are its tangible artefacts and phys-ical infrastructures, its 'scapes' and 'flows' (Urry, 2000). Automobility is a highly paradoxical phenomenon, associated with multiple subjects and desires, eg, effi-ciency, independence, and autonomous mobility (Rajan, this volume; Bonham, this volume). These paradoxical desires, subjects and objects converge in con-crete socio-spatial junctions. These socio-spatial encounters are constrained in many ways, for instance by the management of individuals and vehicles through rules for coordinating and educating the various mobile bodies. The vast market for mobility includes not only the development of artefacts and infrastructures but also a simultaneous cultivation of desires for efficiency, enjoyment, freedom, independence, speed and (auto-)mobility. This market is always constrained, moralized and regulated for various purposes, ranging from governance and citizen surveillance to proactive measures towards public health and environ-ment. A main purpose for making constraints and regulations concerning auto-mobility is to consolidate a functional socio-spatial system for ease of movement and mobility and to avoid serious malfunctions and unintended consequences such as injuries and deaths among individuals and groups of system users. Auto-mobility is an object of ideological work and politicization working through the control of behaviour (Bonham, this volume; Merriman, this volume) and by means of prophylactic anticipation (see below). As an integral part of modern societies, a politics of automobility aims at enabling automotive culture but strives also to improve public health, foster technologically competent citizens – 'automobile selves', and to govern the socio-technical body politic through various means and measures in terms of access, limits, speed, resources, infra-structures, sanctions, etc.

In this chapter, I will focus on the politicization and ideological work aiming at constraining, governing and managing citizens in connection with the Swedish Road Traffic Safety campaign, Vision Zero. This plan for managing road safety was initiated in 1997 and has since been the official Swedish policy, also being disseminated by authorities in other countries such as Austria, Australia, Germany, Ireland and Switzerland. The long-term goal of Vision Zero is that no one will be killed or seriously injured within the (Swedish) road transport system. The vision provides an image of a desirable future where nobody is 'punished' for having made simple mistakes in traffic. The main prin-ciples of Vision Zero are the following:

• *human fallibility* – accidents cannot entirely be eliminated; the traffic system has to adapt to the users and take better account of the needs and mistakes they make;
• *the anatomy of the human body* – a safe road traffic system can alleviate the consequences of inevitable accidents; the basic scientific parameter in the design of road traffic system is the limits of the human body and its vulner-ability, which are taken as standards for the design of systems;
• *reduction of speed* – the most important regulating factor for a safe road traffic system is speed.

The quote in the header, which is taken from this campaign, indicates the characteristic combination in Vision Zero of rational strategies for managing traffic safety with the ethical unacceptability of allowing continuous damages to humans resulting from their exposure to the road transport system. Vision Zero is thus an example of an ideology that is made up of a combination of sci-entific rationality with ethical beliefs. Quantitative notions such as 'zero', 'no-one', 'eliminating the risk', 'vehicle speed', along with various other measures of distributive fairness, are very explicit in the campaign. The dominating rhetorical trope in the campaign is the visionary long-term goal of 'zero' which is operationalized, *hic et nunc*, into concrete strategies that are 'highly pragmatic and scientifically-based' and which, during the first decade following the Road Traffic Safety Bill of 1997, are assumed 'to reduce the number of fatal-ities by a quarter to one third'. Grand utopianism is mixed with everyday prag-matism and managerial accountability. Vision Zero is based on a critique of received statistical determinism and its implicit view on 'fatalities' as calculable and therefore also 'acceptable'. Vision Zero polemically designates death and serious injuries as 'punishments' by the road traffic system against the individ-uals who act fallibly. In contrast to the received and fateful interpretation of statistics, Vision Zero is introduced as an alternative paradigm for the interpretation of numbers, implemented as a strategy for road traffic safety based on a new sense for quantification, a new awareness of the role of numbers and its use in social and scientific political reforms, and, in particular, a return to an atmosphere of idealistic utopianism characteristically envisioned in the notion of Vision Zero. Both in this retrospective critique of statistical determinism and in these prospective visions of a desirable future consisting of risk-free socio-spatial practices, the campaign is characterized by 'quantifrenia' (Porter, 1996), an obsession with numbers, and a desire for both statistical precision in logical terms and a visionary utopianism of a more romantic numeric character.

Automobility will be understood as a socio-technical institution and 'as a product and producer of modernity' (Rajan, this volume, ch. 7).[2] In the subsequent analysis, special attention will be paid to the forms and functions of the quantitative dimensions represented in the campaign. These quantitative dimensions include the following numerical *and* political notions: speed, 'zero tolerance', democracy. The analysis is made in order to outline the different dimensions for quantification and regulation at work in a politics of automobility. I will argue that the return of idealism and visionary utopianism in this campaign takes place in the context of the dominating contemporary rationality of planning, characteristic of what has been called 'the managerial state' (Clarke and Newman, 1997). In this process of domestication and planning, quantification plays a crucial role. The analytic perspectives will be inspired by critical discourse analysis, cultural studies of quantification, and Foucauldian 'governmentality' studies.

Governing by numbers and quantification rhetoric in the culture of modernist planning

The uses of quantification and numeracy in politics and planning have been linked, by various social theorists such as Weber and Foucault, to the particular development of modernity in Western culture. Foucault, in particular, has highlighted the availability of quantitative tools and numerical resources in governance for the practical regulation of populations and for the construction of the body of regulation *per se*, ie, both the population as a body and the concrete human being as a body, as well as for the purposes of moral and ideological normalization in these social constructs (Foucault, 1991; Barry *et al.*, 1996; Dean and Hindess, 1998). The logics of numeracy in modernist planning finds a very apt contemporary example in the planning and performance of the various socio-spatial practices included in the management and performance of road traffic and automobility (Flyvbjerg, 1998; Bonham, this volume). In this chapter, data will be taken from the socio-cultural context of the Scandinavian welfare state, a context which, in many respects, provides an ideal-typical setting for the implementations of quantification on a population basis, given its strong culture of literacy and numeracy such as statistics and epidemiology applied on a comparatively limited population body.

In his historical study of the pursuit for objectivity in science and public life, *Trust in Numbers*, Theodore M. Porter (1995) regards numbers as social technologies and as strategies of communication that are utilized by various social actors as means for planning and prediction (1995: 43–49). '[Q]uantification', he argues, can be seen 'as a technology of distance' (1995: ix) and as 'a way of making decisions without seeming to decide' (1995: 8). The power of numbers becomes empowered with a sense of super-individual and disinterested objectivity which is, he claims, typical of modernity. In the vein of previous theorists of numeracy such as Foucault (1991), Hacking (1990), and Rose (1990), Porter highlights the normative aspects of 'adequate measurement' (Porter, 1995: 28), and points towards the governing aspects of numbers in order to discipline 'people as well as [finding] standardizing instruments and processes' (1995: 28). Quantitative measurement, he claims, is closely linked to governance:

> Numbers create and can be compared with norms, which are among the gentlest and yet most pervasive forms for power in modern democracies. (1995: 45)

Public management takes place largely through the use of 'measurement, counting, and calculation', which counts among 'the most credible strategies for rendering nature or society objective. It has enjoyed widespread and growing authority in Europe and America for about two centuries' (1995: 74). Quantification is an important technology of measurement in the operations of risk in late modern societies whereby the 'calculative rationality' (Dean, 1999) in the form of statistics produces 'truths' about risks and thereby contributes in the activity of normalization (Lupton, 1999).

The scientific ideal of objectivity inherent in repertoires of quantification can therefore be said to be based on interpretation, ie, thinking of numbers as vehicles for prognosis and 'truth' can only be done with some ideological work. The social use of numbers is also political in a more straightforward way. With reference to political theorist Harold Lasswell, Porter claims that the linkages between democracy and numbers are most typical for the American political system, a context where the actors and agencies made 'greater use of quantified, objective knowledge precisely because of its democratic character' (Porter, 1995: 76). In this sense, the Scandinavian welfare states are related to the uses of numbers as measures and standards of fair distribution which was practised in the US, and also related to its tendencies towards the obsession with 'quantifrenia that prevails in the bureaucratic management' (1995: 76). According to Porter, the language of quantification that dominates economy, administration and management, is also the contemporary *lingua franca* in the European Union, where it is even more important for federal purposes than spoken English in 'the European campaign to create a unified business and administrative environment. It aims to supplant local cultures with systematic and rational methods' (1995: 77).

Following Foucault's critical understanding of quantification, Porter notes that numbers are used as an agency for governing people and populations. Numbers are associated with relatively objective entities which in turn tends to objectify their prey: 'Numbers turn people into objects to be manipulated. Where power is not exercised blatantly, it acts instead secretly, insidiously' (1995: 77), for instance through the use of numbers and 'the authority of statistical and behavioural norms, through which an oppressive language of normality and abnormality is created' (1995: 77).

Numbers, according to Foucault, Porter, and others working in the tradition of 'governmentality' studies, are therefore understood not as a neutral body of disinterested knowledge available for social reforms of a scientific character, as is repeatedly claimed in so many accounts advocating modernist planning and politics. By contrast, following the critical tradition, we could say that epidemiology, statistics and others forms of quantification that are used to motivate and sustain social reforms can be understood as discursive and ideological formations which include not only numerical measurements and its inevitable interpretations, but also political ideologies and an imperative of planning. The technologies of quantification are important, effective and persuasive tools for governance, working by means of a quasi-transparent liberal policy of making knowledge available. Additionally, these technologies are used in practices which are explicitly ideological and policy-oriented, and therefore in some sense they also become ideologically 'contaminated' and de-objectified by these events. Quantification is therefore in several important respects ideological, something that methodologically sophisticated statisticians are very well aware of, but something that may evade its uses in social reforms and public information campaigns. A campaign for road traffic safety is perhaps not the most apt context for raising questions concerning the subtleties of statistical interpretation and the limits of scientific certainty.

One important implication of quantification practices as discursive and ideological formations is that the individual person is systematically omitted in a particular way. The individual becomes a 'dividual', to quote Deleuze (1992), by means of forms of calculation executed on bodies of population. The calculation is based on an ethics of personal renunciation and de-personalization, transforming the individual to a number, a dividend or a 'dividual'. Given that quantification is a form of representation that claims currency from its character of being explicit, transparent and visible, the inherent morality and important omissions can also be sought for elsewhere. Following historians of intellectual culture, Lorraine Daston and Peter Galison (1992), Porter claims 'that objectivity in its various meanings is characterized rather by what it omits than by any positive characteristics of its own' (Porter, 1995: 85). In the rhetorical uses of numbers one should in particular, he claims, search for the absences and the missing Other rather than approaching (only) what is explicit and visible. This absence is the unique *in*dividual, the interested and located individual, which is totally contrasted to the idealistic statistical anonymity of numbers where individuals are generalized, normalized or omitted.

Porter identifies what he calls both the virtues and vices of quantification:

> The remarkable ability of numbers and calculations to defy disciplinary and even national boundaries and link academic to political discourse owes much to this ability to bypass deep issues. In intellectual exchange, as in properly economic transactions, numbers are the medium through which dissimilar desires, needs, and expectations are somehow made commensurable. (1995: 86)

These 'remarkable abilit[ies]' of quantification to establish 'shared images' across cultural divides on the one hand explains its formidable success as technologies of reforms, but, on the other hand, also includes processes of equalization and formulation of extreme cases (see below), that tend to defy and hide the various complications. The often successful formula of implementing quantification in economy, administration and management is interdependent with its 'remarkable ability' of hiding complications and details, and of omitting the individuals.

The analysis initiated by Foucault and continued by Porter and others on the culture of numbers and quantification, focuses on some examples of what is called 'technologies of trust', ie, accounting and actuarial systems, and engineering practices such as traffic safety measures linked to technocracy and economics (Porter, 1995; Lupton, 1999; Baker and Simon, 2002). One such technology of trust is the widespread business of risk analysis in medical and technological contexts (Heimer, 2002; Ewald, 2002). Lindsay Prior (2000), in a similar approach, critically analyses the uses of quantification in risk analysis by showing that the notion of risk, derived from statistical and epidemiological sources, is something that belongs to populations and not to individuals (see Green, 1997). The practical uses of risk analysis derived from such sources, on the other hand, exploit any possible links that can be made with individuals, a process in which the sophisticated methodological discussions are often systematically neglected. Priors' analysis shows that numerical calculations of risks, which are often the statistical base for the analysis of traffic safety, are most often used in order to assess and evaluate the health and performance of individuals, and that these risks are thus mistaken for individual risks when, as statistical probabilities, they rather 'belong' to populations.

Governing by numbers and quantification rhetorics are important aspects and tools in any form of numerical representation. Numbers never speak for themselves, although the transparency and self-evidential character of numbers are often taken for granted as an indisputable matter of fact. In particular, these tools are often used in public campaigns and planning measures that aim at cultivating, informing and governing the attitudes and behaviour of the public. This governance is concretized in various forms of allowances, prescriptions and prohibitions of which the governance of traffic and automobility provides a very clear example. Attitudes and behaviours are represented as favourable or non-favourable, legalized sanctions are made by the police, by other traffic users and by norms in the particular communities of risk and safety. Prophylactic anticipation and risk works through governing by numbers and quantification rhetoric.

Politics of automobility

At issue here are the two interdependent and paradoxical features of automobility understood, following Rajan (this volume), as 'one of the principal "technologies" of contemporary liberalism': being immensely flexible *and* wholly coercive in shaping spatial movements through institutions and practices. A politics of automobility takes place in between these extremes of mobilities and socialities in mobile societies, where the agents are constituted as hybrids of humans and other 'inhuman' components, exemplified by John Urry (2000: 14) in his 'manifesto for mobility' as 'material objects, including signs, machines, technologies, physical environments, animals, plants, and waste products'. Urry reaches beyond 'social' as identified with society towards a 'social' understood as mobility/networks/horizontal fluidities (2000: 3) and thereby aims 'to develop through appropriate metaphors a sociology which focuses upon movement, mobility and contingent ordering, rather than upon stasis, structure and social order (. . .) to examine the extent, range and diverse effects of the corporeal, imagined and virtual mobilities of people, for work, for pleasure, to escape torture, to sustain diasporas and so on' (2000: 15–16).

Mobilities occur in time and space through what Urry calls 'scapes' and 'flows'. 'Scapes' are more or less the infrastructures for mobilities, ie, 'the networks of machines, technologies, organizations, texts and actors that constitute various interconnected nodes along which the flows can be relayed' (2000: 35). 'Flows' are that which is mobilized and moved in time and space – humans, desires and risks – concretized in various socio-spatial practices such as driving a car, riding in a bus, bicycling, pedestrian motion, etc. According to Urry, 'transport' is not the more or less 'empty' transit between places. 'Thinking travel as *transport*', Bonham (this volume: ch. 4, emphasis in original) notes in her historical analysis, was 'a key innovation in urban circulation' taking place, in South Australian cities, basically in the post WWII-period. In contrast to transport as 'empty' transit, the transitory activity itself is emphasized by Urry as 'becoming the primary activity of existence; it is no longer a metaphor of progress when it characterizes how households generally are organized' (Urry, 2000: 50). Mobility rather than sociality is writ large in this manifesto as the prime form of social existence in late modern societies. An analysis of the politics of automobility has to take account of 'the interlocking dimensions of automobility' (2000: 57–58) including the manufactured object, the concepts, the patterns of consumption, the machinic complex, the environment, mobilities, subjects and cultures.

'The car's significance', Urry notes, 'is that it reconfigures civil society involving distinct ways of dwelling, travelling and socialising in and through, an automobilized time-space' (2000: 59). In the analysis of automobility, taking place in between the extremes of flexibility and coercion, it is especially important to study the governance and discipline in time-space dimensions, as well as the subject positions placing the actors, and how this can be linked to a theory of reconfiguration of the civil society.

In the politics of automobility various dimensions are quantified, eg, speed, epidemiology of accidents, statistics of risks, numerical rates of human body tolerance towards road traffic exposure, etc. The regulation of automobility as a safe system is geared towards various means and measures such as educating the users, improving the infrastructures and fostering of good behaviour, such as the taming of speed. In the politics of automobility, the various limits of mobility and automobility are approached as objects of identification and standardization. In this rationalizing process, several paradoxes are encountered. For instance, speed is associated not only with enjoyment, autonomy and freedom, but also with accidents, crime, sin, violence, and other 'major problems'. In modernist and rationalist planning, the politics of speed surfaces in legislation and campaigning, in the moralization of speeding, and in subjectification of idealized positions of automobile agents, with or without control of their mobile desires and responsibilities. Governing the politics of speed includes coping with subject's interpretations of times, spaces and desires, while simultaneously promoting speed through the development of safe automobiles, 'tolerant' infrastructures and 'forgiving' transport systems. It is important to note that both these interdependent features of the politics of automobile speed are inherent features of the modernist dreams, desiring both control and enjoyment.

American consumer advocate Ralph Nader in the 1960s critically highlighted some of these interlocking dimensions of automobility in his study of safety and speed in *Unsafe at Any Speed* (1965).[3] His criticism of the manufacturers' negligence of safety measures and his plea for the rights of consumers to negotiate quality in production were and still are very influential for several welfare campaigns in the realm of road traffic as well as for the development of production and design. The notions of the 'prolonged catastrophe' and 'the second collision' are concrete examples of the sustaining influence of Nader's seminal work. So also are his ideas about the standards of quality management that should be applied not only in the factories for automobile production, but also in assessing and evaluating road traffic performance and maintenance. He posits these norms in quality management terms, as 'zero accident frequency' and this can be regarded as a forerunner to the core ideas in Vision Zero, to which we will turn next.

Vision Zero: towards a 'fail-safe' mobile society

Vision Zero, as we have seen above, is a campaign for the management of the 'fail-safe' mobile society that has determined the official policy and planning for safety in road traffic in Sweden since the late 1990s. This campaign was launched in 1997 'as an entirely new way of looking at road safety' but, as we have seen, these thoughts coincided already in the work by Nader. Vision Zero was based on a set of claims that were presented as 'new'. One such claim of novelty was that in the campaign, the emphasis on road safety management should be transferred from the old version of blame allocation directed at the competence of the individual driver, to safety understood as the accomplishment of safe operations within the whole system. In this 'new' form of systemic road traffic safety management, the 'primary responsibility' is therefore with the system designer. So far, this systemic view could be seen as a paradigm for de-personalizing responsibility. But this is not the whole story. The systemic view of responsibility as the quality of an entire system and its design does not mean that the users of the system are free to act as they wish, nor that the responsibility for failures is located solely with the designer. Responsibility also lies with the users of the road traffic system and, in particular, in their conditions as users, understood as their abilities to comply with rules set by the system designers. Therefore the users are in fact acting competently only if they act on the specific command of the system designers, and are therefore as much responsible, if not even more, than they were in the old versions of individual blame allocation. The shift of responsibility in this novel version could therefore be said to be merely rhetorical. Malfunctions and unintended consequences can be attributed to any one of them, the users and the designers, but certainly the users are not exempted from blame.

Another change in the outlook on safety in Vision Zero is the development from the aim of 'trying to reduce the number of accidents' towards the more radical and 'doable' goal of 'eliminating the risk of chronic impairment caused by road accident'. The long-term goal of Vision Zero, we have learned in the header quote above, 'is that no one will be killed or seriously injured within the Swedish road transport system'.

The first claim towards change and novelty involves a representation of responsibility where, at a first glance, the system designers seem to be more responsible than the system users. On a second consideration, this novel distribution of responsibility leads to another interpretation: the system users are now more responsible than ever because their part of the deal is to act according to demands set by the designers. Problems and malfunctions can be attributed as errors in system design or as errors in the performance of the rules and standards set by the system design. The second claim towards change involves a representation of the interpretative strategies of statistics and numbers, and the kind of rationalities that can be used in order to cope with the representations of the potential unintended consequences of road traffic.

Vision Zero constitutes a concrete image of a desired future state of safety and the aim of the campaign is to make this vision into a 'shared image' and a disposition to good performance. This concrete image is a vision of the completely safe ('fail-safe') road traffic system, where accidents cannot be entirely avoided but where the unintended consequences of accidents do not lead to the deaths of humans, nor to serious injuries that impair them for life. Vision Zero aims to eliminate the risks of traffic, not avoiding accidents *per se*, which are allowed by and accepted by this campaign logic as aspects of human error, but avoiding those potentially leading to serious injury and death. Vision Zero invokes a notion of 'realism' in this understanding of the determined character of system use leading to accidents.

In this vision various understandings of 'realism' and 'idealism' are mixed. A 'realist' acceptance of the seeming inevitability of accidents is mixed with attitudes aiming at altering this 'realist' acceptance into a resistance against 'realism', an ethically motivated non-acceptance. 'Realism' is represented in the assertion that accidents do occur and this is implicitly a result of an experiential and statistical mindset that regards accidents as inevitable outcomes of human-system interaction. According to Vision Zero, accidents cannot be completely avoided and one should therefore not focus on trying to avoid them, since this is understood to be out of reach. What could and should be avoided, however, are the kinds and qualities of the accidents leading to deaths and serious disabling injuries. Accidents cannot be avoided, the argument goes, but the consequences of the accidents can be minimized and alleviated by various measures. The will to change the understanding of road traffic safety in this approach is explicitly identified as coping with consequences instead of erring human behaviour. What could and should be managed are not the events *per se*, but their consequences.

Vision Zero is represented not only as an idealistic vision of a desired future state of affairs, but also displayed as being based on a firm scientific foundation – 'a highly pragmatic and scientifically-based strategy'. Anatomy, statistics, epidemiology, mathematical optimization and economic theories of supply-and-demand, as well as use-and-benefit, are among the most important scientific paradigms in this regard that are mobilized as the pragmatic balance to the otherwise dominating atmosphere of idealism and wishful thinking. This scientific basis helps to define what counts – economically, ethically and medically – as non-acceptable loss of health in order to identify and define the limits for the 'violence' that generates such non-acceptable losses.

The main strategic principles of Vision Zero are the following (see above):

- The traffic system has to adapt to take better account of the needs, mistakes and vulnerabilities of road users (*human fallibility*)
- The level of violence that the human body can tolerate without being killed or seriously injured forms the basic parameter in the design of the road transport system (*the anatomy of the human body*)
- Vehicle speed is the most important regulating factor for safe road traffic. It should be determined by the technical standard of both roads and vehicle so as not to exceed the level of violence that the human body can tolerate (*reduction of speed*)

This scientific basis is here established by means of anatomical, pathological and physiological studies of the limits of violence towards the human body. These limits of possible violence are then translated into permissible limits of speed and other systemic conditions of automobile performance. An example of this is that a pedestrian generally survives a head on collision with a vehicle at 30 km/h, but is generally seriously injured or 'killed' after a collision with a vehicle than runs at 50 km/h. Studies in anatomy, pathology and physiology help at identifying these limits of violence which are then translated into the system as its human limitations. Although it is explicitly remarked that speed is 'the most important regulating factor for safe road traffic', there are also other measures taken. Except for focusing on decreasing speed limits, this can be accomplished for instance by the following means: promoting the use of bicycle helmets; physical planning with safety in mind; better driver education; developing a more efficient system for ambulance emergency rescue helicopters; strengthening the role of the consumer as a 'demander' or claims maker in the market of road traffic safety, particularly in residential neighbourhoods; steps taken towards quality assessment and assurance of long distance transport; etc.

There are also other visionary elements in Vision Zero of which some have to do with sight and visuality in a more concrete sense. Visual observation as the basis of epistemology and Western scientific methods has been noted by many theorists (see Urry, 2000: 103). In Vision Zero at least four kinds of visions can be interpreted as being inherent, following some possible interpretations of 'vision' in *Britannica Online*. First, the vision which means to see something as in a dream; second, the act or power of imagination; third, the act or power of seeing; fourth, something that is seen in a vision. The vision that is associated with experience, statistics and the ability to see all kinds of causalities and accidents in traffic is therefore, in the semantic web of Vision Zero, mixed with the dreamlike character of vision as in a revelation of desires or in a futuristic imagination. In the analysis of Vision Zero we can learn that the different kinds of links between epistemology and visual perception listed above are made. In contrast to other forms of epistemological work taking place in other examples of contemporary welfare campaigns, Vision Zero displays elements of combining epistemology and vision that are seldom found, apart from the conventional meaning of sight/vision as founded in induction and experience. In this sense, Vision Zero is an unusual example of planning where vision is allowed a role in different respects.

The psychology of the vision as dreams of the future is also emphasized; echoing the utopian slogans of nineteenth century popular-based movements. The use of the visionary element is not, however, identified as a historical echo of an effective mobilization of the mobile population but is based on the theoretical and psychological foundation stating that the notion of 'vision' in Vision Zero is motivated by the firm belief ('scientifically-based', 'knowledge') that humans and organizations generate action and innovation through the formulation of long-term visions or idealized future conditions that in turn can guide concrete action. This learning is derived partly from management studies and practices where the efficacy of co-workers' long-term goals is emphasized as a tool for increasing motivation (Clarke and Newman, 1997). This step can also be regarded as a return of a kind of idealism in planning, but this return is embedded in contemporary technologies for management and surveillance. Vision Zero is concretized in the goals of eliminating all deaths and serious injuries, but it is operationalized in an entirely different way. At the end of the presentation of Vision Zero the following operationalization occurs:

> In the next ten years, it is estimated that it should be possible to reduce the number of fatalities by a quarter to one third.

Vision Zero is therefore a long-term goal and as such it should not be expected that it will be reached even within the coming decade. Vision Zero in practice could be reduced to more pragmatic expectations. During the years since 1997, annual reports on deaths and casualties in traffic have been evaluated, in the media and in reports by the authorities, in relation to both the visionary and the operationalized goals. These public evaluations have often divided the public into groups that either ridicule the campaign for its idealistic naïveté or defend the important psychological values of maintaining unrealistic visions.[4] Numbers are slippery and open to interpretation, as in all branches of politics. Still, the more radical goal of 'zero' is motivated as the best possible standard for action, more or less irrespective of the pessimism and disillusionment in the analysis of the annual (negative) figures. In this sense we could say that the power at work in Vision Zero is a monodirectional 'one-way traffic' of information from authorities to citizens. At work here are at least two different rationalities of quantification: one that takes statistics as a reliable measure for future action and one that does not trust statistics as such a measure, and instead relies on idealism and wishful thinking.

Vision Zero can be seen as an expression of a utopian democratic socio-spatial politics of automobility that pitches 'vehicle speed' as 'the most important regulating factor for safe road traffic'. Vision Zero is based on 'zero tolerance', a strategy for public management that also has been used in other social problem areas such as crime and drug abuse. Well-known examples in this regard are the New York Police Department and their successful strategies of 'zero tolerance' in crime prevention. By hitting hard on petty crimes they aim at obstructing the socialization processes possibly leading to major criminal activities. Vision Zero identifies speed as *the* major problem in the vision of an egalitarian mobile society based on democratic values (the quantification of opinions in governance, the fair distribution of safety). Such an extreme position, stating 'zero tolerance' as well as zero deaths and zero serious injuries, runs counter both to a statistical rationality and its concomitant determinism (still in operation in the sequential evaluation of the progress reports), and runs counter to a common sense understanding of the prognosis for crisis based on concrete experience in socio-spatial practices. Vision Zero is associated with more idealistic and utopian visions of what politics, planning and prophylactic management can be and what it can accomplish. The 'zero tolerance' element in Vision Zero is not a rejection of quantification as a mode of governance. It is a rejection of the fateful consequences of a road traffic system by setting a very high standard for the evaluation of the performance of the system.

We have also seen that the psychological value of the number 'zero' is very different from the concrete operationalization of the road safety statistics. The formulation of a viable vision zero, from the point of view of its advocates, therefore needs, among other things, to be defended against common experience and against a rationality stating otherwise. This includes the communicative processes of introducing, representing and making viable a set of criteria that explicitly state an extreme position, ie, that the problem and its negative and sometimes dangerous and lethal side-effects cannot be acceptable.

Governing by numbers and quantification rhetorics in Vision Zero

In this section I will focus on some aspects of quantification and numeracy in Vision Zero that have bearing on the general theme of the politics of automobility. Different dimensions of quantification and numeracy, derived from such knowledge areas as anatomy, management, mechanics, psychology and politics, are represented in Vision Zero where they jointly operate as important communicative strategies for regulation and governance. Quantification and numeracy perform many functions in this campaign and the rhetorical aspect is not unlike what can be found in most of the previous, similar information campaigns in the realm of communication on socio-spatial and welfare issues. A detailed analysis, however, points to important differences distinguishing Vision Zero from its predecessors.

First of all, statistics and epidemiology are, not surprisingly, among the most important sources and forms of numerical representations in Vision Zero. Judith Green (1997), in *Risk and Misfortune*, notes that the development of accident prevention during the twentieth century has evolved into a discrete professional activity largely by way of the availability of statistics enabling classification and accumulation of accident data (see Bonham, this volume). The aggregated knowledge on these issues has contributed in transforming the potential for coping with experiential data, thus giving new impetus and meaning to the phenomenon of accidents.

> When aggregated, accidents appear not as unique misfortunes, but as statistically predictable events with identifiable social, environmental, psychological and biological risk factors. (Green, 1997: 81)

In this process of aggregation, numerical categories and dimensions of quantification have constituted important aspects. In the analysis of quantification practices in Vision Zero, I will focus on a selection of those aspects that have bearing on the politics of automobility, namely 'speed', 'zero tolerance' and 'democracy'. The descriptions in the following three areas will then be analysed in a subsequent section.

(1) Speed

In the previous quote from the strategic principles of Vision Zero we learned that:

> Vehicle speed is the most important regulating factor for safe road traffic. It should be determined by the technical standard of both roads and vehicle so as not to exceed the level of violence that the human body can tolerate.

Consequently, the particular theme of 'vehicle speed' as a 'major problem' and 'the most important regulating factor' is reiterated in various information designs and pedagogical formats throughout the text, and also at other places in the campaign at large. Among a list of eighteen possible risk factors in traffic, including drinking-driving, unsafe automobiles, lack of visibility in traffic, non-use of bicycle helmets, etc, speed is repeatedly listed as the most important risk factor. Speed is undoubtedly a quantitative measure but in quantification rhetorics it performs more functions than merely stating an absolute mechanical correlation. In more detailed outcomes of the campaign it is also specified, especially in connection with the presentation of new standards for speed and safety in urban areas, where the speed is often concretely specified as 30 km/h or 50 km/h. In the context where speed is concretized to 30 km/h in urban areas, the argument is made with help of studies in medicine such as anatomy, physiology and orthopaedics that identify limits of external violence to the human body. The 'pragmatic and scientifically-based strategy' of Vision Zero, as it is introduced in the text, is particularly explicit when it comes to speed and violence to the human body-complex of bones, tissues and fluids. The body of a human being can survive crashing with a vehicle in 30 km/h but, as we have seen, will almost certainly be seriously injured or even killed when the vehicle speed is 50 km/h. Speed in these contexts is associated with violence to the human body. Speed is a measurement for violence. Performing traffic in excessive speed is 'violent' behaviour, directed against other people. The use of the word 'violence' implies agency and intention in contrast to the impersonal and contingent forces of chance that could be traced from statistical analysis. Understanding the causes of accidents due to speed by associating speed with 'violence' and agency is therefore a way of making these causes manageable.

In more general formulations on traffic safety and speed, like the one quoted above, speed is first of all identified with a speed that is excessive, ie, not speed as a general and relatively neutral kinetic category, but speed as a tendency for speeding, acceleration and systematic transgression of limits. Speed is therefore marked not as a neutral category, but as a potential problem in need of control. At other places in the campaign, the formulation 'bad speed accommodation' is used, ie, associating speed with a tendency of drivers not to accommodate the vehicle speed in relation to the surrounding socio-spatial context. In both these cases speed is numerically unspecified but marked as excessive and as a negative condition for the maintenance of safe road traffic. Henceforth it is moralized as negative and problematic for the long term goals of road traffic safety.

Speed is also talked about in terms of a will for a general reduction of limits for permissible speed. The response of the system designers to the challenges of road traffic safety is to regulate what they identify as the 'most important regulating factor' and thereafter expect the system user's compliance. As we have seen, the responsibility is not only with the designers, but more importantly with the users/actors who are supposed to perform the established limits. Representing speed in this way as an actor-initiated problem with potentially serious effects for others is a conventional way of coping with problems in the area of traffic safety. This dimension is also very explicit in Vision Zero.

(2)   Zero tolerance

Zero is another quantitative construct which in this context works in many ways, for instance in the interplay between its character as both utopian vision and as pragmatic formula for action. Vision Zero is a campaign for road traffic safety building on the notion of 'zero tolerance'. 'Zero tolerance' means 'no tolerance' and therefore constitutes a die-hard-strategy for coping with problems: No negotiations, no exceptions, no fussing with collective ideals.

Zero is a vision and is therefore an ideal, and this ideal should be actualized and represented by all actors of the system. Zero is here a positive ideal where 'zero' equals the elimination of 'bads'.[5] As a utopian vision, it has a dreamlike character of infinity where the socially shared goals are futuristic, distant and perhaps never even attainable. The fact that Zero is a vision as well as a concrete strategy for action means that there are some interpretive spaces for not demanding 'zero' from 'zero tolerance' here and now. 'Zero tolerance' is a condition for action that is only at work in the moment, while Vision Zero is also a long-term goal with an idealistic character.

Vision Zero not only refers to infinity but also illustrates finality. The finite aspects of Zero refer to the fact that *no* deaths and serious injuries can ever be accepted within the system. The level of accidents should be reduced to 0: 0 killed and 0 seriously injured. The finality also resonates with the character of the casualties and road traffic consequences that should be avoided: being killed and seriously injured are irreversible events and should therefore be avoided.

The 'no one' that should not be killed or seriously injured could be either you or me. It is therefore also part of a technology for constructing a political subject in the process of governing by numbers and ordering the rights of citizenship (see below).

(3)   Democracy

Democracy is linked to numbers. Its governmental arithmetic runs something like: the majority rules and minorities have rights (Porter, 1996). In Vision Zero, the numerical character of democracy in the context of road traffic safety becomes explicit in many different ways. As we have seen with the notion of zero in Vision Zero, this numerical category is both inclusive and exclusive in terms of subject attribution. As systems users and citizens in a safe society, according to a democratic vision of the fair distribution of goods and 'bads', we all have the right of not being 'punished', either killed or seriously injured, in road traffic. This is not only a right resulting from citizens' claims and demands; it is also a shared responsibility that is expected from all system users. We are, according to this scenario, all responsible mobile citizens and should therefore act so that no one in the political body suffers from our negligence. The distribution of these rights belongs to all, not just to a small elite. In the introduction to the document it is also mentioned that Vision Zero is a Road Traffic

Safety Bill that 'was passed by a large majority in the Swedish parliament', thus the outlook of Vision Zero is represented as politically accountable, as being based on criteria of a fair political quantification according to the normative standards set up by a democratic culture and its procedures for fair decision-making. The goal of Vision Zero in the Swedish campaign is constrained by the geographical borders of the national community:

> The long term-goal is that no one will be killed or seriously injured within the Swedish road transport system.

Of course, similar boundaries are maintained as the units of operation in other national road traffic safety campaigns. But the theme of national sovereignty in the Swedish Vision Zero can perhaps be interpreted a bit further. Maybe it helps to understand how Sweden as a national geo-political unit (part of the EU, still not part of the EMU) here is represented as a pioneering public health ideal of 'the safe community', and as a paradise of political consensus, democratic values and social reformist pragmatism based on scientific knowledge.

The democratic theme echoes also in other important ways in this Vision. Critical stances are taken against other ways of quantifying democracy in the area of the politics of automobility. Vision Zero is introduced as a 'new approach to road safety'. The old approach consists of:

> ... trying to encourage the road user to respond, in an appropriate way, typically through licensing, testing, education, training and publicity to the many demands of a man-made and increasingly complex traffic system. Traditionally, the main responsibility for safety has been placed on the user to achieve this end rather than on the designers of the system.

This old approach shows a democracy at work, in which a well-wishing elite of road traffic safety cognoscenti are providing and motivating ('trying to encourage') the public to act in certain ways, while also distributing the responsibility to these actors. The quantitative formula for this operation includes the old-fashioned communicative view on top-down distribution of information and hierarchies of sanction. In contrast to these 'old' strategies, contemporary actors in the road traffic system, according to Vision Zero, are expected to 'negotiate the system to concentrating on how the whole system can operate safely'. Instead of top-down information processing, the alternative consists of dialogue, political mobilization and citizen participation as the expected ways of setting the potentials of democracy at work. This includes a new way of calculating the values of fair distribution. In this system, responsibility is not with singular actors, but with the system at large in which everybody ideally is an active contributor, both as claims-maker and as actor. In this process the politics of automobility is expected to become a prime setting for political action by the citizens. The quantitative dimensions of democracy stress numerical and political processes such as fair distribution, equalization, distributed justification, etc.

Summing up the role of numbers

The different representations of the quantitative dimensions in Vision Zero, actualizing quantitative dimensions in knowledge areas such as anatomy, management, mechanics, psychology and politics, are important aspects of the governance and rhetorics in the general politics of automobility of which Vision Zero is an expression. The quantitative notions used are far from any neutral or disinterested mechanical concepts or statistical 'truths', even when they are presented as such, but suggest also several other interpretive options, including morality, ontology and political ideology. Numbers are slippery and open to interpretation. To sum up the role of numbers, I will finally analyse three aspects of these quantifying practices aiming at illustrating their function in the service of rationalist numerical planning and politics. The political use of numbers is a theme already utilized by Thucydides and Herodotus in their classical political expositions, which continues in our time to be used for the design, implementation and legitimation of power.

The changing status of the accident, for instance in terms of epistemology, ordering and calculability, is, as we have noted, an important condition for the contemporary view of the accident as a form of domesticated and controllable misfortune. Following Judith Green, we can say that the technologies of quantification have changed our outlook on accidents:

> In the late twentieth century there has been a dramatic transformation in how accidents are classified, discussed and managed. Ideally accidents should no longer happen. In an era of ever more sophisticated risk assessment, the accident apparently occupies a rather different conceptual space than it did in the first half of the century: as an event that is predictable, and ultimately preventable. (Green, 1997: 12–13)

Quantification makes accidents both predictable and preventable, in particular for those who believe fully in its logics and efficacy. In Vision Zero this influence is very obvious, although the belief in quantification as an instrument for prediction does not lead to a deterministic view on future accidents. A belief in the technologies of quantification as prognostic prophylactic instruments is paralleled by an explicit critical revision of these same technologies of quantification as instruments of prediction. The result is that Vision Zero includes representations both of a belief and a disbelief in these technologies of prediction. The element that is added here is one which is so often omitted from 'pragmatic and scientifically based' planning, ie, idealistic and visionary utopianism. In this context, however, it is motivated by the cognitive psychological effects of long-term goal oriented action.

Secondly, Vision Zero exhibits clear characteristics typical of managerial culture in which managerialism is located 'as a cultural formation and a distinctive set of ideologies and practices which form one of the underpinnings of an emergent political settlement' (Clarke and Newman, 1997). The politics for safe road traffic and the campaign is based on a 'result-based action programme', which means that every kind of step taken towards the long-term goal is defined on criteria of measurement and motivated by a framework of quantifiable accountability. According to this logic, only those steps can be taken that subsequently can be assessed on a quantitative basis in a system of cost and benefit analysis. While this procedure enables the steps taken to be numerical and therefore calculable, it also excludes other possible measures that will not fit into this scheme of numerical accountability. This way of legitimating political and planning processes in a programme of effective management, is derived from the motivating forces of profitability typical of the private market that John Clarke and Janet Newman (1997), among others, describe. Norman Fairclough in *New Labour, New Language?* (2000), notes the promotional and managerial aspects of contemporary political culture, focusing on changes at the level of political discourse. These changes can also be seen vividly in Vision Zero, which aims to break with older forms of order and power, in its place introducing public consultation, focus groups, negotiation, dialogue and debate, just as New Labour in the UK have done, according to Fairclough. The communicative options open the processes for public participation, quantitatively enlarging the participatory conditions for change by means of citizen mobilization.

Finally, questions about governance are addressed in Vision Zero. With help of the critical influences of governmentality adapted to late modern or advanced liberal societies, we can help to identify Vision Zero in a context of proposed changes in the realm of human conduct. Changing people's attitudes concerning road traffic safety is one such area for the change of conduct (Bonham, this volume). Democracy, citizenship and self-government are all explicit aspects and technologies of Vision Zero that recur in other approaches to power from a neo-liberal perspective. Following Barbara Cruikshank's general argument in *The Will to Empower* (1999), we can argue that the turn towards dialogue and democratic citizenship in Vision Zero is 'less a solution to political problems than a strategy of government' and a mode of exercising power (1999: 1). The technologies of citizenship through various means such as mobilization and empowerment find graphic examples in Vision Zero. This resonates with Deleuze's understanding of 'societies of control' as the replacement of Foucauldian disciplinary societies. A society of control is made up of a numerical language 'that marks access to information, or rejects it' (Deleuze, 1992).

The paradoxes of automobility consist of balancing autonomy in relation to regulation. Through the example of the Swedish Road Traffic Safety Bill, Vision Zero, we can see these paradoxes at play along with the paradoxes of modernist planning based on a belief in calculability wedded to a visionary idealism and utopianism that is critical of quantitative rationality. The return of idealism and utopianism in planning, I argue, is not a return to an earlier period of utopian nostalgia and optimism, but could better be understood as a psychologically motivated co-optation of idealism for the purposes of the administrative practices in the managerial state. Vision Zero is also an example of the international spread of what Pierre Bourdieu and Loïc Wacquant have called the 'new penal state' where absolute expressions such as 'zero' and 'zero tolerance' flourish as new discursive tokens for power (Fairclough, 2000: 77–78).

Notes

1 A presentation in English of Vision Zero is available at http://www.vv.se/traf_sak/nollvis/ tsnollvis3.htm All quotes from Vision Zero in this chapter are taken from this document.
2 This chapter is part of a larger project that adresses issues about risk, safety and responsibility concerning road traffic safety. Other examples and analyses are approached in Forstorp (forth-coming) *Mobilitet och risk. Nollvisionen som diskursiv politik* [*Mobility and Risk. Vision Zero as Discursive Politics*].
3 In the writing of this chapter I have only had access to a Swedish translation of Nader's book. Therefore the English expressions used here are my own and might differ from the original.
4 Resistance to Vision Zero has not been invisible, although not particularly explicit. Singular whistle-blowers have voiced their anger or frustration, but the organized attempts at overthrow-ing the present policy for road traffic safety have not materialized. The goal in 1997 was that the number of fatal accidents in road traffic should be halved within the first decade of its operation (from 640 to 270). In 2003 the number of deaths was reduced, but not yet at the expected level, 519 as compared with 640 in 1996. Even critics against the far-fetched goals of Vision Zero have accepted that the campaign is successful, not at the level of what was expected, but still having effect.
5 In the context of the social and political uses of 'zero' it is impossible to neglect the way this notion is used after 9/11 and in the designation of the space of the former twin towers as 'Ground Zero'. Here 'zero' is used absolutely differently, as a way of designating annihilation, rupture, and finitude in its most negative sense.

References

Baker, T. and J. Simon (eds) (2002) *Embracing Risk: The Changing Culture of Insurance and Respon-sibility*. Chicago: University of Chicago Press.
Barry, A., T. Osborne and N. Rose (eds) (1996) *Foucault and Political Reason: Liberalism, Neo-Liberalism and Rationalities of Government*. London: UCL Press.
Clarke, J. and J. Newman (1997) *The Managerial State: Power, Politics and Ideology in the Remak-ing of Social Welfare*. London: Sage.
Cruikshank, B. (1999) *The Will to Empower: Democratic Citizens and Other Subjects*. Ithaca, NY: Cornell University Press.
Daston, L. and P. Galison (1992) 'The image of objectivity' *Representations*, 40: 81–128.
Dean, M. and B. Hindess (eds) (1998) *Governing Australia: Studies in Contemporary Rationalities of Government*. Cambridge: Cambridge University Press.
Dean, M. (1999) *Governmentality*. London: Sage.
Deleuze, G. (1992) 'Postscript on the societies of control' *October* 59: 3–7.
Ewald, F. (2002) 'The return of Descartes malicious demon: An outline of a philosophy of pre-caution' in T. Baker and J. Simon (eds) *Embracing Risk: The Changing Culture of Insurance and Responsibility*. Chicago: University of Chicago Press.
Fairclough, N. (2000) *New Labour, New Language?* London: Routledge.
Flyvbjerg, B. (1998) *Rationality and Power: Democracy in Practice*. Chicago: University of Chicago Press.
Forstorp, P-A. (forthcoming) *Risk och mobilitet: Nollvisionen som diskursiv politik* (*Risk and Mobil-ity. Vision Zero as Discursive Politics*)
Foucault, M. (1991) 'Governmentality' in G. Burchell, C. Gordon and P. Miller (eds) *The Foucault Effect: Studies in Governmentality*. London: Harvester Wheatsheaf.
Green, J. (1997) *Risk and Misfortune: The Social Construction of Accidents*. London: UCL Press.
Hacking, I. (1990) *The Taming of Chance*. Cambridge: Cambridge University Press.

Heimer, C.A. (2002) 'Insuring more, ensuring less: The costs and benefits of private regulation through insurance' in T. Baker and J. Simon (eds) *Embracing Risk: The Changing Culture of Insurance and Responsibility*. Chicago: University of Chicago Press.

Lupton, D. (1999) *Risk*. London: Routledge.

Nader, R. (1967) *Den livsfarliga bilen*. Stockholm: Rabén & Sjögren.

Porter, T.M. (1996) *Trust in Numbers: The Pursuit of Objectivity in Sceince and Public Life*. Princeton: Princeton University Press.

Prior, L., P. Glasner and R. MacNally (2000) 'Genotechnology: Three challenges to risk legitimation' in B. Adam, U. Beck and J. Van Loon (eds) *The Risk Society and Beyond: Critical Issues for Social Theory*. London: Sage.

Rose, N. (1990) *Governing the Soul: The Shaping of the Private Self*. London: Routledge.

Urry, J. (2000) *Sociology beyond Societies: Mobilities for the Twenty-First Century*. London: Routledge.

Vision Zero (2002) http://www.vv.se/traf_sak/nollvis/tsnollvis3.htm, accessed 12 December 2002.

Automobility and the liberal disposition

Sudhir Chella Rajan

The private car and the public freeway together provide an ideal – not to say ideal-ized – version of democratic urban transportation . . . The watchful tolerance and almost impeccable lane discipline of . . . drivers on the freeways is often noted, but not the fact that both are symptoms of something deeper – willing acquiescence in an incredibly demanding man/machine system . . . It demands, first of all, an open but decisive attitude to the placing of the car on the road surface [and] a constant stream of decisions that [could be regarded as] a higher form of pragmatism. (Banham, 1971)

Individualism is a calm and considered feeling which disposes each citizen to isolate himself from the mass of his fellows and withdraw into the circle of family and friends; with this little society formed to his taste, he gladly leaves the greater society to look after itself. (Tocqueville *et al.*, 1966: 477)

In the West, by and large, we are all liberals now. Instead of ignoring or affecting to deplore this, we should be recognizing and reaffirming it. Or else, you never know, it might one day no longer be true. (*Economist*, 1996)

Automobility, or the entire gamut of practices that foster car culture, qualifies both as product and producer of modernity. Its constitutive visual image is one of dignified convoys of individual cars, vehicles whose solitary drivers can remain separated from each other as they collectively pursue private goals on public highways. As such, this picture captures the salient features of cars in a post-Enlightenment order: the experience of driving, identified by the quiet plea-sures of the open road, speed, power and personal control, neatly complements the functionality of covering distance, managing time and maintaining certain forms of individuation. One might thus portray an ontology of automobility that reinforces its teleology; together, they establish characteristically that which is *modern* and, by definition, permanently desirable.

Although surprisingly few liberals would boast about it, automobility is not only well attuned to the demands of late modernity, it is also perhaps the most important modern development that could fulfil the unremitting liberal demand for individual autonomy. The single consistent theme running through liberal political theory is the ideal of a free person whose actions are her own.[1] Auto-mobility, on its part, has become the (literally) concrete articulation of liberal society's promise to its citizens that they can freely exercise certain everyday choices: where they want to live and toil, when they wish to travel and how far they want to go. The car itself is arguably also a social equalizer, because it can provide any of its users generous amounts of personal space by fostering that 'calm and considered feeling' while expanding opportunities for negotiating external space.[2] Moreover, car ownership is now so common in affluent countries that nearly every 'free' adult has this uniquely constructed form of control over time and space.[3] Without the freedom to roam and live where one wants to, liberals might claim, social hierarchy would perhaps become more significant, and the travails of daily life would be worse in some ways than it was at the turn of the twentieth century, given the greater resource and population pressures in today's urban environments.

Liberalism and automobility would seem to offer each other plenty of nourishment, but what specific ideological tasks, if any, does automobility perform for liberalism? And where does this relationship leave post-liberal positions, primarily those that construe freedom as a trope and reject the emancipatory claims of individualism, universalism, and procedural rationality? In this essay I argue that the car and its accoutrements have collectively become a principal 'technology' of contemporary liberalism, ie, not only has automobility been able to draw sustenance from it, but liberalism itself has become 'locked in' by an enterprise that helps to institute a powerful and far-reaching normalizing ethic through the reproduction of its specific corporeal practices. The impacts of the automobility-liberalism combine, I contend, are important beyond the boundaries of the cultural and economic relations between cars and lifestyles; the fusion exerts an influence on even larger arenas of political ideology.

The bulk of my argument relates to what I find to be an astonishing feature of contemporary liberal political theory: the near complete blindness to automobility in its texts. Liberals might profess loyalty to classical Greek politics at least in terms of the latter's dialogics of mediating human discord between the 'I' and the 'we,' but they appear to be patently uninterested in the socio-spatial *context* of contemporary Western society's most socially demanding private activity. Certainly, there is the occasional pesky reminder from libertarians that automobility amounts to the widespread endowment of autonomy (Lomasky, 1997). But those who would bring liberal political theory into the middle ground of trans-Atlantic respectability pointedly ignore such leanings.

My interest in this regard is directed mainly towards texts written in the tradition of liberal political theory, not those of self-proclaimed 'political liberals' who do literary criticism, cultural studies, or even critical social theory. But I also maintain more generally that automobility is a remarkably thin object of theoretical enquiry across the field. That this is remarkable ought not to require too much explanation. After all, automobility concerns more than just the car-object, it secures a particular form of social and material life for both drivers and non-drivers virtually around the world through its myriad practices, in part through the political economy of the automobile manufacturing and marketing enterprise and the highway and gasoline delivery infrastructure, but also more dramatically through the governmentality of traffic rules, parking structures, licensing procedures, and sundry regulatory institutions. Its 'machine space' produces both driver and non-driver subjects, often stripping the latter of certain claims to citizenship, and places countless requirements on both – licensing, registration, insurance, attention to the road and their private behaviour, risks of accidents, pollution and access to jobs and housing.[4] Particularly in North America, the state's powerful patronage of automobility is unmatched, except when compared with the military, whose own rationale is the subject of much hand-wringing in liberal international relations theory. Just as importantly, an enduring legacy to liberal theory from Mill to Hobhouse and beyond concerns the need to ensure freedom of individual expression in the face of the 'tyranny of the majority', which is perhaps not an erroneous way to portray the vast physical and cultural landscape occupied by the personal car. For political theorists, therefore, automobility might be explored richly in terms of facilitating the universal exercise of individual liberty; the massive public expenditures and extraordinary political power of auto and oil corporations might be read as prefiguring a special variety of accumulation crisis, resulting in unexplored diversions within late capitalism itself; or the peculiar demands it places on drivers and non-drivers alike might raise serious questions about already shaky political concepts involving bodies, high-speed prosthetics, and sovereignty (eg, Connolly, 2002). That automobility and its politics are not problematized as such by any breed of theorist with any degree of detail is itself a matter of substantial critical interest but one that remains beyond the scope of this inquiry; that mainstream liberal political analysis in particular ignores it leads me to employ the question as a wedge to pry open other curious features concerning the family resemblances between the ideas of liberal theory and the practices of automobility.

Liberal pretexts

I begin by exploring two related strands of explanation for liberal indifference towards automobility. First and foremost, liberals are likely to contend that automobility is merely one outcome, among many, of the particular mode of capitalist enterprise and technological development that happen to be fostered by liberal governments and hence calls for no fresh theoretical analysis into its features.[5] The primary goals of political theory, they might say, are to grapple with analytical problems relating to enhancing liberties and not so much with the social and cultural conditions of everyday existence. Worrying about automobility is no more significant than being unduly concerned about the advertising or apparel industry's relevance to political theory. In both cases, as long as there are no non-trivial constraints to the freedom of human agency as a result of these enterprises, their activity has no bearing on politics.[6] But rights-based liberals are not always so reticent about specific sectors and policies, especially when they encounter difficulties drawing fine distinctions between their private and public aspects. In fact the realm of everyday life is rife with politically significant tensions, and political theory – in general, and liberalism in particular – habitually offers elaborate commentary on distinguishing the private spheres of quotidian experiences from their impacts on public affairs. Witness, for instance, the endless debates over the gender and identity politics of reproductive technology and same-sex couples, the furore over smoking in public places, and race/religious practice/citizenship debates in Europe.

In any event, while communitarians and various other detractors criticize liberals precisely for making abstract and disembodied assumptions for building their normative edifices (Taylor, 1985; Walzer, 1983; Sandel, 1998), the fact remains that, until quite recently, they too have remained largely silent on the political significance of automobility's great transformation of the twentieth century. No doubt, serious scholarly work on urban form and its politics has been the mainstay of critical geography for close to a half century, but these studies tend to focus on how space is produced by automobility and how this affects urban politics rather than how automobility enters (and shapes) the political imaginary in the first place. And notable as they are, even Lewis Mumford's famous polemic on the megamachine (Mumford, 1967), David Harvey's analysis of the 'secondary and tertiary circuits of capital' (Harvey, 1982) and Manuel Castells' network society (Castells, 1996) tend to sidestep the political implications of automobility as such, treating it instead as a *phenomenon* with important social, spatial and economic antecedents.[7] Interestingly, then, the contagion seems to extend far beyond liberal circles, which causes one to want to probe into the very sites of automobility that appear to deflect critical thought. What indeed could possibly account for this widespread blindness to the politics of automobility? Might we imagine that the everyday experience of cars and the associated reordering of physical and social space have become so deeply entrenched that Western theorists find it difficult to take automobility seriously as a thematic of intrinsic political importance that needs under-labouring to articulate its ethical dimensions and legitimacy? In other words, is it conceivable that the very commonness of driving might work against its conceptualization as a unique theoretical subject in any other terms than historically or sociologically?

Here, I offer the following conjecture. In the course of a breathtaking century of cultural and social transformation, the car has almost indiscernibly turned into an ordinary part of daily life in contemporary Western life and acquired the quality of a human endowment *and* need, much like a home or clothing. Kenneth Schneider describes a 'social malignancy' wherein 'automobility gradually permeates the daily behaviour of people, the purpose of institutions, and the structure of cities and the countryside' (1971: 22). Automobility has thus gotten constituted as a 'formative context', appearing as 'basic institutional arrangements and imaginative preconceptions that circumscribe our routine practical or discursive activities . . . and resist their destabilizing effects' (Unger, 1987). The formative context of the automobilized world we inhabit and the mutual empathy with other drivers that it sustains together spawn an entire set of dominant beliefs and codes about the nature of social relations and individual desires. Unger suggests that the formative context colours critical imagination itself:

> Until we make the underlying institutional and imaginative structure of a society explicit we are almost certain to mistake the regularities and routines that persist . . . for general laws of social organization. At the very least, we are likely to treat them as the laws of a particular type of society and to imagine that we can suspend them only by a revolutionary switch to another type. Superstition then encourages surrender. (1987: 4)

Reading Unger off Bourdieu's concept of *habitus*, automobility naturalizes us (eg, through our bodily dispositions) into routines of 'false necessity' and thereby itself becomes nearly imperceptible as a social *fact*. And even when critical theorists detect automobility, few new normative claims seem to arise from their debates, because the activity of car use itself has become 'normal'. The dual nature of this normality might indeed divert our critical gaze away from its blurry political forms towards its cultural and economic effects. I return to this idea later.

A second explanatory strand, relating to contemporary liberal theory's particular silence on automobility, is rather more long-winded. Here, I look beyond rights-based liberalism to examine a series of developments in broader liberal projects' recent history. In John Gray's words, the liberal political and intellectual order in Europe and North America, otherwise known as the Enlightenment agenda, 'broke . . . into pieces' at the end of the First World War, coeval with the emergence of socialist ideals and the 'enhancement of the scope and intensity of state activity' for the next several decades (Gray, 1986: 36–37). One could speculate that this was above all a practical response to extant economic crises, but also an ideological reaction to Communism's apparent welfare achievements in the East.

Significantly, this happened precisely during the period of automobility's meteoric rise in the West, which was itself fuelled by the dramatic post-war state-led investments with which we are by now very familiar (Flink, 1988). Early attempts to revive classical liberalism were, one might speculate, conveniently stalled by the intervening welfare state developments whose justification was based on the revisionist accounts of the day. Thus, with the exceptions of Hayek (whose ironically titled *Road to Serfdom* published largely for an American audience was mute on the significance of that state's growing expenditures on highways to protect human liberties) and later Nozick, the most prominent liberal theorists for the next several decades were increasingly anxious to confront the problem of social, political, economic, and subsequently even cultural equality, with 'freedom' increasingly relegated to the background. Rawls' framework to distribute goods fairly by reducing inequalities, while hailed as a landmark of *liberal* political philosophy, was nevertheless less focused on classic liberal concerns relating to freedom and individuality *per se*, even while it lay securely within the neo-Kantian camp. Similarly, it would not be frivolous to claim that there are liberal philosophers today who could be just as easily be labelled feminists (eg, Okin, 1998) and multi-culturalists (eg, Kukathas, 1993; Kymlicka, 1989), their one common intellectual trait being an almost primary concern with expanding the realm of equality (as defined across several different domains) alongside the classical liberal ideal of autonomy.

At the beginning of the twenty-first century, automobility has itself come to occupy a strange place with respect to equality. In Western Europe, East Asia and North America, as I pointed out at the beginning of this chapter, car-ownership has already become 'hyper-equal'; indeed, in the United States, the population of private cars already far exceeds persons licensed to drive them. And while there are still the severely disabled, the old and the destitute who are unable to use this prosthetic for negotiating edge cities and other contemporary capitalist spatial formations, automobile use can scarcely be called an elite enterprise in these societies. At least on the face of it, automobility appears to have the built-in mechanisms to fulfil contemporary liberal society's promise of delivering *both* freedom and equality in several of those places that have embraced capitalist theory and practice.

What I am arguing, therefore, is that mainstream liberal thought appears to have accommodated its own development to meet the emerging demands of its socio-spatial context, namely, the built environment and the social and cultural relations within the metropolitan centres of global capitalism. These demands have integrated issues of social and cultural justice into traditional conceptions of freedom, bounded nevertheless by certain specific notions of what all of these things stand for. Freedom *per se*, at least as the right not to be interfered with, has become less of a primary demand in part because of a judgment that it has *largely been achieved* in the late modern West, with automobility being one of its most conspicuous expressions. In several versions of contemporary liberal thought, there is emphasis on positive freedom – enhancing the capability to act and associated concepts of strong democracy (Berlin, 1969; Barber, 1984; Kateb, 1984) – but, by and large, a quiet sense of satisfaction about autonomy pervades liberal discourse (Rorty, 1989; *Economist*, quotation above).

But if automobility expresses the realization of freedom *and* equality, why are liberals reluctant to shout about it from the rooftops? The short answer is that while liberals literally need the technology of automobility to reveal the experiential 'affectiveness' of liberal values (namely, freedom and equality), they cannot afford to undergo careful analytical scrutiny of those practices once they have abandoned notions of both natural right and utilitarian cost-benefit analysis. In other words, while automobility can usefully express the physical experience of freedom and equality, liberals are wary of validating that experience discursively because of the perils that lie in that direction. After all, it is well established that automobility implies not just the proliferation of cars but also the cultivation of an entire physical, social and regulatory infrastructure to support movement along prescribed routes and modes. It entails vast investments of capital and mammoth social and environmental costs (estimated at roughly $2–5 trillion per year in the US in current terms, see Delucchi, 1997). As I explain more fully in the next section, it is a potential source of embarrassment to liberals that the costs, particularly the risks of causing death to others through accidents and pollution, may well undermine the Kantian principle of treating humans as ends in themselves. Driving is arguably immoral (ie, in violation of the categorical imperative) from the liberal perspective because if everyone in the world were to drive at the same level as, say, the average North American, then the global environmental catastrophe would be complete. Emissions of greenhouse gases and oil demand would be more than double what they are today, implying that the risk of abrupt climate change would be increased several-fold, that global oil reserves would dry up in less than a decade along with numerous other social and political consequences. It is inconceivable that any individual driver would wish to suffer such detriment and liberal political philosophy would have to conclude that driving infringes on the rights of other individuals.

I should of course note that this logic would generally not cause worry to utilitarians, whose cost-benefit calculations are of course the motor behind the entire transport industry. Even the sporadic boosterism for automobility by libertarians (Lomasky, 1997) may be explained in terms of their archaic reliance on natural right theories, ie, the belief that rights are morally prior to any social institution. But most contemporary liberals eschew the latter view because of an avowed commitment to social and environmental justice (see, for instance Gray, 1986: 47–49). And this puts them deep in the puddle when having to explain their implicit endorsement for automobility.

Gewirth's quandary

Alan Gewirth is one of the rare instances of a liberal political theorist tackling the problem at all, and that too only in a casual reference to driving in a minor essay on cost-benefit analysis (Gewirth, 1990). Gewirth is one of the leading philosophers of the twentieth century emerging from the Kantian tradition, so a critical exploration of his argument illustrates quite faithfully the general difficulties that liberal philosophers of various stripes would likely find themselves in, were they to attempt to find moral justification for automobility. Gewirth's analysis on driving needs to be understood within the context of his larger moral theory, which he terms the 'Principle of Generic Consistency'. He bases his political philosophy on a rights-centred framework in which moral right rather than money constitutes the privileged units of inquiry. He proposes that the agent who is committed to acting rationally will be purposive and voluntary in her action, that is to say, will attach value to her action's purpose:

> Action has 'normative structure,' in that evaluative and deontic judgments on the part of agents are logically implicit in all action; and when these judgments are subjected to certain rational requirements, a certain normative moral principle logically follows from them. (Gewirth, 1978: 26)

Freedom, the 'procedural necessary condition of action', and well-being, its substantive counterpart, are the necessary conditions of agency, and every agent should have a claim-right to these goods. Freedom 'consists in controlling one's behaviour by one's unforced choice while having knowledge of relevant circumstances. Well-being . . . consists in having the general abilities and conditions needed for achieving one's purposes' (Gewirth, 1990: 216). Well-being can be assessed in three levels that are progressively less needed for action: basic well-being consists in having essential prerequisites for action and includes life, physical integrity, and so on; non-subtractive well-being includes general abilities and conditions needed for maintaining undiminished one's general level of purpose fulfilment and one's capabilities for particular actions (eg, not being lied to or threatened); additive well-being consists in having abilities and conditions for enhancing purpose fulfilment and capabilities for particular actions (eg, education, opportunities for income generation). Thus, basic well-being is normatively prior to the others; similarly, some kinds of freedom are subordinate to it.

In order to be consistent, the agent will have to generalize freedom and well-being to others, that is to say, accept 'on pain of inconsistency' that all purposive agents have a claim-right to freedom and well-being. Unlike Rawls' argument in *A Theory of Justice* based on inductive justification, where an egalitarian position is justified as the rational choice of a hypothetical agent with no prior conception of the good, Gewirth's theory begins with agents who are mindful of their values and then work their way through dialectical reasoning to the conclusion that all agents must have claim-rights to freedom and well-being.

Since freedom and well-being are derived from the needs of human agency, they determine how we address moral rights that may conflict with each other. Gewirth's moral Cost-Benefit Analysis (CBA) uses the hierarchy of moral rights of persons as determined by prevailing substantive conditions (ie, well-being) to determine what actions should take precedence over others. For instance, the cost of being lied to or robbed is lower than the cost of being killed, insofar as the former actions are necessary ones to guard against the latter. Yet, Gewirth objects to the notion that his system amounts to a 'utilitarianism of rights' on the grounds that his hierarchical ordering and the resulting wide disparities in degrees of importance needed for considering a moral CBA mean that not every situation could be resolved frivolously through some sort of moral calculus. Indeed, some rights could be so important as to be held inviolate.

Using the example of driving, Gewirth argues that although the automobile industry provides many jobs and cars offer the convenience of mobility, they also carry risks of auto accidents resulting in death. 'Hence, by the moral CBA so far interpreted, no automobiles should ever be built, since the cost in deaths outweighs the benefits of employment and convenience. But such a drastic conclusion is surely implausible' (Gewirth, 1990: 221). Gewirth argues that freedom in the 'risk of death' plays a significant role here, since the driver 'mainly controls whether and to what extent his or her life will be endangered' and can take certain actions to control his or her behaviour to reduce the risk of mortal accidents. In other words, although the risk of death from accidents indicates that the costs outweigh objective benefits and therefore implies that no auto-mobiles should be built, it is the freedom of human agency to take risks that should give weight to the primary right to life. Thus, the right to life 'includes the right to control the circumstances that impinge on one's continuing to live', so that the 'driver's control over his or her driving serves to protect rather than threaten the right to life' (Gewirth 1990: 221).

Rather astonishingly, Gewirth does not consider safety risks to others in this analysis, nor does he consider environmental risks and any of the other social burdens discussed earlier in this paper. In other words, he does not ask the critical question: to what extent does the right to (controlling one's own) life impinge on others' rights over controlling their destinies affected by auto-mobility? It is only because the driver controls how he or she could lower risk by driving carefully, that the 'hierarchic priority of the right to life over the right to drive is not refuted by the lethal possibilities of the latter right' (Gewirth, 1990: 221). Since it is statistically borne out that drivers of large vehicles (eg, SUVs and pickup trucks) are more likely to cause accidents injuring or even killing passengers in smaller cars (Toy and Hammitt, 2003), the additive well-being associated with driving a large car must be considerably weaker than the basic right to life. Even more starkly, since the non-driver cannot control the driver's actions, it would follow that her basic well-being is normatively prior to the latter's right to drive. In the case of non-drivers who live in impoverished countries, the situation is still worse. If global warming could further imperil their survival, then surely the wealthy's freedom to drive must have a lower priority than the well-being of the poor, especially when such driving is for relatively frivolous activities as leisure trips and 'cruising'. Similarly, it is unacceptable (within a rights-based framework) to argue that the poor emit commensurate levels of greenhouse gases, given that the rich are responsible for 'luxury emissions', while the poor generate comparably small levels of 'survival emissions' (Agarwal and Sharma, 1999).

Liberal dispositions

My two earlier explanations for liberal reticence on automobility can be sum-marized in one sentence: liberals tend not see the problem because they are steeped in it; they will often not see it because it is philosophically daunting. Yet, while liberals remain coy towards automobility, I maintain that they would probably find it in their interest to support its practices. I suggested earlier that by constituting a major part of the physical fabric of modernity automobility seems capable of sustaining liberalism's drive to reproduce itself and command canonical influence. If this is true, how does automobility's ordinariness in fact provide validation regarding the universalizability of liberal *practice*, even if liberal theory refuses to analyse it as such? And judging by the general reticence towards automobility, one might infer that the practices of automobility have paradoxically caused even non-liberals to become well-disposed towards the practices of liberalism-automobility. In other words, automobility seems to do some important work even for the rest of us, those who are not committed to liberal political philosophy. How then does it shape our critical thought and practice?

In late capitalist societies, most of us, whether liberal or not, must learn how to drive and 'master' the road, engage in elaborate structures of negotiation with other drivers, read road signs and maps, contend with parking, licensing and so on, and perfect these practices day after day. These banal human rehearsals within an automobilized world are not, however, entirely tedious but could even induce a calming influence; they form a habitus that is 'collectively orchestrated without being the product of the orchestrating action of a conductor' (Bourdieu, 1977: 72). The thrill of participating in the ensemble is captured in this description by Joan Didion:

> [She was] not somewhere on Hollywood Boulevard, not on her way to the freeway, but actually on the freeway. If she was not she lost the day's rhythm, its precariously imposed momentum. Once she was on the freeway and had manoeuvred her way to a fast lane she turned on the radio at high volume and she drove . . . She drove it as a riverman runs a river, every day more attuned to its currents, its deceptions, and just as a riverman feels the pull of the rapids in the lull between sleeping and waking. (Didion, 1970: 13–14)

In Didion's and Reyner Banham's autopia, as suggested here and in the epigraph at the beginning of this chapter, respectively, the driver needs to adopt an 'open but decisive' attitude in subjecting her body to high speed excitement in physical space (unlike the collapsed virtual space of Virilio which has no dimensions) with the real possibility of causing and enduring death or serious injury. But that excitement is tempered by the sober charge that the subject imposes on herself, by becoming a trained, alert and dependable body among thousands that *must share these characteristics* on the road. The exhilarating act of driving is thus imbued with the grave responsibility of having to steer safely and respectfully past others, with the vital expectation that the sentiment and capability are mutual.

The active constitution of the subject as a driver in a high-speed and risky world is aided by the pervasive presence of the car's supporting institutions – the highway and gasoline delivery infrastructure, traffic rules, parking structures, licensing procedures, and highway patrol officers; jointly, they serve as 'training wheels' to prepare the individual to become a mature citizen in a material and spatial society. Thus,

> The subject constitutes himself in an active fashion, by the practices of the self, [but] these practices are nevertheless not something that the individual invents himself. They are patterns that he finds in his culture and which are proposed, suggested and imposed on him by his culture, his society and his social group. (Foucault, 1987: 122)

Through this process, driving incessantly reproduces post-Enlightenment metaphors of autonomy, individualism and toleration, while disavowing the possibility in a modern urban order of either a Hobbesian state of nature or

Leviathan control over it. Indeed, it evokes the 'ideal – not to say idealized – version of democratic urban transportation' (Banham, 1971). And yet, contradictions for liberalism abound – in the regulation of 'private' space (eg, seatbelt laws), the proliferation of unsolicited risks (eg, accidents, pollution) and the inevitable creation of barriers to some categories of people (eg, the 'bypass roads' among Israeli settlements in the West Bank). Thus liberal idealism thrives precisely because it declines the opportunity to defend explicitly the 'freedom' offered by the automobile and prefers instead to allow the experience to literally speak for itself.

As I indicated earlier, the negative freedom, or 'freedom from', that liberalism took up from the Enlightenment as its central political headline has become far less significant than positive freedom, or the 'freedom to', under late modern capitalism, which has quite conveniently become the latter's favourite advertising slogan. But of course the individual's desire for more and bigger vehicles or to live among ever-larger open spaces is not really (or solely) the individual's, but is learned from or even imposed by others. Or as in John Meyer's description of American individualism: 'the individual . . . achieves freedom . . . only under the condition that he become isomorphic, or similar in form, to all other individuals in the society' (Meyer, 1986: 84). That is to say, individualism is a 'public, not a private, view of the person, which others are bound to respect and to which a person is obliged to conform' (1986: 84).

Automobility is therefore also the field in which the biopolitics of individualization fully matches 'security' mode of power, that is to say, one in which the daily routines and practices of pleasure of an individual conform perfectly to the demands of an external power, and in the process set in motion the organization of a vast and complex network of social life and spatial relations. But this is not a story about automatons building a web they trap themselves in; that is to say, individual practices are not rendered unreflexive in the face of external power and on the basis of some deep dispositional tendency of driver-subjects to stay on the road. At least not entirely, since the scope of participation does seem considerably constrained and channelled by the very structurating demands created by the field. This follows what Paul Sweetman terms 'habitual reflexivity', in which 'not only has consumption become increasingly individualized, but consumer culture demands reflexivity through its requirement that "individuals of all classes . . . harness their rising expectations to venture along the road to self-improvement" (Featherstone, 1991: 92)' (Sweetman, 2003: 539). While consumerism under late capitalism thrives on such a reflexive habitus, what is significant about automobility is the 'liberalism theology' that is generated by its practices; the freedom to break loose can always be realized simply by getting into one's car and driving off in any direction one chooses. This then is one of the chilling implications of the automobilized concept embodied in the notion current under late modernity: 'We are all mostly liberals now': freedom is a compulsory constraint, it must be exercised along designated modes, and automobility is its major expression which (re)produces normalizing behaviour in the name of progressing individual liberty.

Liberal justice in the automobilized city

> The essence of the police is neither repression nor even control over the living. Its essence is a certain manner of partitioning the sensible . . . characterized by the void or a supplement. Society consists of groups dedicated to specific modes of action, in places where these occupations are exercised, in modes of being corresponding to these occupations and places. In the fittingness of functions, places and ways of being, there is no place for a void . . . The essence of politics is to disturb this arrangement. (Rancière, 2001: 20–21)

A remaining question involves the complexity of making post-liberal gestures within this framework. If autonomy has taken serious refuge in spatial metaphors of automobility (still a working hypothesis, but one that I hope is gaining support through my argument thus far), then how is political movement constrained within the landscapes of liberal-automobilized ideology? I suggest that one promising way to address this question is to continue to work off the metaphor itself.

In the spring of 1992, Los Angeles experienced an 'urban insurrection' (the 'LA Riots' in the dominant media parlance) whose immediate cause was a breakdown in legitimacy in a liberal institution with regard to race justice.[8] The case involved the famous videotaped police beating of Rodney King almost exactly a year prior to the uprising. Rodney King, a black 25-year-old unemployed construction worker with a moderate criminal record, was chased down Foothill Boulevard past midnight, stopped by 15 white police officers, pulled out of his car and severely beaten by four of them for nearly ten minutes. The incident occurred in a residential area and was unexpectedly filmed by a neighbour from his balcony. Following widespread media broadcast of the videotape a criminal case was lodged by the city against the police officers involved in the beating. When the case went to trial, however, the judge moved the case out of Los Angeles to Simi Valley, a suburb with a 'web of cul-de-sacs' (Thomas Dumm in Gooding-Williams, 1993), where the infamous verdict of 'not guilty' was delivered by a mostly white jury.

The palpable public disbelief at the trial's outcome was reflected in multiracial demonstrations outside the Los Angeles police station on the day it was announced. This was followed by a small number of biracial attacks (initiated by a mob of African-Americans attacking white motorists at an intersection), whose frenzied media coverage seemed to precipitate a widespread pattern of looting of primarily Korean-American owned stores but also subsequently of larger supermarkets along downtown and South-Central Los Angeles. The rioting took place for 3–4 days before the widespread presence of the National Guard reserves caused it to stop. While largely depicted in race terms, ie, violence by blacks towards whites and Asian Americans, only about a third of those *arrested* during the rioting were African-Americans, indicating that many other ethnic groups, including Latinos and whites, participated in the general unrest.

While there has been a plethora of commentaries on these events, I want to direct attention towards those features that relate to automobility and liberalism. First, the site of the beating and its apparent trigger are significant. The police chased Rodney King in his white Hyundai for 8 miles because he was presumably speeding. The image of a black man in a white car involved a high-speed chase along the freeways of Los Angeles was to reappear in the case of football hero O.J. Simpson, some 3 years later. In that instance, 'society's presence as viewers had an impact on both the actions of the police following, and also possibly on O.J.'s own actions during the pursuit' (Vanouse and Weyhrauch, 1995), but King and his pursuers were blind to that possibility before the media event. Still both cases established that, as fast as one could drive on the freeway, one was not invisible to the public gaze of normality.

Second, the location of the trial signified the careful adoption of procedural rationality outside the already tainted stance of prejudiced Los Angelenos, within the community of Simi Valley which was assumed to live literally under a 'veil of ignorance'. That Simi Valley is spatially enclosed, racially clean and physically and culturally cut-off from the polluting influences of the city were all important in its choice as venue for the trial. The outcome of the trial, as Thomas Dumm suggests, was therefore predictable: Rodney King was certainly not normal in Simi Valley for whose residents, 'those who are different are far away, spatially; those who invade will be contained and removed' (Thomas Dumm in Gooding-Williams, 1993: 182). The distortion of the visible evidence – rendering it invisible, by converting a moving image into a series of stills – during the trial meant that the verdict was 'an artful product of an aesthetic of rationality – even to the extent it rationalized and upheld an order of socialized irrationality' (Patricia Williams in Gooding-Williams, 1993).

Finally, the actual events of the insurrection serve as key points of reference in our discussion. Two television images are relevant here. First, an interview with 'spectators' and 'shop owners' looking excited and bewildered as they declare that many 'looters came in driving BMWs and Volvos'. The second shows a 'traffic jam of looters' as automobiles of all fashions laden with stolen goods make their way out of the *circumscribed* chaos of mall parking lots to the more ordered world of traffic signals and lanes outside. These droll images in an otherwise tense situation indicate something else about the hyper-automobilized character of Los Angeles: first, the identity of the cars people drove could supersede other markers such as ethnicity, class or gender when the latter are sufficiently blurry; but second and more important, despite the primary loss of legitimacy in the police force and the legal system that characterized the insurrection and was manifested through looting and arson, one kind of order certainly prevailed, namely the entire machinery of automobility. Road and freeway traffic was evidently lane-bound, traffic signals were obeyed including in areas teeming with pedestrian dissidents, and even the incidence of speeding was hardly out of the ordinary. Unlike similar uprisings elsewhere in the world there was practically no suspension of vehicle movement in any part of southern California, despite a couple of dramatic encounters between motorists and angry mobs at street intersections early in the outbreak. In fact even these celebrated cases where drivers were pulled from their automobiles did not typify the uprising; while they represent a lack of security on the road, the pattern of those attacks indicated a separate and localized sentiment early in the disturbances that was coded according to race.

Why were there no more serious threats to the lifeblood of the city at a time of general disaffection with the rest of established urban regularity? There are several explanations, all obvious to an Angeleno and each providing clues to understanding both the character of the rebellion and the prevailing contexts of automobility in California and elsewhere. The network of roads and freeways facilitating automobile movement is too extensive and well structured to suffer significant damage from any kind of onslaught. Not only are there no specific locations that could be easily targeted even in a carefully planned insurgency, the results of any intended disruption to automobility would be harmful to the perpetrators themselves. In fact it is hardly conceivable that something as diffuse and abstractly situated as the freeway system could be imperilled by anything other than a massive, indiscriminate event like an earthquake – like the one that did shake up LA substantially in 1994.

The very layout of urban space in an edge city permits physical access to the built environment only in prescribed forms favouring automobiles rather than virtually any other form of travel. Indeed, a protest demonstration would be impossible on a freeway or even on the myriad 'surface arteries' that frustrate passage by pedestrians. Looting, arson, and urban upheaval of any kind demand a certain amount of 'free' obstreperous movement carried out collectively, and if citizens cannot place themselves in these 'public' spaces because of the physical arrangement of the built environment, then even spontaneous tumult is sequestered to certain areas and patterns.[9]

The exclusion of the pedestrian from much of urban space is only one of the ways in which automobility extends its power. For the citizen actually identifies herself through her own amputation; her desire to don wheels and her acquired skill to navigate space and time as a driver displaces any possible inclination to take to the streets *as* a pedestrian activist. It is after all the speeding citizen-driver who terrifies the pedestrian with her far superior armour and speed on the tarmac. 'Citizenship', in terms of the right to dissent, is then defined in terms of a prescribed set of subjects allowed to express controlled forms of 'no!' within an automobilized society. These may include certain categories of teenage speed-freaks (ie, white, male and college-bound), environmentally conscious bicyclists participating in 'critical mass' events (although this is an ambiguously acceptable group) and the regulated protest march that effectively rents space on the road for a permitted amount of time. Any other type of opposition will have to be anarchist and singular: a sniper, speeding drunk driver or some other criminal fleeing the law.

In short, it is perhaps only the *terrorist*, the shadowy non-citizen, who actually resists the edifice, but even her actions are mostly pathetic, not necessarily because they are always ineffective but because they convey a deep and fundamental impotence. For finally, this rebel is inevitably one without a constituency; at best, she represents the repressed minority rather than the noble revolutionary with *just* cause. Thus it was even in the insurrection in Los Angeles, the disruption though major was powerless, and turned out to be a rather clumsy and formless expression of resistance whose effectiveness was measured by the scale of looting rather than in any other terms expressing the depth of protest.

In the wilderness of Milton Keynes, Southern California or the West Bank, few pedestrians are expected to disarm the smooth flow of (liberal) auto-drivers. But even here one can discern a weak but dual demand to accommodate pedestrians: their existence in fact – whether as recent immigrant workers, the aged, children or potential terrorists – and the growing nostalgia among citizen drivers for a 'community', defined as comic-book towns representing the 'new urbanism' where citizens nod politely as they walk past each other on clean side-walks with potted plants and outdoor cafés. It is this fantasy that the unruly pedestrian confounds, either by jumping across roads and highways that actually have no access for walking or by remaining the stranger that he is. And no matter how much the upright citizen-driver would like to tolerate him, it seems that he will not learn; not even a sound beating appears to correct his recalcitrance.

Somewhere in these logics of late liberalism we can discern a faint echo of black deviants being chased by white police officers who eventually exercise 'reasonable force', juries calmly handing difficult rationalized verdicts to keep out agents of social disorder and the impotent rage of an awkward rebellion being expressed against the edifice. And we take notice of the implied threat in the simple declaration that *we should all recognize and reaffirm the fact that we are now liberals. 'Or else, you never know, it might one day no longer be true.'*

Notes

1 As the *Economist* quote might indicate, liberalism is contested terrain precisely because it claims to be ecumenical, both as philosophy and practice. In this essay, I mostly employ a narrow definition of 'liberalism', referring primarily to a foundational rights-based political philosophy that emphasizes negative liberties and 'market' liberty over institutional context, and upholds a vigilant distinction between the public and private spheres of human activity. For the most part, I ignore libertarianism as well as contemporary American interpretations of political liberalism that confusingly identify it with welfare state policies. The central liberal sensibility I emphasize is one in which individual liberty is the foundation of all human freedom.

2 Recently, there has been a spate of indignant writings by libertarians toward so-called 'automobile-critics' who are themselves accused of being political liberals! See, for example, Loren Lomasky (1995), and James Dunn (1998).

3 In several European countries there is roughly one car per two persons (man, woman or child), whereas in the United States, this ratio is nearly double (about 850 cars per 1000 persons).

4 In the United States, and less but not significantly so in Europe, billions of dollars are expended each year on cars, advertising, fuels, parking, highways and related physical assets. In fact, the true social costs of cars are almost imponderable, given the vast and destructive impacts of auto-mobility on the local and global environment, global security, personal safety, and access (for children, the elderly, the poor and the disabled), spatial aesthetics, and social cohesion (Delucchi, 1997; Pucher, 1999). I borrow the phrase 'machine space' from Horvath (1974), whose eco-centric

analysis of the contradictions of automobility controlling its own destiny appears to me as yet another instance of the disavowal of politics in car culture discourse.

5 While most liberals believe in the evolutionary agenda of the Enlightenment project rather than on ideas of contingency, I am including here the views of progressives in the liberal camp like Richard Rorty (1989) who might suggest that automobility is a contingent product of social and economic history and not dependent on liberal values. Traditional liberals, on the other hand, might treat automobility as an *expected* if not natural outcome of technological innovation fed by the Enlightenment, but even for them, it is no more noteworthy for theory-building than aviation or the Internet.

6 Of course, this line of reasoning is particularly unimpressive in these examples since the cultural grip in each – and of both together – is major, if not ominous. Indeed, with the political economy of globalization becoming an emerging area of liberal concern, one could well imagine them getting folded deep into liberal theory (Beitz, 1999; Caney, 2002).

7 An important exception is Peter Ling's impressive cultural history of automobility in the early part of the twentieth century, which brings to light the conditions of formation of the consumer-driver subject (Ling, 1990).

8 In this section I draw on a number of media reports, Gooding-Williams (1993) and my own interpretation as a native informant.

9 This confounding effect of automobilized (or otherwise deliberately managed) space on political resistance has been commented on elsewhere (Davis, 1990), but also in other contexts, including South Africa during apartheid and the Palestinian territories on the West Bank and Gaza. See, for instance, several issues of *Space and Polity*.

References

Agarwal, A., S. Narain and A.Sharma (1999) *Green Politics*. New Delhi: Centre for Science and Environment.

Banham, R. (1971) *Los Angeles: The Architecture of Four Ecologies*. New York: Harper & Row.

Barber, B.R. (1984) *Strong Democracy: Participatory Politics for a New Age*. Berkeley: University of California Press.

Beitz, C.R. (1999) 'International Liberalism and distributive justice: A survey of recent thought' *World Politics*, 51: 269–296.

Berlin, I. (1969) *Four Essays on Liberty*. Oxford: Oxford University Press.

Bourdieu, P. (1977) *Outline of a Theory of Practice*. Cambridge: Cambridge University Press.

Caney, S. (2002) 'Cosmopolitanism and the law of peoples' *Journal of Political Philosophy*, 10: 95–123.

Castells, M. (1996) *The Rise of the Network Society*. Cambridge, MA: Blackwell Publishers.

Connolly, W.E. (2002) *Neuropolitics: Thinking, Culture, Speed*. Minneapolis, MN: University of Minnesota Press.

Davis, M. (1990) *City of Quartz: Excavating the Future in Los Angeles*. London: Verso.

Delucchi, M. (1997) *The Annualised Social Cost of Motor Vehicle Use in the U.S., 1990–1991: Summary of Theory, Data, Methods, and Results*: Institute of Transportation Studies, UC Davis, California.

Didion, J. (1970) *Play it as it Lays*. New York: Farrar, Straus & Giroux.

Dunn, J.A. (1998) *Driving Forces: The Automobile, Its Enemies, and the Politics of Mobility*. Washington, D.C.: Brookings Institution Press.

Economist (1996) 'The perils of complacency' *The Economist*, December 21st, 1996.

Featherstone, M. (1991) *Consumer Culture and Postmodernism*. London: Sage.

Flink, J.J. (1988) *The Automobile Age*. Cambridge, MA: MIT Press.

Foucault, M. (1987) 'The ethic of care for the self as a practice of freedom: An interview with Michel Foucault' *Philosophy and Social Criticism* 12: 112–131.

Gewirth, A. (1978) *Reason and Morality*. London: University of Chicago Press.

Gewirth, A. (1990) 'Two types of Cost-Benefit Analysis' in D. Scherer (ed.) *Upstream/Downstream: Issues in Environmental Ethics*. Philadelphia: Temple University Press.

Gooding-Williams, R. (1993) *Reading Rodney King/Reading Urban Uprising*. New York: Routledge.

Gray, J. (1986) *Liberalism*. Minneapolis: University of Minnesota Press.

Harvey, D. (1982) *The Limits to Capital*. Oxford: Blackwell.

Horvath, R.J. (1974) 'Machine space' *Geographical Review*, 64: 167–188.

Kateb, G. (1984) 'The resources of American liberalism: Democratic individuality and the claims of politics' *Political Theory*, 12: 331–360.

Kukathas, C. (1993) *Multicultural Citizens: The Philosophy and Politics of Identity*, CIS readings, 9. St. Leonard's, NSW, Australia: Centre for Independent Studies.

Kymlicka, W. (1989) *Liberalism, Community, and Culture*. Oxford: Clarendon Press.

Ling, P.J. (1990) *America and the Automobile: Technology, Reform, and Social Change*. Manchester: Manchester University Press.

Lomasky, L. (1997) 'Autonomy and automobility' *The Independent Review* II: 5–28.

Meyer, J.W. (1986) 'Myths of socialization and personality' in T.S. Heller, M. Sosna and D.E. Wellbery (eds) *Reconstructing Individualism*. Stanford CA: University of Stanford Press.

Mumford, L. (1967) *The Myth of the Machine*. New York: Harcourt Brace & World.

Okin, S. (1998) 'Feminism and multiculturalism: Some tensions' *Ethics*, 108: 661–684.

Pucher, J. (1999) 'Transportation paradise: Realm of the nearly perfect automobile? A review of "Driving Forces"' *Transportation Quarterly*, 53: 115–120.

Rancière, J. (2001) 'Ten theses on politics' *Theory and Event*, 5(3), http://muse.jhu.edu/journals/theory_and_event.

Rorty, R. (1989) *Contingency, Irony, and Solidarity*. Cambridge: Cambridge University Press.

Sandel, M.J. (1998) *Liberalism and the Limits of Justice*. Cambridge: Cambridge University Press.

Schneider, K. R. (1971) *Autokind vs. Mankind: An Analysis of Tyranny, A Proposal For Rebellion, a Plan for Reconstruction*. New York: Norton.

Sweetman, P. (2003) 'Twenty-first century dis-ease? Habitual reflexivity or the reflexive habitus' *Sociological Review*, 51: 528–549.

Taylor, C. (1985) *Philosophy and the Human Sciences*. Cambridge: Cambridge University Press.

Tocqueville, A. de, P. Bradley, H. Reeve and F. Bowen (1966) *Democracy in America*. New York: A. A. Knopf.

Toy, E. and J.K. Hammitt (2003) 'Safety impacts of SUVs, vans, and pickup trucks in two-vehicle crashes' *Risk Analysis*, 23: 641–650.

Unger, R.M. (1987) *False Necessity: Anti-Necessitarian Social Theory in the Service of Radical Democracy*. Cambridge: Cambridge University Press.

Vanouse, P. and P. Weyhrauch (1995) *The Consensual Fantasy Engine*. http://www.contrib.andrew.cmu.edu/usr/pv28/cfe.html, accessed 2004.

Walzer, M. (1983) *Spheres of Justice: A Defense of Pluralism and Equality*. New York: Basic Books.

Part Three
Representing Automobility

No literal connection: images of mass commodification, US militarism, and the oil industry, in *The Big Lebowski*

David Martin-Jones

Dude: 'Walter, I don't see any connection with Vietnam, man.'
Walter: 'Well there isn't a *literal* connection dude.'

Introduction

The majority of material written on the films of the Coen brothers has focused on their status as *auteurs* (Körte and Seessien, 1998; Bergan, 2000; Woods, 2000; Romney, 2001). This trend has ensured that interpretations of their films as products of American national cinema (ie, as expressions of American ideology, or national identity) are in the minority. It has also meant that, especially in the case of *The Big Lebowski* (1997), political subtexts have been either missed or ignored, by film studies academics and film critics. Somewhat typical of the conclusions reached by such an approach is William Preston Robertson's assertion that the film is 'nothing less than a pop cultural potpourri' (Robertson, 1998: 37). Similarly, Carolyn Russell labels the film – when viewed in relation to the rest of the Coen brothers' *oeuvre* – 'an exercise in overbranding' (Russell, 2001: 166). Whilst both writers come at the film from different viewpoints they seem united in viewing its myriad popular influences and intertextual references as ultimately meaningless.

This stance is also supported by Ronald Bergan's claim that: 'There is no compelling reason for *The Big Lebowski* being set . . . at the time of the Gulf War' (Bergan, 2000: 198). Yet this seems a particularly misconceived statement, especially considering the political readings that already exist of other Coen brothers films that lack the specific references to military events found in *The Big Lebowski*. For instance, Carolyn Russell interprets their earlier film, *Barton Fink* (1991) as an analogy for the rise of fascism and the subsequent holocaust of WWII. Indeed, her reading is extremely plausible, even though the only references to these events in the film are oblique images that barely stand out from its stylized, early 1940s *mise-en-scène* (Russell, 2001: 88). If such a case can be made for this film, then why not for *The Big Lebowski*? Although Russell's argument from product overbranding corresponds to contemporary thinking on the use of the auteur's name as a marketing label (Corrigan, 1991), another interpretation is also possible.

This chapter examines the political subtext of *The Big Lebowski*. This subtext critiques the growth of car culture in twentieth century America, and the nation's resultant involvement in overseas wars for oil. The chapter explores the various formal and narrative elements which are used to construct the subtext, piecing it together from its often oblique references to the changing face of postwar America, its urban geography, its economy, and its ideology. In particular it focuses on the way that US foreign policy is determined by Fordism, the automobile, and the need for oil, as it is represented in the film. Thus the film is examined as a work of national cinema that engages with the reasons behind the first Persian Gulf War. With the rapid developments that have taken place in the Persian Gulf since 9/11, this subtext has become much easier to spot than it was previously. This fact, however, does not diminish the importance of understanding its construction.

Exactly how 'deliberate' this subtext is must remain a matter of contention. Undoubtedly the Coen brothers would deny its existence, as they often do when faced with critical interpretations of their work. Indeed, I do not wish to prescribe agency to the Coen brothers. After all, as the debate on auteurism has shown, this would be to uphold the extremely problematic notion of Enlightenment individualism that film studies has variously tried to shake off since the 1980s (Stoddart, 1995). Moreover, as Rajan has shown in this volume, such a stance would align this chapter with the same 'liberal disposition' that is 'product and producer' (Rajan, this volume: ch. 7) of modernity, and the resultant car culture of 'automobility' that accompanies it. I do not wish, however, entirely to detract agency from them either. Rather, this chapter operates in the space opened up by the interaction between recent American films and a certain type of spectator that they consciously, but obliquely, target.

As Nöel Carroll has argued, in the 1970s/80s post-classical Hollywood films were purposefully produced to maximize profits by targeting both a college-educated, film buff audience, and an uninitiated, genre-loving, often adolescent audience. Through allusions to previous films, filmmakers and genres, additional layers of meaning have been created. Thus a 'two-tiered system of communication' (Carroll, 1998: 245) has been established between Hollywood filmmakers and their audience. This particular independent film of the late 1990s could be said to aim at a similarly split demographic, but with a more critical aim in mind than the works of Steven Spielberg, George Lucas, *et al.* In this case, the film's myriad allusions provide clues to the historical meaning of the film's political subtext. Unable to address the issue of American foreign policy in the direct way that a polemical documentary like *Bowling for Columbine* (2003) or *Fahrenheit 9/11* (2004) does, the Coen brothers have inserted a subversive subtext into their film instead.

On the one hand it is tempting to argue that the film functions on several levels due to the astuteness of the filmmakers. On the other, however, the interpretation I offer suggests that a certain audience demographic negotiates a political meaning with the text. This assertion is more in the line with the change of direction in film studies that emerged with the works of Christine Gledhill (1988), Alexander Doty (1993) etc, away from auteurism. Much as a queer reading focuses on certain aspects of a film in order to draw out a queer subtext, so too does this reading function in order to (re)construct the film's political subtext.

Initially clueless

It was around the eleventh or twelfth viewing of *The Big Lebowski* that I realized that something about the opening did not make sense. For some reason the film pointedly placed this otherwise irrelevant *noir* story within the context of America's involvement in Kuwait, in 1991. It deliberately foregrounded this fact at the beginning of the narrative, in both the voiceover and the appearance of President George Bush Sr. speaking on a television in a supermarket. It then, however, delivered a story which apparently bore no relation whatsoever to the Persian Gulf War. I began to realize that something was bubbling away under the surface of this film that went beyond its appearance as 'pop cultural potpourri'. This film wasn't just a postmodern take on Raymond Chandler, it also had a subtext that dealt with America's need to control the global supply of oil.

The Big Lebowski is set in Los Angeles, in the early 1990s. It follows a middle-aged waster, Jeff Lebowski (Jeff Bridges) a relic of the 1960s nicknamed, 'the Dude'. Together with his flammable Vietnam veteran buddy, Walter Sobchak (John Goodman) the Dude spends his life drinking White Russians, smoking pot, bowling and avoiding paying the rent. Due to an initial bungle by two dimwitted thugs employed by the pornography mogul, Jackie Treehorn (Ben Gazzara), the Dude becomes embroiled in a fake kidnapping plot. Three German nihilists are attempting to extort $1m from the Dude's namesake, the Pasadena millionaire Jeffrey Lebowski (David Huddleston). He is the 'Big Lebowski' of the film's title. Entering the world of the wealthy and corrupt the Dude is abused, tricked, drugged and beaten. At the film's conclusion he has achieved next to nothing, his car and home have been trashed, and his friend Donny (Steve Buscemi) has died of a heart attack. All this because someone peed on the Dude's rug. As a story it is still slightly easier to follow than many films based on a Chandler novel, but apparently, mostly entertaining nonsense.

What then, of oil? As I have noted, in its opening sequence the film deliberately informs us that this story is set during America's involvement in Kuwait. Aside from this, however, the film contains only one or two other, oblique references to the first Persian Gulf War. What should we make of these passing references?

At several points during the film, and much to The Dude's exasperation, Walter brings up the subject of Vietnam. In response The Dude angrily confronts him, saying, 'I don't see any connection with Vietnam', and more effusively, 'What was that shit about Vietnam? What the fuck does anything have to do with Vietnam, what the fuck are you talking about?' Similarly, having been informed in the very opening sequence that this is a film set specifically during the time of the Persian Gulf War, and bearing in mind also that the Coen brothers themselves have stated:

> 'We've written the story from a modern point of view and set it very precisely in 1991, during the Persian Gulf War,' Ethan adds, 'which also has a direct effect on the Dude and his friends.' (*Time to Bowl*, 1999: 10)

The viewer might be forgiven for asking, 'What the fuck does any of this have to do with the Persian Gulf War?' Why bring it up at all – either in the film, or the interview – and why state that its context was used so 'precisely', when it seems to have so little relevance to the narrative itself?

From an analysis of the film's opening sequence we can see that the subtext actually examines how the development of America in the twentieth century, and in particular, bourgeois individualism (what we could also term 'automobility'), has encouraged a certain lifestyle to flourish. This is a lifestyle that – as both Dery and Böhm *et al.* point out in this volume – relies upon a steady supply of oil for its continuation. For this reason, the film's subtext suggests, America became involved in a war in the Persian Gulf. Moreover, this war was but the continuation of an already established cold war policy of military intervention in global affairs designed to keep the American market (and therefore, way of life) stable. This policy had already led them into wars in both Korea and Vietnam (Kiernan, 1978: 232). There may not be an immediately apparent, or *literal* connection between the life of The Dude and the Gulf War, but there is a connection.

The film begins with a shot of a tumbleweed rolling across scrub land. On the soundtrack the Sons of the Pioneers sing Bob Nolan's 'Tumbling Tumbleweeds' ('Here on the range I belong, drifting along in the tumbling, tumbleweeds'). On the voiceover, Sam Elliott rambles in the style of a reclining, campfire cowboy, telling a story that occurred 'Way out West'. As the tumbleweed crests the brow of a hill, night falls and the city of Los Angeles appears, sprawling below. A dissolve finds the tumbleweed rolling through the streets of LA, until it finally reaches the sea. At this point we are introduced to the Dude, shopping in a Ralph's supermarket. Here Sam Elliott says:

> This here story I'm about to unfold took place back in the early 90s, just about the time of our conflict with Saddam and the Iraqis. I only mention it cause sometimes there's a man, I won't say a hero, cause what's a hero? But sometimes there's a man, and I'm talking about the Dude here, sometimes there's a man, well, he's the man for his time and place, he fits right in there, and that's the Dude, and Los Angeles.

Behind the checkout a small television shows George Bush Sr. commenting on the need for American intervention in the Persian Gulf. 'This will not stand, this will not stand, this aggression against Kuwait', he states. This was the bullish, official Whitehouse line which led America into war in the Gulf – without consideration of all and any negotiations that could have avoided this seemingly inevitable military conflict – solely in order to establish spurious grounds for an American military presence in the oil rich area of the Middle East (Bennis and Moushabeck, 1992). For Robertson the opening represents:

> . . . an arch statement on America's great Westward Expansion, with Los Angeles being the farthest geographic point in that expansion, not to mention the weirdest and most decadent. And insofar as this is a buddy movie, concerning itself with issues of sex and manhood . . . the arch statement is really about the chauvinism of Westward Expansion, and, indeed, the absurdity of the pioneering American masculine mystique itself. But more than that, it's about the past, and the irony of a land professing a doctrine of newness and expansion that is in reality a vestige of its cowboy past. (Robertson, 1998: 44–5)

This reading seems extremely plausible, especially considering the symbolism of 'night falling on the range', and the immediate replacement of this image with one of the city of Los Angeles. Robertson's reading, however, says nothing of the two initial references to the war in the Persian Gulf. To add some extra depth to this interpretation I will first examine how American expansion and the pioneering masculine mystique are linked.

Following Eric Mottram's argument in *Blood on the Nash Ambassador* (1983), the movement from frontier to city depicted in the film's opening is comparable to the historical shift from the image of the gun-toting, masculine individualist of the nineteenth century frontier, to the automobile driving individualists of the newly emergent twentieth century America. In his analysis of films like *Bonnie and Clyde* (1967) Mottram describes how the image of the car came to extend the western ethos (exemplified in the Billy the Kid myth) by placing the gun on wheels and making it fully automobile. It is this same myth of individual autonomy, supposedly in rebellion against the system, which is deconstructed in the subtext of *The Big Lebowski*.

With the tumbleweed coming to rest on the beach in California, and the colonizing, Westward Expansion literally running out of land, we are invited to question just exactly where this Expansion moved to next. The answer given in the film, through its depiction of several of the main characters, is, Korea, Vietnam and the Persian Gulf. It is these wars (admittedly, amongst others) in which the gun-toting masculine individualist found his twentieth century outlet.

For the film buff viewer the most prominent intertextual reference in this sequence conclusively points to this reading of the film. Bob Nolan's 'Tumbling Tumbleweeds' appears prominently in a very similar sequence in *The Two Jakes* (1990), a film which explicitly critiqued America's need for oil. In this film the distinctive song is heard as detective Jake Gittes (Jack Nicholson) begins to investigate the conspiracy of oil upon which Los Angeles' post-war suburban real estate development was constructed.

As he drives through the San Fernando Valley his car radio plays an advertisement for a new Pontiac car. Gittes changes stations, and 'Tumbling Tumbleweeds' comes on. Gittes is heard in voiceover, reflecting on his latest case:

> Time changes things, like the fruit stand that turns into a filling station. But the foot-prints and signs from the past are everywhere. They've been fighting over this land ever since the first Spanish missionaries showed the Indians the benefits of religion, horses, and a few years of forced labour.

The similarities between the two uses of the same piece of music are apparent. In both instances the frontier-evoking music illustrates how contemporary changes – like the emergence of the filling station under the new Fordist economy – have their roots in America's past, particularly in the colonizing of the land. Far from 'pop cultural potpourri', *The Big Lebowski* uses its inter-textual references and film buff directed allusions to invite the viewer to make the connection between the life of The Dude, his car oriented context, and the legacy of America's past.

From Baron to Barren

Mottram's work on filmic representations of the car is most usefully seen in rela-tion to a much more widely debated issue, that of the role of the motor car in shaping twentieth century America. Several writers, including Antonio Gramsci (1971), David J. St Clair (1986), Peter J. Ling (1990), and James Howard Kunstler (1993) have stressed the importance of Fordism in shaping the geo-graphical, ideological, and economic landscape of America. At the heart of the writing of all these theorists is an examination, and at times a strong advoca-tion, of the thesis that the automobile has had a major impact on the emergence of America as a global superpower. Whilst this is a well known argument it bears briefly rehearsing here.

In 1914 Henry Ford implemented an eight hour working day for a set wage of $5. His rationalization of production in his custom designed Detroit assem-bly plants created a model for mass commodification that would influence first the American, and then the global market economy. The economies of scale associated with the division of the production process into a series of unskilled manual tasks enabled the mass production of a single type of product, as typ-ified by the Model T Ford.

The $5 day ensured not only that workers were content to stay at Ford's fac-tories, but also that there was a large workforce who had extra income to spend on commodities like the motor car. Thus Fordism produced not only the product, but also the market that would buy it. It created a feedback loop which interminably fed consumerism. Moreover, as this process began to spiral out-wards, car production also effected the spatial geography of the United States. The Fordist worker now had access to the necessary capital to buy both car and house. As Urry notes in this volume, these demands from the consumer played a large part in the increasing construction of both highways and commuter suburbs. The increased availability of these facilities, in turn, fed back into the demand for cars, and as more consumers demanded out-of-town housing, the demand for cars rose, and so on. The national geography thus developed around the automobile, and was shaped by Fordism.

WWII led to the economic dominance of Fordism, and to America's global economic strength. America's wartime industries, left undamaged in comparison to its decimated European and Japanese competitors, were relatively unchallenged in the post-war era. For over two decades they enjoyed a period of unbridled production, ensuring economic prosperity for the American consumer. Moreover, as production expanded, so too did the construction of highways and commuter suburbs, along with the new addition of the Interstate.

The fact that America enjoyed such prosperity was mainly due to the Interstate, the economic rationale behind which was military in origin. Whilst it is still debatable whether America's geographical and ideological development were directly influenced by the changes that took place in National Socialist Germany (St Clair, 1986: 149), there were obvious merits to be discerned by the rest of the world in the National Socialist's Autobahn. This was the case both for creating employment during times of depression and for the swift deployment of the military during wartime (Sachs, 1984; Gilroy, 2001). This was so evident that when the argument was put forward in post-war America – notably by people with a vested interest in promoting car production – that an Interstate system would facilitate the evacuation of urban centres and the implementation of military control in the event of a nuclear war, this cold war reasoning met with a favourable response.

The Interstate system, as Kunstler notes, saved the American economy from sliding into recession in the mid 1950s. It became, 'simply the largest public-works project in the history of the world' (Kunstler, 1993: 107), and buoyed up the economy through the 1960s, due to the vast suburban expansion it enabled. Neither Kunstler nor St Clair, however, are naïve enough to believe that the political justification given for this expansive programme – the supposed 'evacuation of cities during a nuclear attack' (Kunstler, 1993: 107) – was anything other than 'window dressing' (St Clair, 1986: 154). Such ideas pandered to cold war paranoia in order to promote the sale of cars for suburban commuters. Whatever the justification, as a consequence of this vast construction work America continued to grow and prosper during the first two decades of the post-war era. The prosperity it enjoyed was facilitated by an Interstate system which, whether directly or indirectly, aligned economic prosperity with an ethos of military mobility. It is here that the ideal of Westward Expansion, the gun-toting individualist, and the apparent need for automobile freedom for the consumer are most clearly conflated.

The extensive programme began by Ford, however, had one small drawback. Building huge roads and stocking them with cars for suburbanites was fine until you ran out of room. Any threat to the oil supply, moreover, could also have disastrous effects. Los Angeles, then, is perhaps *the* point at which the Westward Expansion of the Interstate, necessitated by Fordism, literally ran out of room. Whether, as St Clair notes, this is the city that has been most influenced in its development and design by the existence of the car, or, as Kunstler argues, the geography of LA was decided long before the introduction of the automobile, it remains extremely difficult to get around in LA without a set of wheels (St Clair, 1986: 128; Kunstler, 1993: 207–12).

By the early 1970s, the American economy was beginning to feel the strain of these limitations. Admittedly this was not solely due to reasons of internal stress. The previously crippled European and Japanese wartime economies had rebuilt and were competing with American manufacturers for their domestic markets. Indeed, the competition which these economies brought to the global market also required the transferal of the manufacturing base to developing countries, in order to cut the costs of production. The American economy, based on the self-perpetuating production of both commodity and consumer, had finally reached saturation point. With the loss of its domestic manufacturing base, employment gradually leveled off, demand fell, and stagflation set in. Add to this the fact that America was now importing much of its oil, the crisis effect of the Arab oil embargo of 1973, and OPEC's decision to raise oil prices, and it becomes clear how imperative the need to control a steady oil supply had become for the American economy. This had become an extremely serious issue if the way of life supported by the automobile driven economy was to survive. For this reason, America's intervention in the Persian Gulf nearly twenty years later, in the undiplomatic manner in which it was pursued, is perhaps no big surprise. In fact, George Bush Jr.'s continuation of this policy under the guise of a perpetual, Orwellian styled, 'war on terror' also seems unsurprising, although no less devastating as a result. The question remains, what does all this have to do with *The Big Lebowski*? Just what is the connection?

Characters

The Big Lebowski uses its characters to directly equate the myth of the gun-toting, automobile individual with post-war US military intervention abroad. The 'Big Lebowski', we learn early on in the film, lost the use of his legs whilst fighting in Korea. Yet this character is the most vehemently bombastic in defense of his individual business achievements. As his personal assistant, Brandt (Philip Seymour Hoffman) takes pains to point out, the Big Lebowski is not 'crippled' or 'handicapped', but 'disabled'. This specific term suggests that he is defined by his primary loss, that of the ability to remain automobile. Made vehicularly automobile once more through the prosthesis of an electric wheelchair, the now *re-abled* Big Lebowski exists in the film to critique the effect of the masculine myth of the automobile achiever on the American economy.

We first meet the Big Lebowski through the pictures that adorn the walls of his house. As the Dude is talked through them by Brandt we see the Big

Lebowski posing with prominent members of the Reagan administration. These first glimpses, as we are informed simultaneously of the Big Lebowski's war trauma by Brandt, suggest that the legacy of US involvement in Korea, and the ethos of the automobile achiever, continued to survive in American politics well into the 1980s. When the Dude meets the Big Lebowski, moreover, he states his belief in himself in terms that mirror his belief in his unchallenged automobility. 'I didn't blame anyone for the loss of my legs, some Chinaman in Korea took them from me but I went out and achieved anyway.' This achievement he further addresses in terms which mirror the capitalist demands of the Fordist economy when he tells the departing Dude that he should: 'do what your parents did! Get a job, sir!' Finally, his 'vanity', his daughter Maude (Julianne Moore) points out, is apparent in his decision to keep his trophy wife, Bunny, in a full allowance, despite her obvious lack of any feelings for him. Typically, the image he creates, of his phallic, gun-toting mystique, also extends to his masculine prowess.

This image, however, is gradually deconstructed by the film. The Big Lebowski is shown to be a fraud whose trophy wife stars in pornographic movies, who has little business acumen of his own, who lives on an allowance from his daughter, and who has been gradually embezzling money from the 'Little Lebowski Urban Achievers' trust fund. He appears as an image of the masculine myth of the frontier achiever, artificially made mobile on a set of automated wheels. This is the reality of the disabled America of the early 1990s, the legacy of Fordism necessitating its constant, war-like need to control the global supply of oil.

Walter, the Vietnam veteran, further emphasizes the theme of American military intervention overseas. He also (literally) expresses the excessive rhetoric of the gun-toting individual. Whilst not specifically a war for oil in the same way that the Persian Gulf War was, Vietnam was still a war which, like Korea, enabled the traditional wartime industries (a large proportion of which are automobile orientated) to flourish. A war supposedly to keep South East Asia free from the fabled domino effect, it was also a war to secure a greater share of the world market for American capitalism. As Michael Tanzer (1992: 267) points out, the oil companies Mobil and Shell took full advantage of the war, setting up drilling rigs in Asia. Mobil in fact, were still drilling off the coast of Vietnam on the last day of the war. Through the use of these bullish characters the film illustrates David Riesman's contention that WWII 'had taught Americans the lesson that wars cure depressions and are, as conducted extraterritorially, less unpleasant . . . a tacit agreement that government can control depression, if need be, by war and preparation for war' (Riesman, 1964: 296). Thus the gun-toting myth that colonized America, we are shown, has become a global force in the latter half of the twentieth century.

Finally, the film brings this critique of US foreign policy up to date with the inclusion of the Persian Gulf War and Bush's hawk-like stance on the need to use excessive military force. The continuation of this policy from Vietnam to the Gulf is foregrounded when Walter, the man who argues that, 'Pacifism is not something to hide behind', utilizes Bush's aggressive rhetoric of 'unchecked aggression'. The ideology of the gun-toting frontiersman has so permeated the fabric of American society, however, that Walter uses it to justify seeking recompense for someone peeing on the Dude's rug!

Walter is also used to represent the American support of Israel in the Middle East. This is most evident when he arrives at the bowling alley loudly quoting Theodor Herzl, father of Zionism: 'If you will it, it is no dream.' Walter's devotion to the Jewish religion continues after the divorce from his wife, Cynthia, even though it was his marriage that necessitated his conversion. Walter's blind devotion works as a loose allegory for the American military support of Israel, a cause doggedly pursued by United States foreign policy despite the flagrant disregard of Palestinian rights by the Israeli government. The aggressive individualism of the frontier seen in Walter's unthinking use of the Bush regime's militaristic rhetoric is thus shown to be complicit with America's continued intervention in the Middle East. As an allegorical figure, running his own security firm enables all-American psycho Walter to make use of the skills he learnt in Vietnam. These are shown to be at once ludicrous and extremely dangerous, particularly during the botched pay off deal. Here he drops the symbolically designated Uzi, which fires rounds off wildly in all directions, indirectly causing the Dude to crash his car.

Dream

It is to the image of Saddam Hussein in the 'Gutterballs' dream sequence that I now turn. This is the most crucial image in the creation of the film's iconic subtext. Beginning with the humorously phallic image of a bowling pin flanked by two bowling balls, it immediately flags up its comment on masculinity. The Dude appears and is handed a pair of bowling shoes by Saddam Hussein, from a huge, uniform rack of pigeon holes leading up to the moon. This image encapsulates everything that this masculine myth promotes. It portrays the mass commodification of Fordism, seen in the rows upon rows of identical bowling shoes, which is itself based upon the need to control the supply of oil, as seen in the figure of Saddam Hussein handing the Dude his mass-produced shoes. Following the dream logic of this image, the rack of shoes is topped off by an image of the moon, suggesting the ancient parable of the man who attempted to build a tower to the moon. This impossible mission is a suitable analogy for the limits that face Fordist capitalism, once it runs out of room to maneuvre, in this case due to over-production and the saturation of the domestic market.

An image containing almost all the same ingredients appears in *Three Kings* (1999). Set during the first Gulf War, *Three Kings* explores exactly the same gung-ho, American capitalist abroad (gun toting individualist) myth. Towards the middle of the film, Troy Barlow (Mark Wahlberg), a fortune-seeking American GI from Detroit on a mission to steal Kuwaiti gold bullion in order to buy 'convertibles in every colour', is captured by Iraqi troops. As he is tortured, Captain Said (Said Taghmaoui) informs Troy that his weapons, sabotage and interrogation training were all provided by US special forces during the Iran-Iraq war. The following exchange then takes place:

Said: You are here for save Iraqi people?
Troy: Yes.
Said: (*Incredulous*) Really?
Troy: Yeah.
Said: A lot of people in trouble in this world my man, and you don't fight no fucking war for them.
Troy: You invaded another country, you can't do that.
Said: Why not dude?
Troy: Because it makes the world crazy, you need to keep it stable.
Said: For what, your pick up-truck?
Troy: No, for stability, stabilize the region.

At this point Said forces an unlabelled CD into Troy's mouth. As another Iraqi soldier pours crude oil down Troy's throat, Said says, 'This is your fucking stability my main man'. In this image the official US line, on keeping the region stable, is confronted by a literal rebuttal. Rather like the anonymous, homogeneous bowling shoes in the comparable sequence in *The Big Lebowski*, here the anonymous CD represents the mass commodified product of Fordism, over which the crude oil of Kuwait pours into the mouth of the American 'consumer.' It is not the country, its people, or the 'region' that is the primary objective of the American military, but the stabilization of the price and supply of oil needed to sustain the 'pick up truck' lifestyle. The stability that US foreign policy speaks of is that of consumerism. It is based upon the mass production of goods designed by Fordism, which is itself fuelled by the oil that the US must now import if it is to stay in the global driving seat. Thus, any threat to this global dominance will meet with military force. Put another way, 'This aggression against . . . *American interests which happen to be in Kuwait* . . . will not stand'.

To return finally to the image of Saddam Hussein and the bowling shoes, the Busby Berkeley styled musical sequence that follows is reminiscent of the American cinema of the depression era. Once again the intertextual reference is far from meaningless. It serves to conflate this image of Fordism, mass commodification and the need for oil, with the historical period of the New Deal. This was a time when the automobile economy was deliberately promoted in order to help build America out of recession, through policies that indirectly increased Federal Aid to highway construction programmes (St Clair, 1986). Considering this was the same process facilitated by the construction of the Autobahn in National Socialist Germany, it now seems a little less random that the German nihilists who fake Bunny's kidnapping are members of German 'techno pop' band, 'Autobahn'.

Mise-en-scène

The oil subtext created by the film's depiction of characters and dreams is compounded by its use of the Googie architectural style in its *mise-en-scène*. This style was deliberately chosen by the Coen brothers to enhance the look of their film (Robertson, 1998: 102–4), yet initially it is not obvious why. If we consider what the Googie style represents, however, some interesting answers emerge.

The Googie style was named after the Googie coffee shops of Los Angeles. The term came generically to designate many of the coffee shops and diners which were built all over the USA during the 1950s and early 1960s. The Googie style is easily recognizable because it developed in order to be eye-catching. Googie diners and coffee shops were built as huge advertisements for the goods they sold, buildings designed as signs *specifically in order to catch the eye of the motorist travelling along America's steadily growing highway network.* According to Alan Hess (1985) a typical Googie roadside diner might consist of a huge, space-aged, upwardly-angled roof of concrete, beneath which the entire front of the diner would typically be constructed of glass, illuminating its cherry red plastic seating booths and gleaming chrome interior. It was a design that addressed the passing motorist's glance, stating, 'pull in and consume here'. This automobile-orientated architecture then, developed to meet the demands of the changing suburban/highway geography of post-war America.

More to the point, the construction of the distinctive shapes of the Googie style developed because of the survival of America's wartime industries, and their need for a new outlet in peace time. The building technologies and techniques that developed as a consequence of the war, especially in the use of concrete and plastics, were thus utilized in the domestic market in the immediate post-war years. Yet again we see the development of the automobile culture expand along with developments in military technology. Military innovations of WWII were also celebrated in the architectural motifs employed in Googie, most noticeably in rocket, jet and atomic motifs. In fact, the neon starbursts that recur at several points during the film are extremely similar to the atomic symbols that adorned many Googie styled buildings (Hess, 1985: 130–1). The starbursts were deliberately added to both the interior and exterior of the bowling alley where the Dude and Walter play, in order to suggest a Googie look. They also recur in both dream sequences, evoking further the fears of an era in which vast interstates could be constructed under the pretence of preparation for a nuclear war.

It now seems particularly appropriate that the two diners in which we see the Dude and Walter eating were specifically chosen because they represented the Googie style (*Time to Bowl*, 1999: 14). Placing the film's characters in settings which evoke the post-war boom time further strengthens the subtext's critique of the consumer culture that the narrative apparently avoids.

Bowling

Finally, this brings us to a major theme of *The Big Lebowski*, leisure, and in particular, bowling. The Fordist eight-hour, $5 day and the desire to consume that it evoked, were predicated upon the consumer having both the money and the time for leisure. The consumer lifestyle was based not only upon the automobility of the consumer, but also upon leisure time. In fact, when the Dude is asked by Maude what he does for recreation, his response explicitly conflates the two. He states: 'The usual, bowl, drive around, the occasional acid flashback'. The recreational use of drugs aside, 'bowling' and 'driving around' are both felt to be leisure activities by the Dude. Automobility is thus valued by the consumer in and for itself, not because they believe that it facilitates the work/leisure lifestyle, but because they mistakenly believe it to be its reward.

Unlike Walter, however, the Dude is not a typical Fordist worker. Where Walter represents the frontier cowboy, the Dude, morphing out of the tumbleweed of the opening, represents the frontier drifter. Gridlocked in contemporary LA the 'Fool' (a meaning implied by the term 'Dude' in the nineteenth century) has become the waster. He is a product of the 1960s counter culture that rebelled against the warlike myth of the gun-toting individual promoted during the Vietnam war, and the economic miracles it could supposedly perform. He emerged during the period which witnessed the peak and decline in American economic prosperity, during the late 1960s, and the oil crisis of the early 1970s. The Dude won't work. He is, as the Big Lebowski calls him, 'a bum', a drink and drug consuming drop-out, the antithesis of the ideological aims of *'embourgeoisiement'* (Ling, 1990: 176) implemented by Fordism. The Dude does not adhere to the throwaway ethos of consumerism, as we see in his treatment, or rather in the film's treatment, of his car.

It became evident in the early years of Fordism that a high turnover of car production necessitated a constant displacement, in the mind of the consumer at least, of the previous model with the image of the latest (Riesman, 1964). Since then cars have ceased to be designed or sold for their durability. Rather, cars are marketed as fashionable items in a rapidly changing market. For the Fordist consumer, the replacing of the old with the new is an inevitability. For the Dude, who has opted out of the system, this is simply not an option. Living in a city in which a set of wheels is essential, he is forced to keep on running his dilapidated car, as he simply cannot afford to replace it. His car's gradual destruction throughout the course of the film demonstrates his alienation from the culture he lives in. Shot by Walter's dropped Uzi during the bungled pay off, smashed into a telegraph pole, stolen by a joyrider, crashed into a dumpster, beaten with a crowbar, and finally burned out by nihilists, the car's gradual destruction signals the Dude's downward spiral into pedestrianism, his crushing defeat under the wheels of the infinitely replaceable, automobile economy.

When the Dude's car is recovered by the police, he retrieves it from a crowded police lot. Here cars stretch out of the frame, quite literally, as far as the eye can see. The Dude naively asks the policeman if they have any 'promising leads' as to who stole the car. He replies:

> Leads? Yeah, sure. I'll just check with the boys down at the crime lab. We got four more detectives working on the case . . . they got us working in shifts! (*Laughs*) Leads! Leads!

Effective policing of car crime is impossible in present day LA. Nor is it a main priority, due to the rapid production and turnover of disposable cars. The vast number of cars which have not been claimed from the police lot bear testimony to this fact. If we compare this sequence with a predecessor, from Edgar G. Ulmer's *Detour* (1945), then we can see how much the interim has changed the face of the American landscape. In this film Al Roberts (Tom Neal) suggests to *femme fatale* Vera (Ann Savage) that he dump the stolen car of the man he has accidentally killed, once they reach LA. She responds: 'Why, you dope! Don't you know a deserted automobile always rates an investigation?' Although this is not in any way an accurate historical document, if nothing else these films show how different the public attitude towards cars has become. Thus *The Big Lebowski*'s subtext critiques contemporary consumer attitudes towards the disposable automobile.

In fact, even by completely opting out the Dude loses. His life of complete leisure is that of one who lives on the luxuries which the American economy provides for its workers. What is this type of automated leisure after all, than practice for the Fordist workforce? Bowling is a game in which the consumer racks up a points score by knocking over a set of pins that are then automatically righted, enabling him to knock them over again. This pursuit is the perfect practice for the automated worker of the Fordist assembly plant. The perpetual repetition of a simple, unskilled task is rewarded by the continual, automated arrival of its duplicate, and the accumulated points score of the $5 day. It is for this reason that the picture which dominates the Dude's living room, of President Nixon bowling, is so telling. The president famous for his continued support of the escalating American war effort in Vietnam is pictured enjoying the fruits of the leisure that his militarism enabled, at exactly the time at which the Fordist US economy entered into its time of crisis, the early 1970s.

In short, if we are still looking to pinpoint the connection that the film makes between war in the Persian Gulf and the irreverent noir story of the fake kidnapping of Bunny Lebowski, then it is, in fact, all connected. It may not be a *literal* connection, after all this is not *Bowling for Columbine* or *Fahrenheit 9/11*. As the commercial 'success' of each Coen brothers' film reflects on their ability to make their next film, it is not wise to rock the establishment's boat too much. There is a connection, however. Every facet of the automobile-orientated American life on the screen is directly a product of an ideologically fueled economic policy that has taken America to global dominance in the post-war world, and necessitated its role as global police (read, military) force (see also

Dery, this volume). This is the cause of its interventions in Asia, the Middle East, and we should perhaps also add, South America. The entire American way of life is based upon the war in the Persian Gulf, that's what anything has to do with Saddam Hussein. The fact that this point is relegated to the film's subtext, and is otherwise completely ignored by the narrative, is perhaps testament to the way in which some factions in America were able to effectively ignore (or perhaps, prefer to ignore) the real reasons behind the military events that America was involved in.

Conclusion

The subtext that I have pieced together from these images emerges only when they are viewed in isolation from the film's narrative 'pop cultural potpourri'. It works by referencing previous films that share similar themes and concerns. The second meeting with the Big Lebowski for instance, whilst reminiscent of scenes in both *Citizen Kane* (1941) and *The Big Sleep* (1946) is also, Carolyn Russell points out, 'visually evocative' (Russell, 2001: 146) of a similar scene in *The Magnificent Ambersons* (1942). This is perhaps *the* film about how automobiles irrevocably changed the American landscape, and the values of its suburbanites. Yet the political content of the subtext requires more than just a knowledge of film history. It also requires a knowledge of American history and ideology.

The question this chapter begs is, just how useful is such a subtext? If only the anorak-wearing few like myself will be able to spot it, is there really any point? Since researching and presenting this material at the Automobility conference in 2002 it has come to my attention that Mike Wayne – addressing the film as part of a much broader discussion of political cinema in general – has already attempted to answer this question. Briefly noting the film's allegorical reading of America's involvement in the Gulf War, Wayne concludes that the allegory is ultimately not very effective, as it is so 'unreadable' (Wayne, 2001: 131). He then proceeds to analyse a more effective use of allegory in certain South American cinemas. Undoubtedly this distinction suits his purpose, the charting of the development of Third Cinema in a post-colonial context (for an introduction to Third Cinema see Solanas and Gettino, 1976; Espinosa, 2000; Gabriel, 1976; Pines and Willeman, 1991).

In this context, *The Big Lebowski* does indeed seem something of a failure. When viewed more locally, however, solely in relation to American cinema, it seems a little less so. After all, American cinema has traditionally shied away from overt engagement with politics (Lindhom and Hall, 2000: 32), preferring instead to smuggle political messages into its films (Davies and Wells, 2002: 7). Taking this into consideration, Wayne's work could be said to uphold the somewhat elitist prejudice – that American films are mostly politically disconnected spectacle – on which theories of Third Cinema were initially predicated. The limiting culture industry binary that this stance is in danger of recreating (ie, that popular – especially Hollywood – films are 'bad', and art/avant garde cinemas are 'good') says nothing of the market orientations, or the viewing practices of the audiences of such popular films (Hollows, 1995). As this chapter shows however, if we are to take Carroll's views on the two-tier audience of post-classical Hollywood films into account, then we must realize that there is a certain section of the audience who are able to read the informing allusions of the film's subtext. Indeed, this is a demographic who have been trained to do so since the 1970s/80s.

Admittedly it is up to these viewers to piece together the historical resonances that these filmic allusions create. If aiming at this audience is what makes an American film political, however, then it is indeed a success. Moreover, whether the film's political subtext reached this audience may not necessarily be entirely the responsibility of the film. This is a statement I make despite my own initial difficulties in piecing the clues together. Rather, it is a lack of communication between film and audience that causes its 'failure'. This is a situation created by industry expectations of profit and readability, and the promotion (or lack of it) of an engaged, critical, national film culture. After all, it is easy to say that all American films should be more overtly political, but who is going to pay for them to be made if there is no audience to consume such films? Like many independent films then, *The Big Lebowski* addresses a split demographic in order both to capture a market share of the mainstream audience and to address those able to discover a political critique within an otherwise ludicrous, albeit very entertaining film.

References

Bennis, P. and M. Moushabeck (eds.) (1992) *Beyond the Storm: A Gulf Crisis Reader.* Edinburgh: Canongate.

Bergan, R. (2000) *The Coen Brothers*. London: Orion.

Carroll, N. (1998) *Interpreting the Moving Image*. Cambridge: Cambridge University Press.

Corrigan, T. (1991) *A Cinema Without Walls: Cinema After Vietnam*. London: Routledge.

Davies, P. J. and P. Wells (2002) 'Introduction' in P. J. Davies and P. Wells (eds.) *American Film and Politics from Reagan to Bush Jr.* Manchester: Manchester University Press.

Doty, A. (1993) 'There's something queer here' in A. Doty *Making Things Perfectly Queer: Interpreting Mass Culture*. Minneapolis: University of Minnesota Press.

Espinosa, J. G. (2000) 'For an imperfect cinema' in R. Stam and T. Miller (eds.) *Film Theory: An Anthology*. Oxford: Blackwell.

Gabriel, T. H. (1979) *Third Cinema in the Third World: The Aesthetics of Liberation*. Michigan: Ann Arbor.

Gilroy, P. (2001) 'Driving while black' in D. Miller (ed.) *Car Cultures*. New York: Berg.

Gledhill, C. (1988) 'Pleasurable negotiations' in S. Thornham (ed.) *Feminist Film Theory: A Reader* Edinburgh: Edinburgh University Press.

Gramsci, A. (1971) *Selections from the Prison Notebooks*. London: Lawrence and Wishart.

Harvey, D. (1990) *The Condition of Postmodernity*. Cambridge, MA: Blackwell.

Hess, A. (1985) *Googie: Fifties Coffee Shop Architecture*. San Francisco: Chronicle Books.

Hollows, J. (1995) 'Mass culture theory and political economy' in J. Hollows and M. Jancovich (eds.) *Approaches to Popular Film*. Manchester: Manchester University Press.

Kiernan, V. G. (1978) *America: The New Imperialism, From White Settlement to World Hegemony*. London: Zed Press.

Körte, P. and G. Seessien (eds.) (1998) *Joel & Ethan Coen*. London: Titan.

Kunstler, J. H. (1993) *The Geography of Nowhere: The Rise and Decline of America's Man-Made Landscape*. New York: Simon & Schuster.

Lindholm, C. and J. A. Hall (2000) 'Frank Capra meets John Doe' in M. Hjort and S. Mackenzie (eds.) *Cinema and Nation*. London: Routledge.

Ling, P. J. (1990) *America and the Automobile: Technology, Reform and Social Change*. Manchester: Manchester University Press.

Mottram, E. (1983) *Blood on the Nash Ambassador: Investigations in American Culture*. London: Hutchinson Books.

Pines, J. and P. Willeman (eds.) (1991) *Questions of Third Cinema*. London: BFI.

Riesman, D. (1964) *Abundance for What?* London: Chatto & Windus.

Robertson, W. P. (1998) *The Making of Joel and Ethan Coen's The Big Lebowski*. London: Faber & Faber.

Romney, J. (2001) 'In praise of goofing off' in J. Hillier (ed.) *American Independent Cinema*. London: BFI.

Russell, C. R. (2001) *The Films of Joel and Ethan Coen*. Jefferson: McFarland & Co.

Sachs, W. (1984) *For Love of the Automobile: Looking Back into the History of our Desires* Berkeley: University of California Press.

Solanas, F. and O. Gettino (1976) 'Towards a Third Cinema' in B. Nichols (ed.) *Movies and Methods*. Berkeley: University of California Press.

St. Clair, D. J. (1986) *The Motorization of American Cities*. New York Praeger.

Stoddart, H. (1995) 'Auteurism and film authorship' in J. Hollows and M. Jancovich (eds.) *Approaches to Popular Film*. Manchester: Manchester University Press.

Tanzer, M. (1992) 'Oil and the Gulf Crisis' in P. Bennis and M. Moushabeck (eds.) *Beyond the Storm: A Gulf Crisis Reader*. Edinburgh: Canongate.

Time to Bowl (1999) (Booklet accompanying the DVD of *The Big Lebowski*.) Polygram Video International.

Wayne, M. (2001) *Political Film: The Dialectics of Third Cinema*. London: Pluto Press.

Woods, P. (ed.) (2000) *Joel & Ethan Coen: Blood Siblings*. London: Plexus.

The mimetics of mobile capital

Nicole Shukin

Introduction

In 2002, the Canadian Broadcasting Corporation (CBC) aired a radio mini-series entitled 'The Wayward Bookmobile'. It featured a Municipal Efficiencies Officer whose civic task of retiring a bookmobile begins to unravel under its wayward spell. The Officer's syntax starts switching erratically between literal modes of transportation figured by a traveling library, and literary modes of transmission mobilized by the mimetic powers of books-on-wheels. Over the course of the mini-series the books, sparked by the sign of mobility into what Arjun Appadurai calls 'things-in-motion', auto-animate from mimetic artefacts into virtual subjects (1998: 5). Instead of fulfilling his task of repossessing social excesses associated with the wayward bookmobile, the Officer ends up possessed by the spectral magnetisms of a suddenly radioactive busload: the pig Wilbur (from *Charlotte's Web*), Black Beauty, Bambi, and other popular animal signs.

The wayward bookmobile emblazons a whimsical figure of automobility whose more serious formulations within Fordist and post-Fordist cultures of capital call for rigorous critical engagement. By introducing a mimetic load put into circulation under the articulated signs of mobility and animal life, the wayward bookmobile is suggestive of the specific discourse of automobility that I will work to critique, following in a long line of Marxist and post-Marxist endeavours to demystify the seeming liveliness of things by retrieving the material histories of their capital paths. Rather than taking the automobile as solely constitutive of a discourse of automobility, I analyse it alongside other 'things' promoting the mobility and seeming autonomy of capital: moving assembly and dis-assembly lines, motion pictures, and mobile phones, or what I will call 'telemobiles'. The discourse of automobility I examine is constituted, more specifically, by an exercise of mimetic power which articulates technological mobility to and through animal signs. Contemporary advertisements for sport utility vehicles and mobile phones, analysed within a genealogy of auto-mobility discourse, help me to bring this mode of mimetic power into closer focus. First, however, let me briefly elaborate the framework of mimesis invoked by my title, and how a material politics of mimesis situates me in relation to post-Marxist critiques which discern capital's conditions of existence not only in its economic relations of production but also in its discursive, or mimetic, productivity.

Animalizing mimesis

In *Mimesis and Alterity: A Particular History of the Senses*, Michael Taussig invokes the dizzying scene of 'the ape aping humanity's aping' from Kafka's short story 'A Report to an Academy' (1993: xviii). Before the dazzling confusion of originals and copies captured in the scene of aping, Taussig professes renewed wonder at the mimetic faculty, a faculty he describes as 'the nature that culture uses to create second nature, the faculty to copy, imitate, make models . . .' (1993: xiii). To his credit, Taussig complicates the capacious 'nature' of the mimetic faculty – 'if it is a faculty,' he writes, 'it is also a history' (1993: xiv). My reading of cultures of mobile capital is indebted to Taussig's study of mimesis. Nevertheless, I resist the temptation he holds out to re-mystify aping as a quintessentially anthropological puzzle, or worse, to attribute to it a kind of innocence in 'its *honest labor* [of] suturing nature to artifice . . .' (1993: xviii, emphasis added).[1]

Taussig is not alone in fetishizing what he perceives to be the primal power of mimesis. The temptation to mystify mimesis as a wonder of natural history also punctuates the work of Walter Benjamin. Benjamin risks undoing the politicization of mimetic media he advances in 'The Work of Art in the Age of Mechanical Reproduction' (1968), by pondering mimesis as an intrinsic 'compulsion' threading back through an almost Lamarckian natural history. 'The gift which we possess of seeing similarity,' he writes, 'is nothing but a weak rudiment of the formerly powerful compulsion to become similar and also to behave mimetically' (1979: 69). In a different context, Michel de Certeau diffuses the historical specificity of the resistant practice of *bricolage* ('making do') by sourcing it to an age-old faculty resembling the one described by Taussig and Benjamin, to 'the immemorial intelligence displayed in the tricks and imitations of plants and fishes' (1984: xx). In claiming that from 'the depths of the ocean to the streets of modern megalopolises, there is a continuity and permanence in these tactics,' de Certeau similarly risks reinscribing mimesis as a natural rather than a cultural faculty, a wonder rather than a sign (1984: xx).

Here, by contrast, I emphasize mimesis as a cultural rather than natural power, an ineluctably political 'faculty' charged, in this case, with coordinating the 'second natures' of capitalism. As I hope will become clear in what follows, the idea of mimesis as a primordial intelligence of animal or vegetable origin – the invocation of mimesis as an 'immemorial' bridge between culture and nature – is superbly enabling for cultures of capital. Animal signs are nodal mimetic technologies deployed to manage intensifying contradictions between the material and aesthetic conditions and effects of Fordist and post-Fordist cultures of capital. I will be detailing how animal signs articulated to automobiles, moving pictures, and mobile phones specifically work to naturalize capitalism's mimetic power.

Whereas Marxisms have traditionally focused on the organization of class and of labour time as all-determining of what Marx, in *Capital*, terms 'the magnitude of the value of a commodity,' (1967: 52), I will attempt to theorize capital in relation to its mimetic conditions of existence and its 'organization of mimesis' (Taussig, 1993: 47). In critical response to the privileging of class antagonism as the primary motor driving histories of capitalism toward a socialist future, and to counter the determining role attributed economic relations of production by Marx, several prominent post-Marxists (Althusser and Balibar, Foucault, Laclau and Mouffe) have theorized the discursive conditions and technologies of capitalist cultures. Reading capital exclusively as an 'economy of signifiers', however, as Jean Baudrillard does in his radical 'semiological reading of Marx' and his theorization of *simulacra*, alternately risks reducing the material means of cultural mimesis to a matter of irrelevance (Pietz, 1993: 120). Following from Saussure's claim that '*language is form and not a substance*', linguistic value, like exchange value, begins to assume the appearance of a cultural automobility in semiological analyses (1959: 89). Indeed, what gets lost both in an essentialist insistence on the economic referent and in a semiological insistence on the arbitrary signifier, is the substance of the sign of culture. As Régis Debray argues in *Media Manifestoes: On the Technological Transmission of Cultural Forms*, semiotics frees thought from the '*referential illusion*' only to itself fall prey to a fantasy of pure code; Debray contends that a 'mediology' is needed to remedy the '*semiotic illusion*, in order to again find a strong reference to the world, its materials, its vectors and its procedures' (1993: 50). Toward the specific elaboration of a material politics of mimesis in cultures of capital, I therefore read the animal signs of automobility discourse in close relation to the substance of the cultures they help fashion, or in relation to what I will call 'rendered material'.

The *double entendre* of 'rendering' is evocative of contradictory yet complicit metaphorical and material economies of power, and is particularly apt in relation to a politics of animal signs. For if rendering on the one hand names the aesthetic practice of depicting an object in linguistic, painterly, musical, filmic, or other media (new technologies of 3D digital animation are, for instance, called 'renderers'), it also references an industrial boiling-down of animal bodies and a carnal traffic in animal remains. The double sense of rendering signals capital's ability to mobilize contradictory metaphorical and material economies without inflaming glaring *non sequiturs* between them. For instance, capitalist cultures are able to circulate animal life as an organic (if empty) metaphor of technological mobility at the same time as they pursue the material logistics of a profitable trade in animal proteins; such contradictory stakes in animal life are managed as a productive rather than a troubling illogic. Rather than transcending the terrestrial costs and frictions of exchange, the 'immaterial labour' currently associated with the new global empire of telecommunications and information capital operates similarly, I contend, in productive contradiction with an intensifying material traffic in rendered substances (Hardt and Negri, 2000: 289).[2] I invoke rendering to begin theorizing the complicity of capital's aesthetic and economic texts, and to describe the political character of a 'mimetic faculty' immanent to market cultures.

A 2002 television ad for the Volvo *Cross Country* gives glimpse into the popular mimetic articulation of animal and automobility. The ad, opening with a shot of the *Cross Country* as it speeds North, at dusk, toward an exotic arctic house, focuses in on a female driver with a man asleep in the passenger seat beside her. The woman-car hybrid is the only body moving on the road. Suddenly, a herd of caribou erupt out of the dusk and stream across the highway, a latitude transecting the longitude of the car's movement directly within the cross-hairs of the driver's field of vision. The car comes to a stop: time and motion are for an instant suspended as the scene transacts a magical identification between the migratory animal collective and the *Cross Country*. The car and the caribou commune, it appears, by means of their common 'emotional sensors', in the words of Mark Dery (in this volume), who discusses automobiles' 'affective computing'. The female driver, moreover, is essential to the consolidation of the mimetic moment: woman's biological wiring ostensibly attunes her to the mysterious uni-animality of car, caribou, and driver.

Needless to say, the aesthetic interest generated by crossing animal and automobile (not to mention woman) at this metaphorical juncture is profoundly at odds with the roadkills and other fatal displacements or incisions marking material intersections of capital and nature. Yet the Volvo ad manages against an antagonistic, material politics of automobility through its mimetic identification of animal and automobile, nature and capital.[3] Through the nodal sign of the animal, market culture manufactures a discourse of mimesis which not only incites the animism of the commodity to which it is articulated, but which works more diffusely to de-politicize the catastrophic 'nature' of capital.

In Taussig's reading of the famous RCA Victor Logo 'His Master's Voice,' in which a dog is depicted listening quizzically to the sound reproduction emitted from an early phonograph, he explores how the juxtaposition of animal and machine even more specifically turns a trope of mimetic 'fidelity' (1993: 223). As opposed to the car and the caribou in the Volvo ad, in the RCA Victor Logo it is the testing of canine fidelity against the superior machinic fidelity of the phonographic reproduction which is at stake, calibrating a relation of similarity and difference to manufacture common sense and consensus around the powers of technological reproduction. As Taussig discerns, however, '[w]here politics most directly enters is in the image's attempt to combine fidelity of mimetic reproduction with fidelity to His Master's Voice', according to the twin connotations of 'fidelity' as affective obedience (eg, faithfulness) and as an aesthetic register of precise technological replication (1993: 223). In this organizing trope of mimetic power, technological reproductions so true to life that they pass for originals are tested against the natural fidelities of an animal. Capital's mimetic effects are tested upon an animal's sensory and soulful faculties with both complimentary and comic results, as the RCA Victor Logo shows: the dumb animal is tricked, bewildered by the masterful reality effects of techno-logical reproduction. Thus the animal is simultaneously attributed with a natural talent for sniffing out the difference between the full presence of an original and the imposture of a copy *and* it is discriminately put back in its place when its senses are outwitted by a mimetic machine.

Via a reading of contemporary ads, I will show that discourses of techno-logical mobility incessantly repeat their challenge to an animal figure indis-pensable to the modern organization of mimetic sense. As Taussig puts it, '[t]he technology of reproduction triumphs over the dog but needs the dog's valida-tion' (1993: 213). In what follows, I take up the automobile and the telemobile as metonymic of the mimetic productivity of shifting cultures of capital. While telecommunications capital calls to be treated in its historical specificity, I view telemobility as ideologically continuous with a 'regime of automobility', as the editors describe it in the introduction to this volume. I hope it is clear by now that theorizing automobility from the perspective of a material politics of mimesis, specifically a politics of animal rendering, requires approaching cars, motion pictures, and mobile phones as material artefacts *and* as metaphorical drivers of cultures of capital. As Kristin Ross puts it, 'the car is not only impli-cated in a certain type of mobilization by capital, it is also an active though partial agent in the *reproduction* of that structure' (1995: 19).

I turn, in the next section, to a genealogy of automobility culture, culminat-ing in a close analysis of two ads for the Saturn *Vue* sport utility vehicle (SUV). A reading of a Canadian corporate telecommunications ad campaign, energized by its animal signs, will then help me to situate telemobiles in relation to a regime of automobility. Finally, I return to the notion of 'rendering' to theorize the symbolic and material double-bind in which cultures of capital mimetically trap animals.

Rendering automobility

The birth of Fordism is routinely sourced to the year 1913, when Henry Ford 'set in motion the first example of assembly-line production in Dearborn, Michi-gan' (Harvey, 1990: 28).[4] In reciting Ford's Highland Park plant in Dearborn as North America's 'first example of assembly-line production', the moving lines which the plant in fact mimetically modelled are quietly displaced from histor-ical consciousness. For rarely recalled or interrogated is the fact that Ford mod-elled Highland Park's auto-assembly line upon moving lines operating at least since the 1850s in the vertical abattoirs of Cincinnati and Chicago, with deadly efficiency and to deadly effect.[5] Ford, deeply impressed by a tour he took of a Chicago slaughterhouse – particularly with the speed of the moving overhead chains and hooks which kept animal 'material' flowing continuously past labourers consigned to stationary and hyper-repetitive piecework – devised a similar system of moving lines for Dearborn, but with a crucial mimetic twist: his automated lines sped the assembly of a machine body rather than the dis-assembly of an animal body.[6] The auto-assembly line, so often taken as representative of mass modernity, is thus mimetically premised upon an ulterior logistics of mass animal disassembly which it technologically replicates and advantageously forgets in a telling moment of historical amnesia.

This aporia in the material politics of modern capitalism is even more significant given soaring stakes in animals' tropological currency. Foucault was among the first to discern how the animal ascends as an ordering trope in modernity, marking a shift to 'untamed ontology' or 'life itself' as a new cipher of discursive power, or biopower (1970: 278). Ford's seemingly arbitrary visit to the slaughterhouse serves as an occasion to reopen the suppressed politics of animal rendering, and to provoke a reckoning with Fordism's unsettled accounts. Against the perception that Fordism represents a clearly delineable and now defunct stage of modern capitalism, 'automobility' names a constellation of mimetic power whose productivity for cultures of capital is by no means finished, and which exceeds containment within discrete 'Fordist' or 'post-Fordist' eras. Automobility emerges, but doesn't end, with three early time-motion economies: animal dis-assembly, motion picture production, and automotive assembly. I will implicate the mimetic effects of films and cars, which bring mass culture to life under the biological sign of seamless animal motion, in material histories of animal dis-assembly. A regime of automobility institutes talismanic tropes of animal life *and* drives the material displacement and death of historical animals, a productive contradiction for cultures of capital so long as it is mimetically managed as a relation of supplementarity rather than antagonism, according to the double logic of 'rendering' I've introduced.

Taussig claims that cultures of modernity issue in a 'recharging and retooling of the mimetic faculty [via] new techniques of reproduction (such as cinema and mass production of imagery)' (1993: xix). The mimetic faculty is most radically retooled, arguably, through the technologization of the sign of mobility itself, beginning with time-motion studies of the late nineteenth century. In the 1870s, Eadwearde Muybridge initiated a series of visual studies which found their iconic expression in the photographic breakdown of a horse in mid-stride, a time-motion breakdown of animal movement which Muybridge devised by setting up multiple cameras to take a running sequences of shots. By means of a revolving glass plate projector he called a 'zoopraxiscope', Muybridge was able to reconstitute his famous series of equine stills to create an optical sense of seamless animal motion. Étienne-Jules Marey subsequently devised a 'chronophotographic gun' with sequential filmic cartridges, with which he was able to shoot time-motion studies of birds and other creatures in flight (Collins, 1988: 69). Like Muybridge, Marey pursued and presented animals as prototypical subjects of time-motion discourse and technological mobility.

Moving assembly lines instituted time-motion principles, enabling abattoirs, auto plants, and film houses to treat nature as a series of 'component parts' subject to unprecedented reductions and reconstructions (Tichi, 1987: 64). While the proto-cinematic studies of Muybridge and Marey put animals into new aesthetic circulation as the 'first metaphor' for an emerging mass visual culture, time-motion efficiencies innovated by the vertical abattoir were simultaneously putting animals into unprecedented material circulation (Berger, 1992: 5).[7] When Chicago hosted the Columbian Exposition in 1893, Muybridge's zoopraxiscope was among its many exhibits, displayed alongside other cutting-edge mimetic apparatuses such as George Eastman's portable Kodak camera, flexible film, and Thomas Edison's Kinetiscope motion picture camera, all promising an unprecedented visual capture and reproduction of life-in-motion. Visitors were apt to stray from the attractions of the world fair's White City, however, and venture into the bloody outer attraction of the neighbouring 'bovine city', where an unprecedented technology of animal sacrifice – the moving dis-assembly line – was also on display (Wade, 1987: 32). Over one million people paid a visit to the Chicago stockyards in 1893, the year of the world fair (Wade, 1987). An economy-of-scale breakdown of animal bodies was, for a brief historical moment, glimpsed in geographical as well as ideological proximity to its aesthetic double, the sign of animal life under which the emergent mass media were modelling their mimetic power.

While the time-motion studies of Muybridge and Marey figure prominently among cinema's mimetic conditions of existence, time-motion ideologies first put to material work in the vertical abattoir would come more broadly to shape capital's industrial 'econom[ies] of motion' through the influence of Frederick Winslow Taylor (Tichi, 1987: 77). Emerging in the 1910s as a 'patron saint of efficiency', Taylor used a stop-watch rather than a camera to conduct a different species of time-motion study (Tichi, 1987: 56). Choosing for his subjects not birds in flight but miners shovelling coal, Taylor 'shot' their manual motions and zoomed in upon a series of temporal 'stills' to make perceptible inefficient motions buried in each micro-unit of time. It was through the principles of scientific management propounded by Taylor that time-motion ideologies originating in the study of animal bodies developed implications for an industrial culture of moving assembly lines requiring workers to perform repetitive motions with increasing speed and efficiency.

The co-construal of animal and worker in Taylor's time-motion discourse is revealed in his comparison of the labourer to a trained gorilla in *The Principles of Scientific Management* (1914: 40). The simian encoded in the Taylorist sign of labour transparently laces the discourse of scientific management with a figure of animal mimesis, that is, with the figure of a gorilla predisposed to mechanical aping.[8] While Antonio Gramsci seizes upon the figure of the trained gorilla to interrogate the rationalization of animal nature which Taylor's science of labour presupposes – as testified by a discussion of Americanism and Fordism in his prison notebooks entitled '"Animality" and industrialism' (Hoare and Smith, 1971: 298) – Marxist critiques focusing on the worker as the primary subject of modern capitalism have often neglected to consider the production of its animal prototypes.

It's not difficult to discern the animal sign put into circulation with cinema's seminal trope of *animation*, a trope naming and framing the mimetic effect of organic motion produced through the technological mobilization of still photographs. What is less apparent, however, is the point at which the animal semiotic mobilized by cinema is complicit in and materially contiguous with a contradictory rendering of animals, one mediated by the modern abattoir. For in order for modern moving pictures to do more than trope animal mobility – that is, for cinema's mimetic effects *literally* to develop – they required the tangible supports of photographic and film stocks. It is in the physical convolutions of film stock that a material politics of cinematic rendering is encrypted.

To confront the animation effects of cinematic culture with its complicit material conditions and effects, one needs to tease out the animal ingredients of film stock via a material history of photographic gelatin. In 1873, a gelatin emulsion-coating of 'animal origin' was first widely adapted to photographic uses (Sheppard, 1923: 25). Gelatin is an animal protein extracted from the skin, bones and connective tissues of cattle, sheep and pigs. In 1923, a Kodak emulsion scientist, Samuel E. Sheppard, writes:

> As is commonly known, gelatin and its humbler relative, glue, are products of animal origin, the result of the action of hot water or steam upon certain tissues and structures of the body. . . . The actual material consists of the leavings of tanneries and slaughter-houses – ie, trimmings, so-called skips, ears, cheek-pieces, pates, fleshings, etc. (1923: 25)

The coating of choice for photographic and film stocks today as well as at the turn of the century, gelatin binds light-sensitive agents to a base so that images can materialize.[9] In 1884, when the word *film* was put into commercial use by George Eastman, the word 'referred only to the gelatin coating upon the paper' (Collins, 1990: 49). Even today, the Kodak corporation acknowledges that it is gelatin which is the veritable 'Image Recorder', without which there would not be mass image culture as we know it.[10] Turn-of-the-century dialogues between cinematic innovators such as Edison and supply-side innovators such as Eastman led to the incessant finessing of film stocks capable of yielding specific visual effects (sharpness, high definition, transparency) to corroborate the mimetic immediacy and vitality of moving pictures. The suturing tissue of animal bodies was, through industrial slaughter, exchanged for the 'physiological and biochemical unity' of image life, giving glimpse into the duplicit rendering of animals supporting cinema's conditions of existence (Sheppard, 1923: 25).

I've already implicated the automobile in a material politics of animal rendering by recalling Ford's visit to the slaughterhouse, the visit behind the technological mimicry of auto-assembly and animal dis-assembly lines. Within the triangulated time-motion economies productive of automobility discourse, automobiles and films, in turn, have mimetically modelled one another. As Kristen Ross notes,

> the two technologies reinforced each other. Their shared qualities – movement, image, mechanization, standardization – made movies and cars the key commodity-vehicles of a complete transformation in European consumption patterns and cultural habits. (1995: 38)

Just as cinema renders mimetic effects of seamless animal motion in productive contradiction with its material conditions in mass slaughter, automobiles fetishistically fashion themselves as animal signs while actively displacing animals as historical actors. Ford, who according to James Flink 'longed to rid the world of unsanitary and inefficient horses and cows', set to work to replace the horse, long the organic standard of physical transport (1988: 114). Impressed by the moving dis-assembly lines of Chicago's bovine city and the time-motion efficiencies propounded by Taylor, Ford devised a mode of mass production to usher in a 'horseless age'.[11] In 1908, the Ford Motor Company presented its first mass-assembled vehicle to the public, the Model T. Once the Model Ts and Model As of the early part of the century had effectively displaced organic models of animal traction, the Ford corporation began blatantly promoting its cars as substitute animals. From the Ford *Mustang* and *Pony* of the 1960s, the automobile's intensifying mimetic fidelities led it to challenge wild rather than domestic animals as ultimate models of organic mobility and effortless speed. Ford launched a wild animal series in the 1970s and 80s, with the Ford Mercury *Bobcat* (1978), *Lynx* (1980) and *Cougar* (1983).

While Ford's modelling of the automotive assembly line off of the dis-assembly of animals in the abattoir was technologically defining for industrial modes of production, in 1927 General Motors gained an aesthetic advantage over Ford under the presidency of Alfred Sloan. Sloan established the first Art and Colour Department in the automotive industry, hired Harley Earl as its head, and turned styling into an economic priority (rather than superficial flourish) of automobile manufacture. Earl's previous work on Hollywood film sets allowed him to bring 'celluloid lessons' to bear upon automotive sheet metal (Gartman, 1994: 93). Under Earl, an aesthetic of organicism carried the mimetic capabilities of the automobile head and shoulders over the assembled look of Ford's Model T. Earl is known for producing full-size model cars out of clay to achieve effects of streamlining and organic curvature which conceal the component make-up of mass-assembled vehicles.

As the Ford Motor Corporation pursued a mimetic trajectory from the *Bobcat*, *Lynx* and *Cougar* series of the 80s to its current breed of wild off-road SUV, GM pushed its streamlining aesthetics to the aerospace and fish-inspired 'finned' vehicles of the 1950s. Yet the OPEC embargo and energy crisis of the 1970s forced GM to review its ostentatious aesthetic agenda, and to consider the manufacture of sub-compact and energy-efficient cars. In 1985, GM spawned the Saturn Corporation to this end. Less than two decades later, however, the sub-compact fell to the wayside as Saturn trumpeted the arrival of a new sport-utility vehicle. The Saturn *Vue* was introduced through a $35 million dollar ad campaign running from February to May of 2002.[12]

Time-motion ideologies organizing the moving lines of modern capitalism undergo revision and partial dislodging in the path I've described, from Ford's early assembly lines to GM's Saturn 'experiment' and the post-Fordist era of automobility that it announces (Rubinstein and Kochan, 2001: 2). Capital's relation to nature and labour is revised as Saturn emerges to compete with

Japanese imports and to create a North American answer to a 'just-in-time' model of production in which the material stockpiles, serial assembly, and standardized commodities of Fordist production are viewed as liabilities. The reorganization – or in this case, Saturnization – of Fordism purportedly initiates a radical new symbolic and material time-space economy of capital, a participatory, horizontal relation to the nature and labour of technological mobility. Through an analysis of two 2002 Saturn *Vue* ads, however, I suggest that the rendering of animals marks a productive site of discursive continuity rather than discontinuity in Fordist and post-Fordist cultures of capital. For, while time-motion ideologies organizing economy-of-scale production are recalibrated, what stays in place and arguably intensifies is the mimetic productivity of animal signs, deployed to organize and manage capital's volatile relations.

The *Vue* – 'at home in almost any environment' – is just one SUV among many eager to neutralize political antagonisms of automobility culture. The tagline of Toyota SUVs is 'You Belong Outside'; Ford SUVs, such as the *Explorer*, celebrate 'No Boundaries'. Before it changed its tagline to 'Shift' in September of 2002 (fusing automotive gears and digitized cursors into a single function key of mobility), Nissan's *Xterra* was animalistically rather than fossil-fuel 'Driven'. Yet an unabashed identification of automobile and animal emerges with the *Vue* ads. By equating automobility with the biological ignition of animal life, the *Vue* discourse mythologizes the motive power of the sport utility vehicle and conceals the economy of power regulating a carnivorously capitalistic relation of nature and culture.

Both of the *Vue* ads discussed here are two-page spreads – a spatial sprawl reflective of the territorial largesse they promise SUV drivers. Mimicking an encyclopaedic spread and educational tool, the first ad, 'Inhabitants of the Polar Region', invites cross-referencing between three visual components: an illustrated animal panorama, a black and white numbered cut-out on the upper left hand, and a taxonomic key of animal names on the lower left (see Figure 1). By cross-referencing all three, consumers are engaged in an interactive pedagogical exercise through which they learn to classify the *Vue* within an animal series. Corporate pedagogy teaches lessons in natural history to consumers of the twenty-first century. The aura of childhood instruction evoked by its encyclopaedic address underscores the strategy used by the ad to calibrate automobility: *mimetic* management of the relation of nature and culture. After all children, like animals and 'primitives', have been constructed as natural mimics who learn by copying.[13]

In rendering the *Vue* within a painterly diorama in which a sense of time and motion is at best naively suggested, the automobile appears to be intent only upon the mimetic movement of becoming like the animals around it. Yet what at first glance looks like a flat painterly plane upon which animals and automobile intermingle, on closer inspection can be seen to be a differentiated surface, reflecting unequal levels of mimetic fidelity. A close look at the lower left-hand corner of both ads reveals that the animal illustrations are signed by the hand of 'K. Pendletton'. The mimetic technology adequate to the

Inhabitants of the polar regions

Figure 1: 'Inhabitants of the polar regions.' (Reprinted with the permission of the General Motors Corporation).

Figure 1: *Continued*

representation of animal life, in other words, is the relatively rude naturalism of hand-painted art. The *Vue*, on the other hand, asserts its difference through the enhanced mimetic technology it introduces into the visual ecology: the *Vue* is a computer-rendered image whose super-natural mimetic fidelity makes the hand-drawn images of the animals appear rough-hewn in comparison. The taxonomic discourse of species identity articulating the *Vue* and polar animals is thus simultaneously disavowed by the ad's discriminating organization of mimesis. An 'anthropological' discourse of mimetic progress embedded in the ad actually demotes the animal life among which the *Vue* is represented as belonging.

As with the RCA Victor logo analysed by Taussig, the *Vue* ad mimetically invokes an identification of animal and machine fidelities while simultaneously producing a differential which renders animal biologies inferior and obsolete. The animals are demoted not just through the discrimination of the *Vue*'s superior fidelity, but also by virtue of a structure of temporal difference insinuated in the ad's organization of mimesis. Despite the valorization of the animal as an organic metaphor of automobility, or rather because of it, animals are consigned to being 'originals' predating, and never matching up to, their technological doubles. The museological semiotics of the ad's diorama positions wild life as predecessors of the *Vue*, curatorially consigning all but the Saturn animal to a painted past, even to extinction (that several of the animals listed on the taxonomic key are endangered predicts their imminent 'pastness'). The anachronistic, nostalgic image of biological science embalmed in the encyclopaedic text at once animalizes the *Vue* and reinforces the solo currency of the sport-utility body, whose cutting-edge verisimilitude projects it alone as a presence in the present. An evolutionary narrative of survival of the fittest is thus retooled along a trajectory of mimetic prowess. The *Vue* succeeds organic animals by virtue of its representational 'liveness' as well as by virtue of the anthropological discourse of time encoded in the succession of mimetic styles (Simpson, 1999: 88);[14] there is what Johannes Fabian calls a 'denial of coevalness' insinuated within what at first looks like a synchronic tableau of coexisting wild life (1983: 31).

The sport utility vehicle, finally, performs its total autonomy: the *Vue* is de-linked from any visible historical operator. The SUV's powers of self-ignition detach it from reliance on exterior motives or production histories – there are no treadmarks showing the path from factory to wilderness. Yet the darkly tinted windshield at the same time makes it impossible to determine whether there isn't in fact a human inside the vehicle. The inability to confirm either the presence or absence of a human operator introduces an aspect of surveillance into the ad, which further contradicts the animal nature claimed by the *Vue*. If the *Vue* is immanent to the list of animals on the taxonomic key, its tinted windshields contradictorily hint at an invisible human presence – an imperial eye – overseeing the animal panorama. A discourse of surveillance in the shape of an implied eco-touristic gaze hides behind the windshield (and less subtly in the name '*Vue*') to locate the transparent yet sovereign act of consumption within the capitalist ecology. The ad exquisitely suggests that knowledge acquisition and economic buying power are inextricable modes of consuming nature.

No contradiction seems to trouble the *Vue*'s bid to belong to two profoundly disparate bioregions at once: in a second ad, different colour codings operate like moulting coats allowing the *Vue* to coordinate with any environment. The now red *Vue* peacefully coexists with 'creatures of the evergreen forest'. In 'Creatures of the Evergreen Forest', as in 'Inhabitants of the Polar Region', the mimetic discourse of species is carefully ordered according to a historical succession of rendering technologies (pictorial naturalism versus digital supernaturalism) and, by extension, between shades or grades of mimetic fidelity. The very mimetic differentials which work in the interests of capital, however, are precisely those which run the danger of switching and slipping into antagonistic view. The mimetic code securing the identification of capital and nature turns upon the discursive proximity of animal and automobile, a proximity which charges their articulation and calibrates differentials. Yet this very same proximity risks igniting confrontation rather than exchangeability, exposing incommensurable differences as opposed to productive and controlled 'differentials' between animals and automobiles.

Even as the *Vue* ads siphon enormous affective energy off of an image of ecological biodiversity, then, they risk exposing the violence of automobility culture. Emblematic of the violence at the material intersection of automobile and animal is the roadkill. But automobility antagonizes animal worlds in countless ways: through gridlocks of roads and seismic lines which transect animal habitat, through unparalleled access to and therefore displacement of remote locations (the institution of the 'wild' within national parks and nature sanctuaries historically performs the paradox of automobility, a technology of access which contaminates and displaces the pristine nature that is its ideological destination), and through the accidents (eg, Exxon Valdez) as well as the normative everyday of fossil fuel culture. While mimetic differentials controlling signs of identity and difference in the *Vue* ads work to manage against antagonistic material histories of automobiles and animals, the ads cannot guarantee their ability to master the political volatility of the proximities they pose.

Rendering telemobility

Late capitalism has been associated with a shrinking, swirling *mise en abîme* of mobiles inside of mobiles, mimetic media inside of mimetic media. Zooming in from the 'globe-mobile' where few sites, if any, remain immune from the effects of capital, one narrows in on arteries coursing with automobiles, and inside the automobiles, mobile phones, whose digitized human subjects can dial the globe-mobile and call up screens on which they spiral back out to the worldwide web. Rather than constitutive of the 'regime of automobility' theorized in the introduction to this volume, the car is just one of its metaphorical and material technologies. A regime of automobility is increasingly driven by new technologies of capital which, in different yet familiar ways, articulate a discourse of mobility and neoliberal cultural and economic autonomy to and through animal signs. 'Telemobility' is what I call this rearticulated regime of automobility.

Post-Fordist technologies of 'electronic connectivity', in Timothy Luke's words, again recharge and retool capital's mimetic productivity (2002).[15] Tele-mobility revamps what J. Hillis Miller calls, in this volume, 'old dreams of magic communication' by invoking a talismanic discourse of animal telepathy – mesmerizing, hypnotic, magical. A fetish for what Akira Mizuta Lippit calls the 'electric animal' – ie, the 'communicative powers of animal magnetism' – reappears in telecommunications culture to provide a figure for the immediacy of exchange promised by electronic and digital technologies, and spiriting away their material means (2000: 101). Exchange is increasingly configured in terms of an instantaneous, telepathic communication pitched, like an animal signal, either above or below a human radar. Telecommunications media pose as otherworldly mediums by staging communication as an *'animalséance'*, to borrow from Derrida, in which coded messages travel transferentially across sending and receiving poles (2002: 372).[16] If the technological mobility promised by cars is metaphorized as a biological animal drive, in telecommunications culture the 'act of communication' is aestheticized under the sign of animal affect to assume the appearance of an immaterial, effortless bolt of code (Debray, 1996: 45).[17]

As the case of Telus Mobility Inc. can be provoked to show, however, the retooled animal metaphors of telecommunications culture are no less innocent of bloody material histories. In this section, I will analyse the concerted ad campaigns of Telus Mobility – one of Canada's largest wireless corporations – in view of the productivity and popularity of their animal signs. The animal magnetism of Telus mobile phones and wireless services is a focal trope of ad campaigns which tap a discourse of the 'electric animal', a discourse revolving around the notion that animals and figurative technologies or devices of com-munication are in essence the same.[18] The work of John Berger encourages this substitutability by suggesting that 'the first metaphor was animal', conjuring metaphor as originally animal and animals as originally metaphorical (1992: 5). Against the naturalization of metaphor encouraged by Berger, I implicate the animal metaphors in the campaigns of Telus Mobility in a material politics of mimesis, a politics of rendering.

On the web page for Taxi Advertising and Design of Toronto, the agency behind Telus Mobility's prolific ad campaigns, one reads: 'Learn how frogs, bugs and ducks transformed a wireless company into one of the most valued brands in the telecommunications industry'.[19] Indeed, a seemingly infinite visual string of flora and fauna thread together Telus ad campaigns, unified by their hall-mark photographic 'nature': crisp, colourful, and often comical animal and plant species on clinically white backgrounds, with the Telus tagline 'the future is friendly'. Telus's brand ecology enlists exotic animals associated with South-ern latitudes, species imported into the de-contextualized white space of tech-nological culture. Frogs, chameleons, monkeys, parrots, turtles, sloths, and penguins by turn enliven a range of telecommunications wares and services. Yet rather than being fresh and innocent, the mimetic species which regularly feature in Telus ads – monkeys, parrots, chameleons – carry affective residues from colonial discourses of mimesis. The 'honest labour' of making mimetic sense which animal signs are again called to perform is not honest at all, but works to naturalize a neocolonial order of telecommunications capital through an organization of mimesis inherited from colonial regimes of power (Taussig, 1993: xviii).

Although its animals are presented as a new pictographic sign language transcending cultural and political boundaries to inaugurate the limitless telecommunicability of a global marketplace, Telus's choice 'spokescritters' are in fact saturated with virulent historical associations.[20] Telus's circulation of monkey signs, for instance, risks affectively reactivating North American stereotypes of black culture as simplistically mimetic, and of Africans as 'simianlike', given the omnipresence of monkey signs within nineteenth and twentieth century discourses of biological racism construing black people as closer in kind to lower primates than to people (Gates, 1987: 236).[21] The racial typing of animal signs and animal mimicry can be traced back to broader histories of colonialism and to Europe's efforts to keep mimesis in 'some sort of imperial balance' by mapping slavish copying onto non-white, non-Europeans, as part of their construction as apish and in need of development (Taussig, 1993: xv). While Telus' monkey signs play innocent, I aim to pressure them into exposing what they would efface: the violent neocolonial relations of race, labour, and nature through which telecommunications capital renders new technological mobilities.

The visual sharpness of the animal signs in Telus advertisements signifies the technological fidelity promised by its telecommunications media, a fidelity that is again and again proven against an animal's acuity in the style of the RCA Victor logo. In a 15-second television spot created by Taxi in 2001 – 'Introducing photo caller ID' – a hedgehog carefully approaches a Sanyo 5000, the first mobile phone with a full-colour screen. The phone's screen is upright, facing away from the viewer and towards the hedgehog. Suddenly the hedgehog bristles, stops, and retreats; the ad cuts to the phone's screen where its photo ID feature shows the caller to be a skunk. The live hedgehog is daunted by the superlative fidelity, or 'liveness', of the skunk confronting it on the screen (Simpson, 1997). The phone's technological virtuosity promises more than just visual and auditory transmissions; it promises (threatens?) to communicate smell as well, to shower the receiver with nature's sensorium. In the arena where animal and technology are put to such a biological test of verisimilitude, the hedgehog cedes to the overpowering mimetic fidelities of telecommunications media.[22]

Cary Wolfe writes that 'the discourse of species . . . is rearticulated upon the more fundamental ur-discourse of the "organization of mimesis" by the world system of global capitalism in its postmodern moment' (1999: 145). Nowhere is it more clear that animal signs encipher an ur-discourse of mimesis than in a series of 2004 ads for the Telus camera phone, a multimedia phone coupling

Figure 2: 'Inexplicable? Send-a-pic-able.' (Image reprinted with the permission of the Telus corporation.)

photographic with telephonic capabilities. The mimetic species which feature in this series of ads are vivid lizards, chameleons whose photosensitive skin becomes the splitting image of its surroundings. In each ad, a lizard is shown blending in with the object next to it, an object which is often, but not always, a camera phone. In one exception, a chameleon is shown 'becoming' a blue-swirl lollipop in time-motion stages, stages mirrored by the hyphenated caption: 'In-ex-plic-able? Send a pic-able' (see Figure 2). This Telus ad cries out to be read in the context of a biological discourse of mimesis elaborated by Roger Caillois in his 1938 essay 'Mimicry and Legendary Psychasthenia'. Caillois turns to the study of mimetic insects to carve out a fascinating theory of mimesis as an animal 'pathology' (1984: 17). Insects mimicking the appearance of leaves, twigs, or stones demonstrate, for Caillois, a vertiginous 'luxury' or excess leading animate life to approximate inanimate life, stasis, and even death. He christens this animal death wish '*le mimetisme*' (1984: 25). The playing dead of insects and animals signals not a survival mechanism protecting an organism against predation, Caillois contends, but a perverse death drive which he formulates as a 'temptation by space', or an '*assimilation to the surroundings*' (1984: 28, 27). Telus ads reveal a similar fascination with the notion that mimetic animals are instinctively compelled to become thinglike – whether in stages, as with the lollipop lizard, or instantly, as with a chameleon in a different ad which has become of a piece with shards of colourful porcelain lying around it.

Yet as Denis Hollier notes, 'Caillois does not find it worthwhile to remind us that [an insect or animal] can only play dead because it is alive. His entire analysis proceeds as if playing dead and being dead were one and the same' (1984: 13). The 'vital difference' which Caillois overlooks also marks the difference between the aesthetic discourse of biological mimicry mobilized by Telus camera phone ads, and a politics of rendering (Hollier, 1984: 13). In reading the Telus discourse alongside the work of Caillois, what comes into view is how a bio-logical discourse of mimicry operates to naturalize mimetic effects motivated by capital, effects which Marx strove to politicize with his theory of commodity fetishism: the animation of things and the reification of nature. The discourse of animal mimetism at play in the progressive thingification of the Telus lizard dangerously poses the becoming-animal of capital and the becoming-capital of animals as a biological compulsion, rather than as a fatal transfer of 'life' exacted through the exercise of mimetic power.

The naturalization of capital via a discourse of mimesis also appears in a 2002 Telus ad promoting various gifts for the Christmas holidays (see Figure 3). Above the caption – 'Avoid the re-gift. Ask for a cool phone' – sit a pair of squir-rel monkeys, an original beside a reproduction. The latter is in the petrified shape of a lampstand, a not-so bright idea as soon becomes clear. The live monkey looks with dismay at its kitschy sidekick, less than ecstatic at receiving yet another commodity whose attempt faithfully to ape its future owner is precisely why, as a gift, it misses the mark. The clunky lamp, belonging to an outmoded era of stationary goods tethered to fixed power outlets, is no longer a fit, the Telus ad suggests, for the cordless, wireless mobility of the animal.

An old mimetic catalogue of mechanical reproductions has been superceded by a new mimetic order of electronic and digital reproduction. The ad suggests that the monkey makes a better mimetic match with a Telus 'cool phone', which bears far more than the lamp's physical family resemblance to another simian; a cool phone is no mere analogue. The secret kinship of monkey and phone is that of an invisible shared code, a new kind of mimetic relationship from within which the relation between biological originals and faithful copies is made to look glaringly and garishly obvious. The ad self-consciously distances mobile phones from the now stale charms of analogue reproduction, promot-ing a new order of telepathic communion which transcends crass mimetic correspondence.

Telus repeats the above scenario, with a difference, in a 2003 holiday season ad: 'The perfect gift for those who have everything'. Instead of the mismatch of a squirrel monkey and an imitation lamp, however, the 2003 ad depicts the mis-match of a live piglet and a pile of piglet imitations (a stuffed piglet, a piggy bank, etc.). Instead of suggesting the gift of a Telus Mobility 'cool phone', moreover, this ad suggests the gift of a camera phone. Whereas the 2002 ad with the monkey brings the Telus ur-discourse of aping into view in a way that the ad with the piglet does not (pigs not canonically connoting mimesis the way monkeys have been made to do), Telus's periodic deployment of North Amer-ican domestic animals such as pigs, goats, and rabbits marks an even more loaded mimetic moment. If parrots, chameleons, and monkeys model an era of mechanical reproduction, piglets model electronic and digital culture as the reproduction, or rather creation, of life itself. While the simian inscribes a canonical discourse of mimesis as a gestural, apish mirroring-back, the piglet marks a new biopolitical motion to transcend representationality itself. The

167

Avoid the re-gift.
Ask for a
cool phone.

✗ Phones from as low as $24.99†
Let everyone know what you really want. Ask for a
TELUS Mobility phone with 1X capability, the latest
in wireless technology, and other cool things like:

- Colour screens
- Games
- Access to fun downloads like ringtones and images*
- 2-Way Text Messaging capability

Available at TELUS Mobility stores, authorized
dealers and retailers. To find out more visit
telusmobility.com/student or call 1-888-810-5555.
The future is friendly.®

Figure 3: 'Avoid the re-gift.' (Image reprinted with the permission of the Telus corporation.)

image of the piglet communicated by the camera phone is not a cultural copy, but a first nature emerging pink with presence from its digital birth. By mocking analogue culture's dated ability to reproduce life mechanically, this Telus copy raises the mimetic claims of telecommunications culture to the constitution of new life itself.

Yet even as telecommunications culture aesthetically detaches itself from mechanical reproduction to take ownership of an animal code of life (and own-ership of the perpetual recreation of first nature that mastery promises), the electric piglet almost too easily supplies its own double: the bacon-breeder or gene machine subjected to unprecedented degrees of material and reproductive management in advanced capitalist culture. The dewy piglet's historical body-double mediates the meat life of capitalism to the tune of 21,148,704 pigs per annum in Canada alone.[23] Rather than posing a problem for its discourse, however, Telus's camera phone ad seems to confidentially invite a realization that in the new biopolitical world order, capital's conditions of production have fused with the conditions of life itself.[24] Aesthetics and genetics have become one doublesided currency of advanced capital via its iconic control of animal code.

In a different ad cluster, Telus nevertheless returns to the species most representative of its discourse on mimesis: monkeys. Again, the telecom model of sending and receiving poles across which animal signals effortlessly bounce – a model which edits out the '*violent* collective process' of material transmission (Debray, 1996: 45) – is configured by way of two monkeys. Shown crouching behind a cluster of bananas, or tossing bananas back and forth between them, the monkeys play upon the ludic resemblance of banana and telephone until they themselves evolve into the cool phones of the caption-titles.

The 'primate ethograms' favoured by Telus can be pressured to speak, however, to the violent neocolonial relations of telecommunications capital they work to render transparent (Haraway, 1989: 139). For its deployment of simian code inadvertently links Telus to a racist primatology geopolitically organizing mobile phones' material conditions of existence, and marks the site where telecommunications capital can be made to incriminate its own mimetic productivity in the vicious politics and economics of Congolese coltan, civil war, and bushmeat. Coltan is a semiprecious and highly conductive mineral ore used in tantalum capacitors, micro-components in computers and electronic products such as mobile phones, pagers, and camcorders. While coltan is legitimately mined in Australia, Brazil and Canada, it is more cheaply extracted, by virtue of deeply entrenched neocolonial plunder economies, in the eastern Congo. A 2002 UN Report has linked civil war in the Congo to the illegal trade supplying multinational mineral corporations and telecommunications manufacturers with coltan, and rebel army groups with a lucrative source of military funding (United Nations, 2002).

As Donna Haraway argues, primatology stories cache a communications fantasy, a fantasy 'about the immediate sharing of meanings' (1989: 135). The telecommunications fantasy rendered by the simian signifiers of Telus ads accommodates, nightmarishly, the brutalizing artisanal mining of Congolese coltan which materially mediates it. Coltan attracted mainstream attention in Europe and North America when impoverished Congolese miners began eating the lowland gorillas which Dian Fossey had infamously championed. In 2001, when a group of Belgian NGOs organized a worldwide campaign – 'No blood on my mobile! Stop the plundering of Congo!' – it was the blood of the endangered lowland gorilla rather than that of the Congolese (over three million of whom have died in a civil war funded by telecommunications capital) which most stirred international concern.[25] Rather than enmiring telecommunications culture in the material politics of its labour and nature, however, the monkey signs in Telus ads are designed to do just the opposite: to configure a fantasy of painless, telepathic exchange within which the incommunicable costs of tele-mobility remain perfectly invisible, absorbed by geopolitical black holes such as the Congo.

Conclusion

What looms with the *mise en abîme* of mobiles inside of mobiles in automobil-ity discourse is a convoluted folding of capitalist culture in upon itself, and the spawning of unpredictable and disturbing forms of mimetic excess in its linked symbolic and material economies. As the ability to distinguish between nature and capital dwindles within the globe-mobile of market culture – that is, as nature increasingly ceases to be produced in any form able to contend mean-ingfully with capital's dual rendering of nature as empty signifier and as mate-rial resource – capital rushes to produce a semblance of non-capitalized wild life. Market cultures increasingly speculate in signs of non-capitalized nature even as they accelerate machinations to convert all nature into capital. In this, capitalism enacts in macro the paradox that the automobile enacts in micro: capitalizing away the difference of nature that is in part its 'destination', its dis-cursive conditions of future surplus.

Even when 'nature is gone for good', then, capitalism cannibalizes itself to ensure a future (Jameson, 1992: x). Through its recycling of nature signs and re-renderings of already capitalized material resources, a perennially undead nature can be kept, as Derrida puts it, in 'interminable survival' (2002: 394). While cannibalism of its symbolic economy gives rise to *simulacra* and an endless reprocessing of aesthetic effects (accentuated by the ability of new digital renderers to mimic painterly, photographic, and filmic effects), cannibalism of its material conditions makes all of capitalism into a giant rendering industry, into the sorting and reconstitution no longer of any so-called 'first nature' but of nature as post-consumer product, capitalized in advance. Global outbreaks of mad cow disease in livestock over the past two decades in Europe and North America, attributed to the practice of recycling the remains of ruminants back into the capitalist food chain (feeding rendered material back to livestock to speed protein to market), have recently brought attention to capitalism's specific economy of 'animal cannibalism'.

Yet politicization of the harrowing, increasingly involuted conditions of cap-italism's existence is diverted by managing its aesthetic and material economies in a relation of disavowed supplementarity. The gap or illogic patrolled between its symbolic and carnal conditions and effects is superbly productive for capital. It is the illogic of automobility discourse itself, which drives the sign of culture in strict disavowal of its material conditions and effects. A politics of rendering counters by forcing into antagonistic proximity symbolic and carnal economies normally staggered in differential relation to each other, with the aim of collapsing one of the discursive conditions of capital. Moreover, a politics of rendering resists dreams of alterity still riding upon mimesis by showing how the mimetic faculty, so fetishistically formulated as an animal sign, is immanent to cultures of capital.

Caught in the double bind of rendering, there seem few modes of political intervention capable of breaking capitalism's mimetic loops to produce other animal signs. Irregularities and excesses of rendering – pathological products of the closed loop itself, such as mad cow disease – have thrown the harrowing involutions of capital's mimetic productivity into exposure, but they are not (yet?) a formulation of political struggle. The politics of rendering remains, at this point, a question asked from within a double bind, haunting representation from the 'infernal' other side of mimetic management (Derrida, 2002: 394).[26]

Acknowledgement

My interpretation of the Telus ads in no way reflects the views or intentions of the Telus corporation, which has granted me permission to reproduce them.

Notes

1 Though he does specify its instrumentality for colonial discourses, as well as tracks important reversals in which western culture becomes the object of non-European representations, Taussig nevertheless invites a transhistorical, transcultural view of mimesis which risks dissolving the cultural specificity of mimetic power.

2 In their description of the new imperial order of global capitalism, Michael Hardt and Antonio Negri announce that the 'passage toward an informational economy' is accompanied by a shift from material forms of labour to forms of 'immaterial labour' (2000: 289).

3 I use 'antagonism' as it is theorized by Ernesto Laclau and Chantal Mouffe, who contend that on-going struggle, eg, antagonism, over the meaning and matter of culture is an ineradicable condition of politics (1985).

4 James Flink also claims that 'the Ford Motor Company innovated modern mass-production techniques at its now[sic] Highland Park plant' (1988: 37).

5 'It is uncertain where or when the overhead assembly line originated,' writes Louise Carroll Wade in *Chicago's Pride: The Stockyards, Packingtown, and Environs in the Nineteenth Century*, 'but many Cincinnati and Chicago plants had them by the late 1850s' (1987: 62).

6 It is interesting to find the technological mimicry between the two moving lines brought to attention by Canada's federal Department of Agriculture in a bi-weekly bulletin on the meat packing industry: 'The modern meat plant operates in a fashion similar to Henry Ford's original production of Model T Fords, with mass production of identical products to create economies of scale; however, the assembly of automobiles is a building-up process, whereas the meat packer performs a breaking down process' (http://www.agri.gc.ca, accessed March 2002).

7 In his seminal essay 'Why Look At Animals?' John Berger writes: 'The first subject matter for painting was animal. Probably the first paint was animal blood. Prior to that, it is not unreasonable to suppose that the first metaphor was animal' (1992: 5). The politics of metaphor, of mimesis, disappear in this primal scene of rendering.

8 The sign of the monkey is, as I will explore later in this paper, racially saturated, suggesting that Taylorism contributed to biological discourses of race as well as to what Étienne Balibar theorizes as 'class racism' (1991: 204).

171

9 As the Gelatine Manufacturers of Europe assure on their web page, '[g]elatine is also indispensable for digital photography. The ink-jet printer paper coated with gelatine guarantees brilliant colours and clear shapes.' (http://www.gelatine.org/en/gelatine/applications/134.htm, accessed December 2004).

10 On its web page, the Kodak corporation pays homage to the historically understated role of emulsion coatings in image production, under the heading: 'Emulsion, the Image Recorder' (www.kodak.com/US/en/corp/aboutKodak/KokakHistory/filmImaging.shtml, accessed 20 November 2003).

11 *Horseless Age* was the title of one of the first periodicals devoted to automobile culture (Flink, 1988: 18).

12 The ad campaign was given to Hal Riney of Publicis Groupe, San Francisco. The ads discussed here appeared in 2002 issues of *Martha Stewart Magazine* and *Outside Magazine*.

13 As Taussig notes, 'controlled mimesis is an essential component of socialization and discipline, and in our era of world history, in which colonialism has played a dominant role, mimesis is of a piece with primitivism' (1993: 219).

14 Mark Simpson theorizes 'liveness' – associated with what he describes as a 'logic of the specimen' – in relation to North American taxidermy in his essay 'Immaculate Trophies' (1999: 77).

15 Within what Luke calls 'digital Fordism,' the new 'telematicized car' features satellite radio and GPS services to provide consumers with 'net connectivity on the road' (2002).

16 Derrida himself betrays a fascination with what Lippit calls the 'electric animal', describing the look of an animal as '[t]he gaze of a seer, visionary, or extra-lucid blind person' and the mesmerizing contact with an animal's gaze as an *'animalséance'* (2002: 372).

17 Debray is fiercely resistant to the spiritualization of telecommunication: '*No more than there is any innocent medium can there be painless transmission*' (1996: 46).

18 In the very title of his book – *Electric Animal: Toward a Rhetoric of Wildlife* – Lippit announces his perpetuation of the long-standing idea in western philosophical and psychoanalytic discourses that the animal is more of an undying code than a mortal subject of history.

19 www.taxi.ca (accessed January 2004).

20 See Telus's assurance of its respectful handling of its 'spokescritters' on its web page (http://www.telusmobility.com/about/company_background_ff.shtml, accessed January 2004).

21 Henry Louis Gates recuperates a black critical praxis from the racist currency of the sign of the monkey, by theorizing 'the Signifying Monkey' as an 'ironic reversal of a received racist image in the Western imagination' (1987: 236).

22 The hedgehog ad can be viewed on line (http://www.strategymag.com/aoy/2001/taxi/telus/, accessed January 2004).

23 2003 slaughter numbers posted by the Government of Canada on their agriculture website, under 'Hog Statistics at a Glance' (http://www.agr.gc.ca, accessed March 2004).

24 Hardt and Negri describe the current mode of production of 'empire' as 'biopolitical production, the production of social life itself' (2000: xiii).

25 Among those affected by the sign of endangered animal life was Hollywood movie star Leonardo DiCaprio, who gave his high-profile support to the Dian Fossey Gorilla Fund when it mobilized a campaign to protect lowland gorillas by pressuring to have coltan mining certified (ie, legalized).

26 Derrida describes current conditions of animal life as 'an artificial, infernal, virtually interminable survival, in conditions that previous generations would have judged monstrous' (2002: 394).

References

Appadurai, A. (ed.) (1988) *The Social Life of Things: Commodities in Cultural Perspective.* New York: Cambridge University Press.

Balibar, E. and I. Wallerstein (1991) *Race, Nation, Class: Ambiguous Identities.* London: Verso.

Benjamin, W. (1968) 'The work of art in the age of mechanical reproduction' in H. Arendt (ed.) *Illuminations*, trans. H. Zohn. New York: Harcourt, Brace & World.

Benjamin, W. (1979) 'Doctrine of the similar' trans. K. Tarnowski, *New German Critique*, 17(Spring): 65–69.

Berger, J. (1992) 'Why look at animals?' in *About Looking.* New York: Vintage.

Caillois, R. (1984) 'Mimicry and legendary psychasthenia' trans. J. Shepley, *October*, 31(Winter): 17–32.

Canadian Broadcast Corporation (2002) 'The wayward bookmobile' radio broadcast, aired on *Richardson's Round-up*, November 20–December 1.

Collins, D. (1990) *The story of Kodak.* New York: Harry Abrams.

de Certeau, M. (1984) *The Practice of Everyday Life*, trans. S. Randall. Berkeley: University of California Press.

Debray, R. (1996) *Media Manifestos: On the Technological Transmission of Cultural Forms*, trans. E. Rauth. London: Verso.

Derrida, J. (2002) 'The animal that therefore I am (more to follow)' trans. D. Wills, *Critical Inquiry*, 28(Winter): 369–418.

Fabian, J. (1982) *Time and the Other: How Anthropology Makes its Object.* New York: Columbia University Press.

Flink, J. (1988) *The Automobile Age.* Cambridge, MA: MIT Press.

Foucault, M. (1970) *The Order of Things: An Archaeology of the Human Sciences.* New York: Pantheon.

Gartman, D. (1994) *Auto-Opium: A Social History of American Automobile Design.* New York: Routledge.

Gates, H.L. (1987) *Figures in Black: Words, Signs, and the 'Racial' Self.* New York: Oxford University Press.

Gramsci, A. (1971) *Selections From the Prison Notebooks*, ed. and trans. Q. Hoare and G. Nowell Smith. New York: International Publishers.

Haraway, D. (1989) *Primate Visions: Gender, Race and Nature in the World of Modern Science.* New York: Routledge.

Hardt, M. and A. Negri (2000) *Empire.* Cambridge, MA: Harvard University Press.

Harvey, D. (1990) *The Condition of Postmodernity.* Cambridge, MA: Blackwell.

Hollier, D. (1984) 'Mimesis and castration' trans. W. Rodarmar, *October*, 31(Winter): 3–15.

Jameson, F. (1992) *Postmodernism, or, The Cultural Logic of Late Capitalism.* Durham, NC: Duke University Press.

Kafka, F. (1971) 'A report to an academy' in N.N. Glatzer (ed.) *Franz Kafka: The Complete Stories.* New York. Shocken.

Laclau, E.O and C. Mouffe (1985) *Hegemony and Socialist Strategy: Toward a Radical Democratic Politics.* London: Verso.

Lippit, A.M. (2000) *Electric Animal: Toward a Rhetoric of Wildlife.* Minneapolis: University of Minnesota Press.

Luke, T. (2002) 'Braking with bytes: Telematics as a new politic economy' Paper presented at Automobility conference, Centre for Social Theory and Technology, University of Keele, September 2002.

Marx, K. (1967) *Capital: A Critique of Political Economy, Vol. I*, ed. F. Engels, trans. S. Moore and E. Aveling. New York: International Publishers.

Pietz, W. (1993) 'Fetishism and materialism: The limits of theory in Marx' in E. Apter and W. Pietz (eds) *Fetishism as Cultural Discourse.* Ithaca: Cornell University Press.

Ross, K. (1995) *Fast Cars, Clean Bodies: Decolonization and the Reordering of French Culture.* Cambridge, MA: MIT Press.

Rubinstein, S.A. and T.A. Kochan (2001) *Learning from Saturn: Possibilities for Corporate Governance and Employee Relations.* Ithaca: Cornell University Press.

Saturn *Vue* (February 2002) 'Creatures of the Evergreen Forest' *Outdoor Magazine.*

Saturn *Vue* (March 2002) 'Inhabitants of the Polar Regions' *Martha Stewart Living.*

Saussure, F. de (1959) *Course in General Linguistics*, ed. C. Bally and A. Sechehaye, trans. W. Baskin. New York: Philosophical Library.

Sheppard, S.E. (1923) *Gelatin in Photography.* New York. Van Nostrand for Eastman Kodak Company.

Simpson, M. (1999) 'Immaculate trophies' *Essays in Canadian Writing*, 68(Summer): 77–106.

Taussig, M. (1993) *Mimesis and Alterity: A Particular History of the Senses.* New York: Routledge.

Taylor, F.W. (1914) *The Principles of Scientific Management.* New York: Harper & Brothers.

Tichi, C. (1987) *Shifting Gears: Technology, Literature, Culture in Modernist America.* Chapel Hill: University of North Carolina Press.

United Nations (2002) *Final Report of the Panel of Experts on the Illegal Exploitation of Natural Resources and Other Forms of Wealth of the Democratic Republic of the Congo.* October, 2002.

Wade, L.C. (1987) *Chicago's Pride: The Stockyards, Packingtown, and Environs in the Nineteenth Century.* Urbana, IL: University of Illinois Press.

Wolfe, C. (1999) '*Faux* post-humanism, or, animal rights, neocolonialism, and Michael Crichton's *Congo*' *Arizona Quarterly*, 5(2): 115–153.

Traffic, gender, modernism

Andrew Thacker

Introduction

'Transportation is civilization', trumpeted the modernist poet Ezra Pound in 1917 (Pound, 1973: 169). This is a slogan worth juxtaposing alongside his more familiar injunction to 'Make it New', since literary modernism welcomed certain forms of transport as a modern sensation *par excellence*. Taking your pet turtle for a walk in the city, as the *flâneur* did in 1840s Paris to show distaste for the increased pace of life, was an option no longer available in a city like London in 1914, the year when one form of literary modernism made its mark. As Susan Buck-Morss states: 'For the *flâneur*, it was traffic that did him in' (Buck-Morss, 1986: 102). But, for the modernist writer, urban traffic offered many new perceptual possibilities. This chapter examines how the tropes of movement and flux in modernism and modernity can be understood by connecting them with the material technologies of transport.[1] Not so much the *flâneur*, then, but more the *voyageur* is the more typical figure of early twentieth century modernism in Britain. The chapter, therefore, offers a deliberate contrast to the depiction of the automobile in contemporary American culture, discussed in the chapters in this volume by David Martin-Jones and Mark Dery.[2]

The chapter begins with a brief overview of responses by British and Irish modernist writers to the impact of the motor-car, before considering one writer, Virginia Woolf, in more detail. The chapter then considers a single text – Martin Amis's *London Fields* – as a later cultural reaction to the fact of automobility. While Amis is not strictly a modernist writer, his text is indebted to a similar problematic to that found in modernism, particularly in relation to how the experience of the automobile constructs specific forms of (gendered) subjectivities.

Modernism and transport

Discriminations between the different cultural experiences offered by modern transport are noticeable in a wide range of modernist texts. 'That railways are inadequate appears/Indubitable now' (Davidson, 1909: 101). These are not the words of a frustrated commuter in 2006 but those of 1890s poet John Davidson in 'The Testament of Sir Simon Simplex Concerning Automobilism', a poem first published in *The New Age* in 1908. 'Simplex' was a brand name briefly used by the Mercedes motor company in the early years of the twentieth century. Davidson's poem contrasts two modes of transport and finds the political significance of cars preferable to those of trains. Railways are condemned for being 'democratic, vulgar, laic' because they marshal together all classes and sections of society: 'Bankers and brokers, merchants, mendicants,/Booked in the same train like a swarm of ants'. Motor-cars, however, emphasize the individual over the mass, for although 'the train commands, the automobile serves'. The 'privacy and pride' of the car expresses the 'Will to be the Individual' rather than the 'Will to be the Mob' inherent in rail travel. Davidson's debt to Nietzsche is very apparent in this poem, and it is interesting to note how modes of transport not only represent political or semi-philosophical points of view but are also associated with one sense of modernity. If railways are negatively identified with democracy and socialism ('The socialistic and the railway age/Were certainly coeval'), then both the mode of travel and the political ideal are seen as outdated: 'I call Democracy archaic, must/As manhood suffrage is atavic lust/ . . . whose analogue/In travel was the train, a passing vogue.' The car, however, looks forward to a new age of individuality, freed from antiquated notions of equality. With the car, 'A form, a style, a privacy in life/Will reappear', and this new quality of experience will, as with much in English culture, be linked to a sense of the past: 'Now with the splendid periods of the past/Our youthful century is proudly linked' (Davidson, 1909).

Although formally this poem belongs to the urban ballads popular among Davidson and others in the 1890s, it is modernist in the way that a new technology is associated with a typical experience of modern life itself. Davidson's celebration of the privacies of the motor-car emphasizes the discriminations that it is important to make when considering the impact of forms of automobility upon social life. In a rich and suggestive account of the myth of speed in modern culture Jeffrey Schnapp has argued that 'accelerated motion' may be one of the 'heroic themes' of modernity, but it was not an invention of the modern era. Schnapp traces the cultural history of speed back to pre-motorized forms of transport such as horse-drawn coaches and suggests that 'the entanglement of modern notions of subjecthood with experiences of accelerated motion' derives from these origins (Schnapp, 1999: 4). What is distinctive about the phenomenon of speed in the early twentieth century, according to Schnapp, is the consolidation of two forms of automobility around 1900. The first is a 'thrill-based culture of velocity' associated with cars, and later planes, where the model of individuality is that of the driver as author or controller of the experience of movement. The second is when forms of transport such as buses and trains signify the conveyance of commodities, or subjectivities construed as commodities (Schnapp, 1999: 18). Davidson's distinction between the mobilities of cars and trains thus broadly supports Schnapp's argument.

While agreeing in general terms with Schnapp's argument, I think that the detail of much modernist writing shows a rather more complex set of responses to movement and automobility. Davidson's paean to the pleasures of the car points to the contemporary political resonances of the new machinery, which Schnapp does not really consider, with the car representing a rampant individualism that the liberal E. M. Forster, for example, found repugnant. In Forster's novel, *Howards End* (1910), the ownership of motor-cars symbolizes the crass mercantile spirit of the Wilcox family. More than this simple identification of a mode of transport with a political individualism, we can note how Forster's view of the motor-car is coloured by a perception that its mobility is part of a more general facet of modernity; the car is a key instance of what Forster laments as the new 'civilisation of luggage' or a 'nomadic civilisation' (1910: 256).[3]

Movement between and across various spaces is a key feature of modernism and modernity, and one significant way of interpreting this motif of a modernity of flux is via the emergence of modern systems of transport, such as the motor-car, the electric tram or bus, or underground trains. Analysing the significance of transport in Britain in the early years of the twentieth century enables us to understand the spaces of modernity in a more materialist fashion, as called for by the geographer Neil Smith (1993). We can also consider how the quotidian experience of moving around the metropolis provided a key impetus to the experimental qualities of cultural modernism.[4]

The impact of the motor-car in the early twentieth century was pronounced; one early commentator in 1902 proclaimed that the motor-car 'will revolutionize the world. . . . All our conceptions of locomotion, of transport, of speed, of danger, of safety will be changed' (Pennell, 1902: 185). Artists and writers were quick to recognize the revolution of modern transport. The painter Fernand Léger noted how movement through a landscape by automobile or express train initiates a new set of sensory relations to the space perceived by the artist: 'The condensation of the modern picture, its variety, its breaking up of forms, are the result of all this. It is certain that the evolution of means of locomotion, and their speed, have something to do with the new way of seeing' (Léger, 1914: 135). For Léger the new ways of seeing resulted in Cubism but by 1914 this opinion was widely accepted among other artists, with the Italian Futurists being perhaps the most notable modernist group to embrace the euphoria of the automobile. In the first manifesto of Futurism in 1909 Marinetti, for example, famously used the motor-car as an emblem of the accelerated pace of modern life. The founder of the Vorticist group, Wyndham Lewis, sniffily but perhaps accurately dismissed his modernist rivals, the Futurists, as 'Automobilists', while proclaiming that the Vorticist group 'blessed' another transportative technology, the 'restless machinery' of English shipping (Lewis, 1914: 22–3).

As well as the general social revolution of technologies like the motor-car, the impact upon literature was also noted. The influential critic I. A. Richards complained in *Practical Criticism* (1929) that 'No one at all sensitive to rhythm, for example, will doubt that the new pervasive, almost ceaseless, mutter and roar of modern transport, replacing the rhythm of the footstep or of horses' hoofs, is capable of interfering in many ways with our reading of verse' (Richards, 1964: 318). Richards has a footnote to this comment citing T. S. Eliot in support of his claim that the 'internal combustion engine may already have altered our perceptions of rhythms' (1964: 318). Eliot had himself already linked modernity and modernism to transport when in 1921 he compared the music of Stravinsky's *The Rite of Spring* to the 'the scream of the motor-horn, the rattle of machinery, the grind of wheels, the beating of iron and steel, the roar of the underground railway, and the other barbaric noises of modern life' (cited in Gordon, 1977: 108). It is this attention to the machinery of modernity, barbaric or euphoric, and its impact upon literary modernism that interests me. For it demonstrates how modernist writing must be located within the movements between and across multiple sorts of space. This is a movement through new material spaces and by means of new machines of modernity, and which grounds a more abstract sense of flux and change that many modernist writers attempted to articulate in their texts. Forster, for example, has one of his characters bemoan 'this continual flux of London' (Forster, 1910: 184). I suggest that we must understand the notion of 'flux' in relation to material motion through specific spaces and geographies.

For example, the motor-car and its quality of mobility are used in a revealing fashion by James Joyce to explore the colonial modernity of Ireland in the early twentieth century. In 'After the Race', one of the seemingly slighter stories in *Dubliners* (1914) Joyce uses the setting of a motor-car road race in Dublin to consider elliptically the modernity of Ireland. The Gordon Bennett race, held on the 2nd July 1903, was the first major road race to be held in Britain or Ireland. In Joyce's story the cars represent a sense of European modernity to which Dublin, as a colonial city of the British Empire at this time, cannot easily be assimilated. The cars come 'scudding in towards Dublin' from the surrounding countryside and, as onlookers gather to watch them, Joyce carefully indicates what these cars represent: 'through this channel of poverty and inaction the Continent sped its wealth and industry' (Joyce, 1992: 35). The speed of the cars represents a power and financial status that Joyce perceived lacking in Dublin; equally, the movement of the cars is in contrast to the 'inaction' of his native city. Famously, Joyce had claimed that the aim of the stories in *Dubliners* was to render visible the debilitating 'paralysis' of Dublin (see Ellmann, 1983: 163). In 'After the Race' this paralysis is also depicted in the character of the Irish protagonist, Jimmy Doyle, a well-educated but feckless young man who is the friend of Charles Ségouin, the wealthy French owner of a car which has just finished second in the race. Doyle is about to invest a large sum of money in Ségouin's motor business, and Joyce seems to suggest, as the story concludes with Doyle losing miserably at cards with Ségouin's friends, that this investment will most likely lead to 'poverty and inaction' rather than 'wealth and industry'.

Along with his money, and being seen by Dublin friends 'in the company of these Continentals', Doyle is excited by the car journey itself: 'Rapid motion through space elates one' (Joyce, 1992: 37). This is clearly a form of Schnapp's 'thrill-based culture of velocity' and the motor-car, a blue French model, represents European modernization and capital to Doyle; his pleasure in the power of the technology becomes linked to a delight in modern life itself as the 'journey laid a magical finger on the genuine pulse of life and gallantly the machinery of human nerves strove to answer the bounding courses of the swift blue animal' (Joyce, 1992: 38). Despite the characterization of Doyle as a rather shallow enthusiast for motoring, the excitement of the car's 'rapid motion through space' is clearly linked by Joyce to a European modernity to which he, as a writer, aspired. Joyce, it seems, is much more attracted by the whirl of modern life than Forster. Partly, Joyce associates this flux with a modernity that the paralysed Dublin of his youth signally lacked, but while Joyce is sympathetic in his writing to the fluidity of modern life, this is grounded within a deeply historical understanding of the social and political geographies of modernity in Ireland (see Deane, 2000). 'After the Race' indicates, in miniature, how Joyce's sense of modernity was informed by a politics of space; how far, asks Joyce, is the urban space of Dublin capable of grasping the elation of rapid motion while remaining a colonial city?

For the remainder of this chapter I want to concentrate upon two other writers who interrogate the complex sensations generated by automobiles. Both Virginia Woolf and Martin Amis understand modernity in terms of a sense of movement that can be closely associated with the technology of the motor-car. But in their differing representations of automobility we see something of how the autonomous pleasures of rapid motion are marked by conflicting senses of gender and desire.

Woolf

In her early short story 'The Mark on the Wall' (1917) Woolf writes that 'if one wants to compare life to anything, one must liken it to being blown through the Tube at fifty miles an hour – landing at the other end without a single hairpin in one's hair!' and that it is this kind of experience that 'seems to express the rapidity of life' (Woolf, 1973: 44–5). Throughout her writings images of transport are employed in this analogous way for the sensations – the 'rapidity' – of modern life. The context for interpreting Woolf's images of automobility is not colonial, like Joyce, but more marked by gender relations and the interrogation of subjectivity.

The significant presence of modern vehicles in Woolf's work is a theme that critics such as Rachel Bowlby (1997) and Gillian Beer (1990) have already opened up for discussion. The motor-car, from the late 1920s onwards, is depicted positively by Woolf as an agent of spatial freedom in contrast to the negative way that cars are figured in *Mrs Dalloway*. Overall, I want to suggest that the motor-car functions in three ways for Woolf: first, it helped her conceptualize the relations between space and place, articulating a geography of modernity in terms of an exhilarating sense of movement; second, this movement helps fuel a set of images of identity and subjectivity in flux; and thirdly, it emphasizes how the external material world informs inner psychic space, and vice-versa.

In July 1927 the lives of Virginia and her husband Leonard were drastically changed by the purchase of a motor-car. This was enabled by the financial success of *To the Lighthouse*. Leonard notes how the car, a second hand Singer bought for £275, produced 'a great and immediate effect upon the quality and tempo of our life' and that 'nothing ever changed so profoundly my material existence . . . as the possession of a motor-car' (Woolf 1967: 177–8). The effect upon Virginia Woolf was equally dramatic, as she testified in her diaries. On 11 July she notes that an 'absorbing subject . . . has filled our thoughts to the exclusion of Clive & Mary & literature & death & life – motor-cars. . . . We talk of nothing but cars' (Woolf, 1982: 146). Throughout the summer and autumn of 1927, and through into their holiday in France by car in 1928, Woolf's diaries and letters enthuse over the car. This represented something of a *volte-face* for Woolf who, only three years earlier, had complained of the dire effects of the lowering price of motorcars: 'The cheapening of motor-cars is another step towards the ruin of the country road. It is already almost impossible to take one's pleasure walking' (Woolf, 1986: 440).

The ownership of the car brought with it, in Henri Lefebvre's (1991) terms, a *spatial practice* of great freedom that offered a different pleasure to that of walking. Interestingly, this practice was characterized by being a *passenger* rather than a *driver*, since Virginia Woolf never passed her driving test. This supposedly subsidiary relationship to the motor car did not prevent Woolf from celebrating motoring freedoms: 'This is a great opening up in our lives. One may go to Bodiam, to Arundel, explore the Chichester downs, expand that curious thing, the map of the world in one's mind' (Woolf, 1982: 147). Woolf's attitude here partly chimes with how commentators have discussed the 'golden age' of motoring in the 1920s and 1930s in Britain, specifically for the commercial and professional middle-classes who were the group with the highest ownership of cars. Motor-car ownership was also higher in the southeast of England than in other areas of the country (O'Connell, 1998: 85). The motor-car represented independence and an 'opening up' for the middle-classes, a chance to go on 'tours' and day-trips into rural areas, freed from the restrictive timetables of the railways or buses. Only a few years earlier, in 1923, Woolf contemplated exploring the Sussex countryside by taking 'a motor bus ride along the downs . . . [to] see . . . Arundel' (Woolf, 1981: 259). Numerous publications in this period, such as *Country Life*, carried columns offering advice to urban middle-class drivers wishing to tour the countryside; one 1929 book entitled, *Car and Country: Week-End Signposts to the Open Road*, offered tips on how to find 'hidden villages' and avoid 'the industrial patch' (see O'Connell, 1998: 154–5). The sites to which Woolf expresses a desire to travel in the car are also of interest. Car travel in this period enabled the middle-classes to visit places that were distinct from the growing mass-market holiday sites for the working classes, such as the seaside location of Blackpool. It also enabled what the historian O'Connell calls a 'form of commodification, that of selected aspects of "English" heritage and landscape' (1998: 79) such as sites of natural beauty or historical interest.

The motor-car also resonates with a set of personal meanings that combines the social and geographical freedom of the car with the psychic space that was so significant for Woolf. In the revealing phrase used in her diary – 'the map of the world in one's mind' – we see the coalescence of different forms of space: psychic, cartographic and geographical. This representation of space, where the boundaries between different spaces are constantly broached, is an extremely important one in the development of Woolf's fiction. The car may have signified individual freedom for Woolf, a feeling shared by other people of her class in the 1920s, but it also captured her personal sense of the pleasures and perils of moving through the spaces of modernity, and is discernable as a significant presence in some of her texts of this period.

Woolf closely associated the dark blue Singer with her writing, for as she notes, 'The world gave me this for writing *The Lighthouse*'. Over the coming weeks, when the Woolfs moved down from London for the summer to Rodmell, the car assumed a central role in their lives. Early in August she notes, 'We have motored most days' (Woolf, 1982: 151). Woolf's entry for 10 August continues the eulogy to the emancipation introduced by the car:

> Yes, the motor is turning out the joy of our lives, an additional life, free & mobile & airy to live alongside our usual stationary industry . . . Soon we shall look back at our pre-motor days as we do now at our days in the caves. (Woolf, 1982: 151)

The car epitomizes an 'additional' life that contrasts with the sedentary practice of writing, with Woolf implicitly linking the mobility of the car to the modernity of the times. In a letter to Lytton Strachey she amusingly suggested that the horrors of the Victorian period were perhaps 'explicable by the fact that they walked, or sat behind stout sweating horses' (Woolf, 1977a: 418). The technology of the car is a form of 'industry' that associates the individual with modern times, and shows how the very fact of movement itself, as well as the places one visits, became a key pleasure for Woolf. Not only does the car modify the quotidian life of Woolf but, in offering an 'additional life', it emphasized one of her key themes, that of the instability of a unitary self.

Woolf's desire for travel is also linked, in her mind, to resisting her depression. In 1926 she prescribes herself a series of measures to stave off depression: 'first, incessant brain activity; reading, & planning; second, a methodical system of inviting people here . . . third, increased mobility . . . With my motor I shall be more mobile' (Woolf, 1982: 112). Movement is the key to fighting off depression and a sense of restriction, with the motorcar being a physical embodiment of 'incessant brain activity'. In 1924 she thought she might cure a minor depression by 'crossing the channel' to Dieppe, or 'by exploring Sussex on a motorbus' (Woolf, 1981: 308). Woolf's awareness that she needed 'increased mobility' when unhappy was also a reaction to her unpleasant memories of the 'rest cures' she undertook in 1910 and 1912 (see Lee, 1997; Showalter, 1987). Woolf had also by this time started her relationship with Vita Sackville-West, who was a 'flamboyant' driver with whom she often travelled by car and who had given Woolf an early driving lesson (Lee, 1997: 509). Soon after their first meeting Sackville-West visited Woolf in her 'large new blue Austin car, which she manages consummately' (Woolf, 1981: 313). Female motorists had increased a little throughout the 1920s, although they were often decried for only being interested in cars as fashionable objects of consumption. In 1927 the magazine *Motor Trader* remarked upon a 'fashion for driving cars' amongst women, only to compare it dismissively with women's interest in 'a new fashion in hats or frocks' (O'Connell, 1998: 67). Rather than a fashion statement, however, Woolf told Sackville-West that the description of her driving in *Orlando* (1928) showed 'the most profound and secret side of your character' (Woolf, 1977a: 469). Woolf also linked the androgyny explored in *Orlando* with her Singer motorcar in letters to her sister, Vanessa: 'I can't believe your amazing stories of the Male and Female parts of the Renault. Do the French sexualise their engines? The Singer I know for a fact to be hermaphrodite, like the poet Cowper' (Woolf, 1977a: 463).

When describing the motor car in *Orlando,* Woolf's writing eschews a more fluid style for a jagged, plain prose designed to capture the piecemeal nature of the motorist's perceptions of the surrounding scenes. Driving through south-east London, Orlando sees fragments of text, adverts for shops: 'Applejohn and Applebed, Undert-. Nothing could be seen whole or read from start to finish' (Woolf, 1992: 200). This description is very much in agreement with the sociologist Simmel's observations upon the disjointed, visual relationships that dominate in modern cities where people mainly move in machines and not of their own volition (cited in Benjamin, 1983: 37–8). Here Woolf reflects upon how motoring is at the root of this process of heterotopic disintegration. Now it is not the texts of shop signs that are fragmented, but the human body and mind that becomes like 'scraps of torn paper tumbling from a sack'. The implication, Woolf writes, is that 'the process of motoring fast out of London so much resembles the chopping up small of identity which precedes unconsciousness and perhaps death that it is an open question in what sense Orlando can be said to have existed at the present moment' (Woolf, 1992: 200–1). Orlando only reassembles herself when she leaves the city and starts to see 'green screens' of countryside against which 'the little bits of paper fell more slowly', which gradually lead once more to the illusion of unity. This image of a divided self clearly echoes the historically distinct selves of Orlando's lives over the centuries of the book, but it is significant that the motion of the car produces this particular spatial dissolution of identity.

The association of multiple subjectivities with motoring is also found in a short and cryptic essay composed by Woolf around the time in 1927 when she and Leonard first enjoyed driving around Sussex. 'Evenings Over Sussex: Reflections in A Motor Car' does not explore the spatial form of the text so radically as the passage in *Orlando*, but it does utilize the trope of multiple selves. The essay starts as a kind of topographic account of the Sussex landscape and its towns, but quickly widens the focus to that of the spatial history of the region.

Interestingly, however, the viewer is not fixed in one spot, as in many traditional topographic forms of writing. Woolf thus shuns a discourse of place to capture a sense of touring through a space and its histories. Looking at the landscape also undermines the integrity of the subject who gazes out: 'I cannot hold this – I cannot express this – I am overcome by it – I am mastered' (Woolf, 1993a: 83). As in *Orlando*, travelling through the countryside in the motorcar occasions this proliferation of selves: 'relinquish, I said (it is well known how in circumstances like these the self splits up and one self is eager and dissatisfied and the other stern and philosophical), relinquish these impossible aspirations; be content with the view in front of us' (1992: 83).

From the 1920s onwards Woolf became more aware of the cultural ramifications of transport as a key bearer of modernity, and sought to integrate the spatial experiences of travel into her writings. This is seen in, for example, the major essay, 'Modern Fiction'. When Woolf searches for an analogy in the material world to the creation of modern literature, in the 1925 version she substitutes the motor-car for the bicycle of the 1919 version (Woolf, 1993b: 5). Another famous incident employing motor transport from this period occurs in *A Room of One's Own*, when the narrator looks from her London window and sees a man and a woman get into a taxi (see Bowlby, 1997: 35–9). The cab then glides off 'as if swept on by the current' of urban life (Woolf, 1977b: 92). This is the prompt for Woolf's famous and controversial articulation of androgyny, where the sexual division of mental life is now unified. Like her hermaphrodite Singer, Woolf seems to invest the taxi with the capacity to unsettle established categories of thought. The social space of transport in the city is linked to the fluidity of the androgynous mind; the movements of the car suggesting a life that shifts through space, unfixing the sexual identities housed in the brain. The internal space of the mind and the external space of the city streets once again interact, rhythmically, to produce Woolf's theory of androgyny.

Within Woolf's geographic imagination the figure of transport produces a kaleidoscopic sense of the modern self that she embraced for its potential to unsettle fixed structures of power. With Woolf, then, we discover a modernism committed to exploring and expanding what she called 'that curious thing, the map of the world in one's mind'. In her fiction of the late 1920s the speeding second-hand Singer certainly aided her exploration of the many rhythms of modernity.

Amis

John Davidson's praise for the car would have found its apogee in contemporary Britain, where in the early 1990s there were 23.6 million cars, one for every 2.4 people.[5] But perhaps instead of uncritically celebrating the 'privacy and pride' of the car, Davidson's opinions might have been tempered by the estimate that present vehicle speeds in London are almost identical to those of horses and carts at the start of the twentieth century (Bashall and Smith, 1992: 37).

The traffic jam, one consequence of this growth of car ownership, is now the norm for many metropolitan journeys and is used as a structuring device in Martin Amis's *fin de siècle* novel of 1989, *London Fields*. In a text concerned with charting the death and slowing-down of all manner of experiences – the death of love, of the century, of the novel *et al.* – the car as a mode of transport carries a great deal of symbolic weight. Very early in the novel, the narrator drives through the 'cobweb' of London in a high performance car. The brief journey produces 'Giddiness and a new nausea, a moral nausea' (Amis, 1989: 3), brought about by the 'force' and power of the car; a quick spin becomes a metaphorical spin, registering the 'mass disorientation and anxiety' (1989: 64) that the narrator later notes to be the defining characteristic of the contemporary millennium. Clearly this nausea is unlike the thrilling culture of speed discerned in early twentieth century automobilists such as the Futurists and represents the more stressful side of a modern subjectivity. Interestingly, this car has an early 'A-to-B device' for mapping one's urban jaunt in advance, a device never employed in a novel that is mostly concerned with the experience of lacking a clear direction for development.

Car transport functions in two ways in Amis's novel: as an image of isolated subjectivity that is fearful rather than thrilling; and to emphasize the frustrations of moving through contemporary urban space. The distance travelled from Woolf's understanding of the motorcar as a prompt to a rethinking of identity is here very noticeable. We can also point to the gendered differences between Woolf's celebration of female freedom via the car, and Amis's focus upon how a certain form of masculinity is tied to the possession of a certain form of car. The stress, for example, upon Keith Talent's 'heavy Cavalier' indicates the lonely life of this individualized mode of transport: Keith would never willingly be a passenger if he could help it. Keith's masculinity is linked to *control* over the car; defined in this way, however, the lack of control and freedom produced by traffic snarl-ups only exacerbates an alienated form of modern subjecthood. If Joseph Conrad once memorably commented in *Heart of Darkness* that 'We live, as we dream, alone', characters in *London Fields* live, as they drive, alone. Urban anomie is heightened by technologies that reinforce isolation: the video sex relationship that Keith and Nicola Six 'enjoy' only replicates other forms of social alienation. These include death itself, which Amis notes, is something we all experience but, 'in different lanes, at different speeds in different cars' (1989: 119).

Commenting upon certain forms of what he terms 'dead public space', Richard Sennett, in *The Fall of Public Man*, notes how certain spaces, such as that of La Defense in Paris, only exist as conduits through which to move (Sennett, 1977). As Jennifer Bonham shows, 'efficient movement' for automobile traffic became the dominant form of spatial organization in many cities around the world during the twentieth century (Bonham, in this volume). Such spaces as La Defense derive from motion, and the use of such areas impedes richer social relations, asserts Sennett. These spaces parallel 'the relations of space to motion produced by the private automobile' (Sennett, 1977: 14). Cars are not now used to tour and view the city; rather they promise freedom of movement and individual control, somewhat in the way Davidson predicted in his poem. City streets are transformed into spaces to be pumped through in vehicles, and yet the massive freedoms promised are blunted by the experience of driving as a perpetual scene of stress and frustration. Sennett argues that this anxiety,

> comes from the fact that we take unrestricted motion of the individual to be an absolute right. The private motor-car is the logical instrument for exercising that right, and the effect on public space, especially the space of the urban street, is that the space becomes meaningless . . . unless it can be subordinated to free movement. The technology of modern motion replaces being in the street with a desire to erase the constraints of geography. (Sennett, 1977: 14)

In essence when geography is subordinated to the demands of the automobile, we are disconnected from the space around us: as Sennett comments elsewhere, 'the driver wants to go through the space, not to be aroused by it' (Sennett, 1994: 18). The human relationships embedded in the spatial organization of society reinforce the figure of the driver as an isolated individual.

In *London Fields* contemporary urban life is often figured in this way as a debilitating state of alienation. The very body of London cannot be comprehended anymore since the 'metal-lined, reinforced, massively concrete' streets are 'illiterate' and 'illegible': 'You cannot read them any more' (Amis, 1989: 367) laments the narrator. If this indecipherability springs from the subordination of social space to the principle of motion, movement itself is ruled by the clogged experience of urban life in the novel. In a key passage Amis's narrator discusses how the temperaments of world cities are reflected in the nature of their traffic. Two features summarize London: doubleparking (which Keith Talent does as a matter of course even if spaces are available), and the 'inferno' of gridlock. The paradox of the unrestricted freedom of the car-driver, writes Amis, is that 'if everybody does it then nobody gets around, nobody gets anywhere' (1989: 326). Here we note a significant difference from the experience of traffic in the modernist period, where flux and hurry often signify an uneasy celebration of the technological power of modernity and the new. Technology in *London Fields* is almost always negative, either commodified (Amis is careful to use brandnames throughout) or with aggressive potential, as with the automobile:

> Four times in last few days I have sat tight in the car, gridlocked under the low sun, with no way out, while jagged figures discover what the hard machine can do to the soft: what the hood of the car can do to the human nose and mouth. . . . Traffic is a contest of human desire, a waiting game of human desire. You want to go there. I want to go here. And just recently, something has gone wrong with traffic. Something has gone wrong with human desire. . . . In traffic, now, we are using up each other's time, each other's lives. (Amis, 1989: 326)

This passage attempts to show the impact of changes in the usage of material space by automobiles upon human relationships. It was estimated in the early 1990s that three quarters of cars entering London remain parked there all day

(Bashall and Smith, 1992: 40). The social organization of street transport thus stifles the very aspect of human experience it was meant to enable: the desire to move to some other place, and the distance required for all desire to operate, is thwarted and time itself is copiously but futilely consumed. The traffic jam is dead social space, an arena where the social desire for human connection is blocked, much as Keith and Guy in the novel are kept from proper conjunction with Nicola. The characteristic nineteenth century *fin de siècle* experience of a languid, winding-down in the pace of life reappears at the end of the twentieth century in the image of Keith Talent taking fifteen minutes to cross one junction on the Great Western Road. Movement amid 'horrorlorries' and 'horrorcars' is described as 'thwarted hurry' (Amis, 1989: 439), the use of clumsy noun constructions emphasizing at the level of style an experience of spatial frustration. It is no surprise that Keith, at one point, feels 'as frazzled as London traffic' (1989: 358). It is a fair description of Amis's own prose style in the book, with its short stubby sentences, its refusal to indulge in complex clause structures, and the use of cumulative lists of descriptive phrases, all replicating the disjointed, crabby motion of traffic across the congested metropolis.

Conclusion

This chapter has examined a range of twentieth century literary engagements with the experience of technologized transport. It has suggested that the sense of modernity as flux, famously summed up by Marshall Berman, following Marx, as a state where 'all that is solid melts into air', can be cognized more comprehensively by reference to particular spatial histories of transport systems such as that of the motor car (Berman, 1983). Automobility, as Schnapp argues, produces and emphasizes a very modern form of subjectivity, where the driver is an autonomous individual and the passenger is a supposedly inferior form of modern selfhood, part of 'the mass'. But, as we have seen, certain writers queried this familiar distinction between the individual and the mass, autonomous versus dependent subjectivity. Virginia Woolf was a perpetual passenger who found this automobilist experience one of a 'free and mobile' life, rather than a diminishment of subjectivity. This, I have suggested, indicates the significance of the gendered construction of automobilist identities. The connection between a stunted masculinity and the thwarted movements of the car driver in Amis's *London Fields* also demonstrate how the form of subjectivity found in automobility needs to pay close attention to questions of gender. Juxtaposing Woolf and Amis in this way is not intended to set up some dialectical opposition between the car as freedom and frustration, or between modern and post-modern forms of automobility. Instead, it indicates the complex range of cultural representations that automobile subjectivity has taken across the century: understanding these images must take account of the historical and geographical differences within and across modernity. For example, it should be noted that much of Woolf's pleasure derives from car journeys through *rural* settings; Amis's *London Fields* concerns the automobile exclusively in an urban context. The irony of the book's title is pertinent in this context – there are certainly no fields to spin through on a day out here.

The discussion of more contemporary experiences of automobility in Martin Amis and Richard Sennett once again confirms the intrinsic link between the car and the spatial construction of identity. Movement through space in the car as an experience of individual autonomy is shown to be problematic; this is a direct consequence of how the impact of the automobile has restructured social space, especially in the city. In Foucauldian fashion the expansion of individual autonomy represented by the automobile has resulted in a restriction of these very same liberties. Now all drivers sometimes feel like mere passengers denied the elation of rapid motion, and the desire embodied in the experience of the automobile seems continually thwarted. Perhaps only by recovering something of Woolf's pleasure in being a passenger of dissolving identities can this excitement be recaptured. But that, of course, would mean eschewing the car for the bus or the train, thus raising much wider questions about how the governance of space and geography must engage with the problems of contemporary automobilities (see Bonham, Merriman, Rajan, and Forstorp, in this volume).

Notes

1 Obviously, other forms of movement, such as the circulation of commodities, are also important for understanding modernity. Benjamin's work in *The Arcades Project* is crucial in this respect, where the *flâneur* is a key figure for understanding the flux of modern commodities in the city. However, this chapter concentrates upon the physical transits of transport and the attendant psychic shocks of automobility.

2 Without a lengthy excursus upon the terminology of modernity and modernism, it is useful to indicate that since my background is in literary studies I use the term *modernism* to refer primarily to a distinct period in literary history, roughly from 1850 to 1950. Woolf's texts, on which I concentrate in the first part of the paper, are acknowledged as central in characterizing how modernism is defined. Martin Amis, on whom the second part of the paper focuses, cannot be termed a modernist writer, even if he has been influenced by earlier modernists such as Joyce or Woolf. I am, however, wary about defining him as a *post-modernist* writer. This is because I am becoming more convinced that the distinction, in the sphere of cultural representation at least, between modernism and postmodernism, is rather unhelpful and lacking in nuance. Writers such as Woolf and Amis might, instead, be seen as offering differing (and sometimes similar) forms of response to the historical and geographical trajectories of modernity. For a useful discussion of this kind of view see Brooker (2002). My usage of the term *modernity* is (still) indebted to the work of Marshall Berman and David Harvey: it refers to a particular kind of experience of change, of newness, of anxiety and excitement. The automobile, particularly as represented in the writers I investigate here, seems to be a key object for understanding the meanings of this variety of modernity.

3 For further discussion of automobilities in *Howards End* see Thacker (2000).

4 Ford Madox Ford, for example, in *The Soul of London* (1905: 43) concludes his chapter on 'Roads into London' by drawing a link between the 'pathos and dissatisfaction' of gazing out of a train window at incidents from daily life that one never sees completed, and the desire for stories to have an ending.

5 Society of Motor Manufacturers and Traders, reported in *The Guardian*, 22.10.93.

References

Amis, M. (1989) *London Fields*. Harmondsworth: Penguin.

Bashall, R. and Smith, G. (1992) 'Jam today: London's transport in crisis' in A. Thornley (ed.) *The Crisis of London*. London: Routledge.

Beer, G. (1990) 'The Island and the Aeroplane' in H.K. Bhabha (ed.) *Nation and Narration*. London: Routledge.

Benjamin, W. (1983) *Charles Baudelaire: A Lyric Poet in the Era of High Capitalism*, trans. H. Zohn. London: Verso.

Berman, M. (1983) *All That is Solid Melts into Air: The Experience of Modernity*. London: Verso.

Bowlby, R. (1997) *Feminist Destinations and Further Essays on Virginia Woolf*. Edinburgh: Edinburgh University Press.

Brooker, P. (2002) *Modernity and Metropolis: Writing, Film and Urban Formations*. Basingstoke: Palgrave.

Buck-Morss, S. (1986) 'The *flâneur*, the sandwichman and the whore: The politics of loitering' *New German Critique*, 39: 99–140.

Davidson, J. (1909) *Fleet Street and Other Poems*. London: Grant Richards.

Deane, S. (2000) 'Dead ends: Joyce's finest moments' in D. Attridge and M. Howes (eds) *Semicolonial Joyce*. Cambridge: Cambridge University Press.

Ellmann, R. (1983) *James Joyce*. Oxford: Oxford University Press.

Ford, F.M. (1905/1995) *The Soul of London*, ed. Alan G. Hill. London: Everyman.

Forster, E.M. (1910/1983) *Howards End*, ed. O. Stallybrass. Harmondsworth: Penguin.

Gordon, L. (1977) *Eliot's Early Years*. Oxford: Oxford University Press.

Joyce, J. (1992) *Dubliners*. London: Penguin.

Lee, H. (1997) *Virginia Woolf*. London: Vintage.

Lefebvre, H. (1991) *The Production of Space*, trans. D. Nicholson-Smith. Oxford: Blackwell.

Léger, F. (1914/1966): 'Contemporary achievements in painting' in E.F. Fry (ed.) *Cubism*. London: Thames and Hudson.

O'Connell, S. (1998) *The Car and British Society: Class, Gender and Motoring, 1896–1939*. Manchester: Manchester University Press.

Pennell, J. (1902) 'Motors and cycles: The transition stage' *The Contemporary Review*, 1 February: 185–7.

Pound, E. (1973) 'Provincialism the enemy' in W. Cookson (ed.) *Selected Prose 1909–1965*. London: Faber.

Richards, I.A. (1964) *Practical Criticism: A Study of Literary Judgement*. London: Routledge.

Schnapp, J.T. (1999) 'Crash (speed as an engine of individuation)' *Modernism/Modernity* 6(1): 1–50.

Sennett, R. (1977) *The Fall of Public Man*. London: Faber.

Sennett, R. (1994) *Flesh and Stone: The Body and the City in Western Civilization*. London: Faber.

Showalter, E. (1987) *The Female Malady: Women, Madness and English Culture, 1830–1980*. London: Virago.

Smith, N. (1993) 'Homeless/global: scaling places' in J. Bird, B. Curtis, T. Putnam, G. Robertson and L. Tickner (eds.) *Mapping the Futures: Local Cultures, Global Change*. London: Routledge.

Thacker, A. (2000) 'E. M. Forster and the Motor Car' *Literature and History*, 9(2): 37–52.

Woolf, L. (1967) *Downhill All the Way: An Autobiography of the Years 1919–1939*. London: Hogarth Press.

Woolf, V. (1973) 'The mark on the wall' in *A Haunted House and Other Stories*. Harmondsworth: Penguin.

Woolf, V. (1977a) *The Letters of Virginia Woolf: Vol.3*. ed. N. Nicholson and J. Trautmann. London: Hogarth Press.

Woolf, V. (1977b) *A Room of One's Own*. London: Granada.

Woolf, V. (1981) *The Diary of Virginia Woolf Vol. 2*. ed. A. Oliver Bell and A. McNeillie. Harmondsworth: Penguin.

Woolf, V. (1982) *The Diary of Virginia Woolf Vol.3.* ed. A. Oliver Bell and A. McNeillie. Harmondsworth: Penguin.

Woolf, V. (1986) 'The cheapening of motor cars' in *The Essays of Virginia Woolf Vol.3.* ed. A. McNeillie. London: Hogarth Press.

Woolf, V. (1992) *Orlando*. London: Vintage.

Woolf, V. (1993a) 'Evening over Sussex' in *The Crowded Dance of Modern Life Selected Essays vol. 2*. ed. R. Bowlby. London: Penguin.

Woolf, V. (1993b) 'Modern fiction' in *The Crowded Dance of Modern Life Selected Essays vol. 2*. ed. R. Bowlby. London: Penguin.

Wyndham Lewis, P. (1914) 'The melodrama of modernity' *BLAST*, 1: 143–145.

Part Four
After Automobility

Virtual automobility: two ways to get a life

J. Hillis Miller

Pixels as automobility

In this chapter, I try to think out the difference between two forms of imaginary automobility, one associated with the now fading age of the book, the other associated with the new electronic age. Reading a novel and surfing the net are two forms of automobility or of what several of the chapters in this book call 'motility' (Latimer and Munro, this volume). I sit in my chair reading a book or facing a computer screen and travel by my own autonomous effort. In both cases I move outside myself into virtual realities that may make me sometimes forget entirely where I 'really am'. What is the difference between these two forms of automobility? In thinking about this I have been immensely aided by the other chapters in this volume. They have taught me much about the history and sociology of actual automobile use. They have also taught me much about the socio-economic and political conditions presiding over the current shift from a print and manufactured-commodities culture to an information culture. This shift is turning even automobiles more and more into moving media and information centres, and ultimately toward being 'smart cars', quasi-robots guided by 'smart roads'. The driver will then become a passenger like any other. All on board will be able to continue working on the computer, sending emails, listening to iPods, or playing computer games, just as they would at home or in the office. This would 'happily' combine actual automobility, movement through space, with virtual automobility or motility by way of computer chips. I agree, as Nicole Shukin argues in this volume, that the shift from books to computers is not 'progress'. It is a lateral movement from one technology to another within a hegemonic capitalism that is recklessly destroying the planet. Ross (1999) talks about a striking statistical study showing it takes almost as many tons of energy (15 to 19) to fabricate a PC as to fabricate a car (25 tons). So much for the idea that the pixilated culture will be disembodied or free from the need to exploit natural resources! I have elsewhere investigated at some length the question of 'the death of literature' (Miller, 2002, esp. 1–23). The book epoch is slowly fading, as various digitized media gradually replace books in the daily lives of most people. Books, however, will be around for a long time yet. In addition, 'literature', not in the sense of printed novels, poems, and plays, but in the sense of the 'literary', that is, tropological and fictive-performative uses of language and other signs, is migrating to those other media: radio, film, television, popular music, computer games, advertising, and television news. The 'literary' will never die, but it is transmigrating.

My focus is on the effects of two capitalist technologies on the subjective life of the 'consumer', in this case the book reader as against the player of computer games. Most people agree that telecommunication technologies are transforming capitalism and therefore the life of those who live under capitalism. Telematics are making capitalism more radically transnational, much more difficult to control by a given nation's laws and powers. Just-in-time or *kanban* methods of design and production can combine parts and know-how from all over the world to put together a finished product, whether it is an automobile or that powerful instrument of motility, a personal computer, or, for that matter, a printed book or magazine.

One of the abbreviations used in emails and chatrooms, so I am told, is 'gal': 'Get a life!' It is a wonderfully subtle and nuanced exhortation or putdown. It suggests, not too gently, that the person to whom it is addressed does not have a life at this point. He or she has manifested that by some behaviour or speech obnoxious to the exasperated interlocutor. The latter says, 'Get a life!'

Why doesn't that person have a life already? Presumably because he or she is too hung up on conventional judgments, values, and behaviour. To 'get a life' means, I take it, to abandon prescribed values and behaviours, to live freely, according to self-generated norms that defy convention. To have a life is to have integrity, independence, and originality. The myth of free automobility associated with motor-cars is a version of that ideal. Of course the performative command, 'Get a life!' is often an invitation not to independence but to joining the speaker's way of life, just as using an automobile, as many of the chapters in this volume show, is a form of subservience, not of unlimited freedom. 'Get a life!' then means, 'Give up your present life and join me and my way of life'. It is a quasi-religious injunction. Jesus promised that if you joined him you would get a life, and get it more abundantly. 'For whosoever hath', said Jesus in the parable of the sower, 'to him shall be given, and he shall have more abundance: but whosoever hath not, from him shall be taken away even that he hath. Therefore speak I to them in parables: because they seeing see not; and hearing they hear not, neither do they understand' (Matt. 13: 12–13). Like the parables of Jesus, 'gal' is addressed to those that have ears and can hear or eyes that can see and understand. The code is inscrutable to those not in the know. The injunction 'gal!' it happens, is a set of letters with an ironic meaning of its own. 'Gal' is somewhat derogatory slang for 'girl'. To understand the cryptic, 'gal!' or to crack its code is already to belong to a somewhat esoteric community, a community apart, perhaps a community of dissensus.

My questions are the following: Is the sense of what it means to have a life, a genuine identity or selfhood, changing with the ongoing shift from a paper-based culture to a pixel-based or pixilated culture? If so, just how? Are new forms of community developing that define in new ways what it means to have

194

a life? Are they perhaps communities of true dissensus, that is, unique, self-enclosed, incommensurate groups, with singular goals and norms? Is the way we live now, or want to live, different from the way we used to live? If one wanted to get a life today would one do it differently? These questions have often been asked. Many answers have been proposed in recent years. I still find it not all that easy to get clarity that satisfies me. This essay is another try.

A large literature on these topics already exists, including some things I have written myself (Bukatman, 1993; Dery, 1996; Turkle, 1997; Negroponte, 1999; Miller, 1999; Derrida and Stiegler, 2002; Derrida, 2005; Miller, 2002a; Miller, 2002b; Dery, in this volume). David Crystal's fascinating *Language and the Internet* has an eight page closely-packed bibliography, even though it limits itself to the question named in its title (Crystal, 2001). 'It is not the aim of this book,' says Crystal firmly, 'to reflect on the consequences for individuals and for society of lives that are lived largely in cyberspace' (2001: 3). This is just what I want to reflect on. Crystal does not really, strictly speaking, obey his prohibition, with anything like crystal clarity. The consequences for individuals and for society cannot be separated from the effect of the Internet, as Crystal puts it, 'on language in general, and on individual languages in particular' (2001: 3). Crystal's bibliography includes such items as Diane F. Witmer's and Sandra Lee Katzman's 'On-line smiles: does gender make a difference in the use of graphic accents?' (Witmer and Katzman, 1997).

Horace reading

Let me propose a thought experiment. I want to juxtapose the 'lives' of two teenagers, one at about 1946, the other today. Both, it happens, are, in my imagination of them, male. Whether that makes a decisive difference is a large and complex question, on which I shall only briefly touch. I think it does make a difference. Our culture interpellates males and females, boys and girls, to behave differently in their ways of submission to reigning communication technologies, whether of paper or of pixel. I doubt if the difference is primarily biological. Witmer and Katzman (1997), however, found relatively little difference between the way men and women use online smiles, so one must be wary of jumping to conclusions about this.

I call the first of my virtual personages, 'Horace', in memory of Horace Greeley (1811–72), an earlier American paper man. I call the other 'Jim', or 'Jimjim' to his family and friends, for no particular reason. I had thought of calling Jimjim Jimjane, to express the uncertainty of his or her gender, as he or she is called to express it by the Internet. The evidence I have, however, suggests that the particular cyberpersonality I have in mind is more likely to be male. Though the avatars people adopt in cyberspace may often be deliberately uncertain or ambiguous as to the gender of the user, Jimjim says, speaking of the computer game he habitually plays: 'From SubSpace specifically, I only know about four female players well. I know of a few more, something like 10 or 20 [out of eighty or more], but I don't know them well. There aren't very many girls that play SubSpace, and I'm sure some of them don't like to tell people they are, since it sometimes leads to bad situations' (personal communication to author). Jimjim's sister and female cousin, also teenagers, are also computer-adept, but they use cyberspace in quite different ways from Jimjim. His sister also studies computer science, but she is interested in programming for neuroscience research. She uses AOL Instant Messenger primarily to talk online with friends she has known since high school. Jimjim's cousin works for a small company that creates websites for local businesses. She is a gifted computer artist, whereas graphic design does not interest Jimjim much. The cousin and a friend, also female, created an online newspaper with a distinctly radical political bias. I conclude that different teenagers live in cyberspace in quite different ways. It would be an error to try to generalize a single cyberpersonality. It is difficult, perhaps impossible, to invent a plausible imaginary cyberperson who combines all these uses of the Internet, while being in addition gender-blind. Each cyberperson is to some degree singular, sui generis.

The first of my imaginary teenagers is alone around 1946 sitting in an easy chair reading a book. He is reading Emily Brontë's *Wuthering Heights* for the first time. Ever since Horace taught himself to read at age five, so he would not have to depend on his mother to read *Alice in Wonderland* to him, he has spent as much time as people will allow him to do reading books. He also makes model airplanes and 'ham' radios. He is pretty much a loner. Decisive moments in his life are often encounters with books. An example was his first reading of Dostoevsky's *Notes from Underground*, when he was a sophomore in college. 'Ah Ha!', he said to himself, 'At last I have found someone like myself. This man speaks for me. "I am a sick man. . . . I am a spiteful man. I am an unattractive man. I believe my liver is diseased". Wonderful! A soulmate at last'.

This imaginary personage was a perfect example of what Simon During calls 'literary subjectivity' (During, 2000). Not only did Horace 'love literature' and spend a lot of time reading it. His sense of himself, of who and what he was, was also to a large degree, though of course not completely, determined by the literary works he read. He was called to be what he was by literature. He was a child of the print epoch, or rather of what Jacques Derrida calls the paper age. No television then. No computers. No World Wide Web. Radio, yes. This young person listened to 'Amos and Andy', 'Easy Aces', and 'The Lone Ranger'. Horace remembers hearing hectoring speeches by Hitler broadcast for an American audience in incomprehensible – but very impressive – German. The house had a telephone, but this virtual person does not remember using it much, certainly not for long distance calls, which were a big event in the house, when they happened.

Horace was surrounded by various forms of paper. These were piled up around him, not only the paper of all those books, but the paper of his birth certificate and the rest of his 'identity papers', the paper on which he wrote his student 'papers' and examinations, at first in longhand, then, the papers that is, on the typewriter. In addition, there was the paper on which he wrote rather infrequent letters, infrequent, that is, until he fell in love and wrote reams of love letters when separated from his beloved, paper on which he kept a mawkish diary, all those papers on which he signed his name or inscribed his initials, for example in that diary or on the fly-leaves of the books he owned, and so on.

Horace was a paper man, a bookworm. Paper was inseparable from his identity. Paper was a prosthetic extension of himself, or rather it was a kind of self outside himself. Paper, or what was written on it, called, exhorted, demanded, or beseeched, with an irresistible force, that he be what he was. If he had commanded such eloquence, not to speak of having had command over the French language, he might have said what Jacques Derrida says in 'Paper or Me, You Know . . . (New Speculations on a Luxury of the Poor)', an interview of 1997: ' "I who can sign or recognize my name on a surface or a paper support"; "The paper is mine"; "Paper is a self or ego"; "Paper is me" ' (Derrida, 2005: 56). For such a person, unless an agreement or commitment is 'put on paper', it is not binding. It is not for real. Reading works of fiction, in any case, was Horace's chief form of virtual automobility.

Jimjim at the computer

What a difference when we turn to Jimjim, the second virtual person in my thought experiment! Let us imagine him today. He is seated at his computer, at three o'clock in the morning. He is doing five things at once. He is playing a collective computer game called SubSpace with a group from various countries. He is listening to MP3 songs. He is using AOL Instant Messenger to carry on an email conversation with a friend. He is at the same time engaged in a multi-person interchange with a chatgroup through IRC (Internet Relay Chat). He is also doing homework for his university classes.

Jimjim is a computer science student at a public university. He has been using computers since he was five or six. By a year or two later he was making changes in his mother's computer (the only one to which he had access). Strange things happened when she turned it on, a message on the screen or a new screen saver. He was an early player of computer games. He would play for eight or ten hours at a time, stopping only for meals, when forced to do so. He showed early on an interest in changing or reprogramming game programmes. He has never read a programme manual in his life and is scornful of those who do. The abbreviation 'rtfm' ('read the fucking manual'), one of the items in David Crystal's list of Netspeak codes, would have elicited from Jim a scornful snort or a smiley with a lifted eyebrow or wink: ;-), or perhaps the sarcastic smiley: :-]. Jimjim long ago gradually began to use email and chatmail to communicate with friends. He then began to play online games with them, thereby tying up the telephone line in his home for hours at a time. Allowed to do so, he sleeps all day (literally) and stays up all night (literally), using the computer. He eats primarily junk food, when he can get away with it. In short, he is a computer geek.

197

J. Hillis Miller

He is even a hacker, in the benign sense of someone who likes to hack or alter programmes, to get down as far into the kernel of the programme as he can and do things to it. He already took a basic programming course in high school. Now, in college, he has his own computer, a PC. He keeps it on all the time. He uses it about four fifths of the time he is in his college room, that is, at least eight hours a day. He has downloaded roughly 1700 MP3 songs and listens to them all the time when he is using the computer. A high point for him was receiving the Mandrake version of Linux as a birthday present. The attraction of Linux for him is its power and openness to being programmed, also the way using it gives Jimjim entry into an elite group of fellow geeks. He passionately believes in open source and in total freedom on the Net. This spills over into his general political views, such as they are. He is, I suppose you would say, a libertarian. He has risen up through the ranks of the online game called Sub-Space (played by three quarters of a million people worldwide). He is now a SuperModerator (SMod) in SubSpace. His 'job' includes 'enforcing the rules, watching for cheaters, being nice to the players, hosting events, things like that' (personal communication). SubSpace is by now, as Jimjim admits, a relatively archaic computer game, somewhat primitive in its graphics. Newer games have a great diversity of subject matter, truly amazing complexity, superb animation, and wonderful sound effects and music. Not all are, like SubSpace, shoot-'em-up games of violence, but a considerable number still are. In SubSpace the weapons are spaceships.[1]

Jimjim has a wide range of friends, mostly casual ones, he has met online, chiefly through SubSpace. Most are from the United States, but a few are from Germany, Australia, Canada, Brazil, and some other countries. A few of these relations are relatively close ones, for example with a girl he met online and has met in person only once. He also uses, as I have mentioned, several chatpro-grammes (IRC [Internet Relay Chat], AIM [AOL Instant Messenger], and ICQ, the latter two one person at a time, the former a multiparty chatgroup). The client he uses for IRC is mIRC, a British operation (www.mirc.co.uk). He has never got much into MUDs or MOOs, though some of his friends have. He chats partly with family and friends from high school, but also with the much wider circle of people he has met online.

If Horace got a life from books, Jimjim, it seems clear, gets his life, or much of it, from his active participation in Cyberspace. This is his extravagant form of virtual automobility. Three features of this participation seem especially salient:

1. Jimjim, when he is online, is usually doing several things at once: listening to MP3s, engaging in several different chat conversations, playing or watching some game, doing homework, etc. 'When I'm using the computer', he says, 'I'm probably going to be talking to someone using AIM, as well as using IRC and playing/watching some game (Most likely SubSpace). I also spend time programming, doing homework, and watching anime, although not as

198

much. I tend to be doing more than one of the above things at the same time, as well' (personal communication). This reminds me of a citation in David Crystal's *Language and the Internet* from someone who said: 'it is possible to do calculus homework and have tinysex [Whatever that is; it is something you do on a TinyMUD; I'm not sure I want to know (JHM).] at the same time, if you type fast enough' (Crystal, 2001: 187).

2. Jimjim is, somewhat self-consciously, a different person or persons on-line from the one he is in face-to-face encounters with family and friends. He uses avatars or imaginary names on line. What he says about this is striking in its resistance to the idea that he actively invents these alternative selves. He just becomes a different person. 'I have avatars in a sense, I guess. That is, I use names other than my own online, but I don't invent personalities for them. I suppose that I act differently online than I do when I talk to people face to face, but it's not something I invent, it's just how I normally act' (personal communication). This statement is amazing in its candour and in its self-analytical power. Jimjim could say what Rimbaud said, in one of the famous 'Lettres du voyant', 'Je est un autre', 'I is another'. It's not a matter of invention or choice. It just happens, perhaps as an effect of the medium itself. On-line, Jimjim becomes another person or persons. This means that Jimjim is not a single person, but a strange sort of interior civic community of persons. Is this a community of dissensus? I think it could be argued that it is.

3. Jimjim self-consciously belongs to a different community or communities online from the ones he belongs to outside cyberspace. He uses, to some degree at least, a special language or languages online. He uses smileys often and shorthand sometimes, but mostly writes like he talks. 'Yes', he says, in answer to a question about whether he thinks of himself as belonging to a separate cyberspace community, 'the people I know and talk with online are in a distinctly separate group from the ones I talk to and see offline' (personal communication). Jimjim, in short, is, part of him at least, a cyberperson or rather cyberpersons, just as Horace is a paper person. Jimjim knows around eighty people through his participation in the SubSpace community, twenty or twenty five of these fairly intimately, if you can still use that word for something so disembodied, so spectral. He plays SubSpace and at the same time, laterally, so to speak, carries on Chatgroup conversations with numbers of these friends, in what is called an 'in-game public chat'. A subgroup of the larger group within Jimjim's particular domain of SubSpace happen to be Brazilians. Though Jimjim does not know Portuguese, one member of his group does know both English and Portuguese. That member translates back and forth, and so keeps the game going. The online community to which Jimjim belongs is therefore not only transnational. It is also multilingual. The hegemony of English in Cyberspace should by no means be taken for granted. The number of websites in Chinese is, I am told, increasing exponentially, and will likely exceed those in English during the next decade.

Conclusions: what's the difference?

What, if anything, can I conclude from this thought experiment?

First conclusion: There is no use whatever either in handwringing or in triumphalism. These are two extreme judgments of getting a life in cyberspace that we have all probably encountered. On the one hand, the change from paperpersons to cyberpersons has already occurred or is irreversibly under way. Nostalgia will butter no parsnips. On the other hand, the triumphalism, that sees the electronic revolution as justifying a whole-scale bookburning and as ushering in a millennium of peace and transnational plenty, is equally, and symmetrically, wrong. It ain't the end of the world, but it ain't the happy end of history either. The challenge is to take stock of what is happening and to recognize the new possibilities and the new responsibilities that living in cyberspace brings. It would certainly be a disaster, for reasons I shall specify, to try to reform Jimjim, to enforce on him a 'literary subjectivity', or to close down his chatgroups and his online computer games, or to police and censor the Internet generally, as is the case, so I am told, in the People's Republic of China. Some real danger of that may exist these days in the United States, as civil liberties come under widespread unconstitutional threat.

Second conclusion: The paper age is by no means over. It will probably last a long time to come, just as manuscript culture lasted into the print age. On the one hand, Jimjim reads or used to read a lot of literature, chiefly science fiction. He mentions Neal Stephenson, Roger Zelazny, Larry Niven, among others. And of course Jimjim has his identity papers too, though more and more these are being replaced by cards that have an electronic component. Horace, on the other hand, has grown up to become, you guessed it, a university professor. He now writes on the computer, after beginning with longhand, shifting to the typewriter, then back to longhand, finally straight from that to computer composition. He uses email all the time. It has changed his life. He also uses the Web in his research, searching online bibliographies, reading online versions of books, reading, occasionally, online journals, and so on. He does not, however, use chatgroups or play computer games. His 'other lives' are still lived primarily through reading books that are physical objects you can hold in your hand. To some degree, however, Horace is, perhaps more than he realizes or is willing to admit, a cyberperson as well as a paperperson. If Jimjim listens to MP3 songs all the time, Horace listens to classical music much of the time, even when he is reading or writing. He plays it on the CD player in his computer and now on his iPod. If Horace writes literary criticism, Jimjim writes poetry and fiction. He is admirably adept at expressing himself clearly and succinctly, as the quotations from him indicate. Far from being made illiterate by the computer, Jim has, through constant practice in emails and chatgroups, acquired an impressive clarity and force in his use of language. For some people at least, those with a gift for language, using email and ICQ is splendid training in doing what you want with words. I conclude that much overlapping in the two kinds of selfhood and community-belonging, the two kinds of virtual automobility, exist and will go on existing for the foreseeable future. I can, responsibly, choose to belong to both worlds, as long as I am willing to take the consequences for that mixed existence, or double life.

Third conclusion: Though major differences exist between the two types of persons, they are also in one striking way alike. Both literature and cyberspace are forms of secular magic, to borrow a phrase from Simon During. Just what do I mean by that? During (2002) has admirably traced the history of magic shows and entertainments, from Greek and Roman antiquity to the Renaissance and then down to the early twentieth century. He has discussed the relation of magic to literature as part of this history. He is interested primarily in works like E. T. A. Hoffmann's *Kater Murr* or Raymond Roussel's *Impressions d'Afrique*. Such works have a more or less direct relation to magic shows. During does not explicitly observe, however, that all printed literary works, whether or not they overtly refer to magic practices, can be thought of as a species of magic. Horace's form of virtual automobility, like Jimjim's, is a species of secular magic. A work of literature is an abracadabra or hocus pocus that opens a new world. During has something to say about the way cinema extended magic shows, for example by being based in part on magic-lantern projections that were long a part of magic stage presentations. Eventually cinema put stage magic out of business. Movies had the stronger force, a bigger Zumbah, to borrow Harold Bloom's borrowing of an expressive African word for magic energy (personal communication to the author).

During also does not observe that modern communications technologies, from trick photography, to the telephone, to cinema, to radio, to television, to recordings on disks, tapes, or CDs, to the computer connected to the Internet, fulfill in reality old dreams of magic communication, at a temporal or spatial distance, with the living or with the dead. I can, any time I like, hear Glenn Gould play Bach's *Goldberg Variations*, with fingers long turned to dust. I can even hear Alfred Lord Tennyson reciting his poems. Talk about raising ghosts!

As Laurence Rickels has shown (1988: esp. chs. 7, 8; 1989), in the early days of both the telephone and the tape recorder, people believed they were hearing the voices of the dead (usually their mothers) behind the voices of the living, or through the static, on a telephone connection or a tape recording. These teletechnologies have gradually displaced not only magic stage assemblages, but also that other fading form of secular magic: literature. Radio, cinema, television, CDs, VCRs, MP3 gadgets, iPods, computers, and the Internet have become our dominant far-seeing and far-hearing conjurers, sorcerers, prestidigitators, animators of talking heads. These devices are, in short, our chief purveyors of magic shows and virtual motility. They have incalculable power to determine ideological belief, just as books did in the age of the book, the paper period.

Fourth conclusion: Just what can be said, on the basis of my thought experiment, of the differences between paperpersons and cyberpersons? Some of the differences are, to me at least, quite surprising. I would not have thought of them if I had not performed my thought experiment. To some degree they suggest that it is better to be a cyberperson than a paperperson.

Horace is to a considerable degree more private, more alone and lonely, than Jimjim. Reading a literary work, or even writing one, not to speak of writing a commentary on one, is a solitary activity. It is even to some degree narcissistic, as a passage in Anthony Trollope's *An Autobiography* suggests. In this passage Trollope is speaking of the way he was ostracized as a youth at Harrow because he was a day-pupil at an elite boarding school and had little pocket-money or good clothes. He says that since play with the other boys was denied him, he had to make up his own solitary play for himself. 'Play of some kind was necessary to me then, – as it has always been', he says. Trollope's solitary play took the form of what today we would call 'daydreaming': 'Thus it came to pass that I was always going about with some castle-in-the-air firmly built within my mind. Nor were these efforts in architecture spasmodic, or subject to constant change from day to day. For weeks, for months, if I remember rightly, from year to year I would carry on the same tale, binding myself down to certain laws, to certain proportions and proprieties and unities. Nothing impossible was ever introduced, – not even anything which from outward circumstances would seem to be violently improbable.' Sounds somewhat like one of those long-continued computer games, does it not, except that Trollope played by himself? Trollope himself makes an explicit assertion that his published novels were a transformation of his youthful habit of daydreaming. Speaking of that bad habit, Trollope says, 'There can, I imagine, hardly be a more dangerous mental practice, but I have often doubted whether, had it not been my practice, I should ever have written a novel. I learned in this way to maintain an interest in a fictitious story, to dwell on a work created by my own imagination, and to live in a world altogether outside the world of my own material life' (Trollope, 1996: 32–3). All writers and readers of novels are addicted to this 'dangerous mental practice'.

Jimjim, on the contrary, is actively engaged with other people in those chatgroup interchanges or in playing SubSpace. He is not nearly so much narcissistically alone. The Internet and many things reachable through it pride themselves on being 'interactive'. 'Interactive' is a leitmotif of the Net. A tremendous amount of linguistic exuberance and creativity is required for the various uses of the Web Jimjim habitually makes, day after day, for many hours a day. As David Crystal's *Language and the Internet* shows, new languages or idioms within standard English are rapidly being created by Internet users. Moreover, insofar as Jimjim is what he is through selves he becomes on the Net, he is actively engaged in a remarkable process of self-fashioning.

Reading a book, however much it requires active response and even intervention, is a more or less passive, receptive activity. Horace sits alone in his easy chair letting the words of *Wuthering Heights* do his magic dreaming for him. He is much more likely than Jimjim, therefore, to have his selfhood determined for him by way of his 'literary subjectivity', whereas Jimjim is creating his selfhood or selfhoods, even though he is subject, of course, to the 'rules of the game'.

If belonging to a community of friends and associates is a good thing, the normal situation for human beings, Jimjim much more obviously has that through his decisive participation in cybergroups than does Horace alone with Emily Brontë, or, earlier in his life, resisting all attempts by his mother to persuade him to 'go out and play with the other children', when he was deep in *The Swiss Family Robinson* or some such book. Moreover, these cybercommunities really do, after all reservations have been made, seem to constitute separate subcultures not straightforwardly subservient to the dominant national culture. Each develops, to some degree, judgments, values, and ethical standards of its own. This might be allegorized in the way so many computer games involve the creation of imaginary states with their own laws and customs.

Are cyberspace communities of dissensus possible?

Communities in cyberspace are therefore, to some degree at least, communities of dissensus, places where perhaps some independent political thinking may be possible. This, in my view, is an extremely good thing. Diversity and independence are, or should be, major aspects of any country's national and transnational character. The need for this is particularly acute in the United States today, at a time when the call to think like everyone else, on pain of being accused of disloyalty, is so much a part of the 'wartime' mentality. A terrifying example of that, terrifying to me at least, was a television ad for the travel industry that was broadcast in the United States after 9/11, when the air travel industry was in trouble. It shows bits of a speech by George W. Bush echoed in robot fashion by a series of individuals or groups associated with the air travel industry. The point of the ad was to persuade viewers that it was patriotic to travel in the aftermath of 9/11. 'Americans are asking, "What is expected of us?"' Bush was shown saying, and the others repeated in somnambulistic echo, 'Americans are asking, "What is expected of us?"'; 'Americans are asking, "What is expected of us?"' What is expected of us is that we should travel for our country and to save the travel industry. It's our patriotic duty. 'And we will', says Bush in another clip, echoed again by airline personnel: 'And we will', 'and we will', 'and we will', in hypnotic entrancement of the viewer, who is by this time glassy-eyed and in no condition to travel. This was a sitting president of the United States allowing his talking head to be used to make a commercial pitch! Jimjim's chatgroups or computer games sound pretty healthy to me, by comparison. That ad has today (2005) long since disappeared from United States television screens.

I judge, on the basis of the conclusions I have drawn from my thought experiment, that it is better to be Jimjim than Horace. Matters are not quite so simple, however. For one thing, both Horace and Jim are exhorted, interpellated, called upon in various ways to be what they are by many other ISAs (Ideological State Apparatuses) than just literary works for Horace and the Net for Jim. School, television, cinema, newspapers, magazines, not to speak of police and politicians, all play a role.

Horace now, sixty years after 1946, watches television, including network news, but he also seeks out Cursor.org, an alternative news source on the web. Jimjim watches much less television than Horace does, though probably more movies, but of course those MP3s are not innocent of ideological content either. The literary works that have made Horace what he is are, to be sure, to a considerable degree canonical purveyors of Western ideology, for example, assumptions about middle-class courtship and marriage in Anthony Trollope's novels. Nevertheless, even canonical works are also in part critiques of reigning ideologies. That is certainly true for *Wuthering Heights*. That novel is hardly a straightforward argument for patriarchal gender hierarchy or for bourgeois marriage and family life. Trollope's novels too, though more covertly, are critique as well as indoctrination of Victorian ideologies. Trollope by no means approved wholeheartedly of the way his contemporaries got a life or 'lived now', to echo the title of his *The Way We Live Now* (1874–5).

On the other side of the ledger, again, Jimjim's computer games are not innocent. They often glorify war, as in the many space battle games, such as SubSpace, or they set up imaginary countries that are at war with other countries, in perpetuation of nationalist ideologies that globalization may, or should, be weakening. Lots of violence is present in some, though by no means all, computer games. The geeks who make them up are not isolated from mainstream youth ideologies. The Internet, moreover, has rapidly been co-opted by business interests. Like *Wired* magazine, it is now a tool of capitalism. It is hard to use the Net without being subject to commercial bombardment by flashing 'cookies' and other appeals to consumerist greed.

A game of SubSpace, on the one hand, and *Wuthering Heights*, on the other, are, to put it mildly, quite different virtual realities in which to live. The difference, however, is not that one is violent and the other a canonical assertion of traditional humanistic values. *Wuthering Heights*, like the Bible or like the work of Homer, Sophocles, Dante, Shakespeare, or Toni Morrison, is full of shocking violence. Nor is the difference one of the relative gender stability in canonical literature as opposed to gender ambiguity in cyberspace. *Wuthering Heights* was written by a woman, Emily Brontë, who published under a male-sounding pseudonym, 'Ellis Bell', and who used a male narrator, Lockwood, who records the narration of Nelly Dean, as well as declarations spoken to Nelly by Catherine Earnshaw and Heathcliff, or letters written by Isabella and others. The reader becomes in turn, in imagination, all these virtual people. Talk about avatars and the adoption of alternative personalities!

I have written so far, to some degree, as though *Wuthering Heights* and a game of SubSpace were just different forms of a universal imaginary automobility, each appropriate to the media of its own age. This is of course not the case. The adept reader of *Wuthering Heights*, Horace for example, creates, on the basis of the words on the page, an inner space. For this novel, the inner space through which the reader 'moves' is made up of a Yorkshire landscape, the two houses and the 'Chapel of Gimmerden Sough', in their locations in relation to one another in that landscape, and the interiors of the two houses, Wuthering

Heights and Thrushcross Grange. The latter are specified in terms of windows, doors, and interior spaces within interior spaces. The reader cannot actually see what the author had in mind. He or she can only improvise an imaginary space by means of the words. The consequence is that these spaces and the virtual movements the reader makes through those spaces probably differ quite a bit from one person to another, or even from one reading to another by the same person. This form of virtual automobility is, moreover, relatively passive. It is relatively independent of 'body language', of small muscular movements of hands, legs, and torso. The latter are essentially necessary in order to play computer games. I do not know that empirical investigations of this have ever been attempted. It would be an important project. Some authors and some readers have provided maps of a given novel's scene. These exist for Trollope, for Hardy, for Conrad, for Faulkner, and no doubt for others. Films made from novels are further evidence. My reaction to such films is often, but not always, to say, 'No, no! It's not like that. You have got those rooms all wrong.'

SubSpace, like all computer games, is quite different. SubSpace is an example of the well-known current shift from verbal media to graphic media, as instruments for the generation of imaginary spaces and of virtual automobility within them. Just what is the difference? I shall specify two of the most important. The graphic spaces of computer games, like those of cinema or television, are laid out before the viewer's eyes. He or she has relatively little freedom for the free exercise of imagination in making an inner space. Second difference: computer games, as we know, are 'interactive'. The game-spaces become internalized. The keyboard, joystick, and screen come to seem extensions of the player's body, just as is the case in a different way for the book a reader holds in his or her hands, and just as various chapters in this book stress the way the automobile comes to seem an extension of the driver's body (see especially Mark Dery, in this volume). Virtual movement through a game space is unlike the minimal eye movements and page turnings of the book reader. It requires active muscular and somatic movements of hand and body. It demands high skill in hand-eye coordination. You don't just sit there and read. You have to do something. Often, if you do not do something fast and do it right, you will be killed: 'Game over!' A novel just waits there for me to read it. I conclude that verbal virtual automobility and graphic virtual automobility are radically different.

The ultimate result of my thought experiment is that it is better to be a cyberperson than to be a paperperson, though the issue is complex, as I have tried to show. It appears to be a basic feature of human beings, at least as presently socialized, that they need virtual realities or magic shows of some sort or other. These have immense effect on the way people lead their lives, on the way people think, feel, and interact with their fellows, even on the way they decide to go to war or on how they vote. Many of the United States and British soldiers in Iraq have no doubt been brought up on computer games. Clips of soldiers breaking into Iraqi houses, or of smouldering cars, debris, and body parts after a car bomb has gone off, shown repeatedly on television news broadcasts, at least in the United States, look suspiciously like moments in certain computer games.

Virtual realities, it may be, determine the way 'real realities' are presented by the media. By a remarkable piece of serendipity, I encountered, as I was writing this essay, an article in *Wired* by Bill Werde that tells how one company, Kuma, is making 'reality games' based on events in Iraq and Afghanistan, for example the capture of Saddam Hussein, or the killing of his two sons, or the rescue of soldiers trapped in a March 2002 firefight in Afghanistan. 'About a month after a battle', says Werde, 'Kuma will release a videogame version with tactics, weapons, and terrain reconstructed thanks to the sort of research normally reserved for, well, journalists' (Werde, 2004: 104). These games allow a single player to perform the role of a soldier involved in these events, and, in virtual reality of course, changing what actually happened. These games build, no doubt, on the identification television viewers may already have felt when these events were shown as news. 'The look of the games owes much to the news as well', says Werde. 'Every mission is introduced with a simulated TV spot, and military analysis is provided by retired Marine major general Thomas L. Wilkerson, who explains tactics, such as why the US needed those TOW missiles [to get Hussein's sons]' (Werde, 2004: 105). Real events as shown on television news and virtual events in computer games become less and less distinguishable. Each contaminates the format of the other, and, as we know, form is meaning. The medium is the message. Our behaviour and judgment in the real world are strongly influenced by the view of things computer games enforce, just as used to be the case with that older form of magic shows, printed novels, and just as is still the case for those addicted to novels, like Horace. Can it be that George W. Bush plays computer games? We know that he watches American football on television and that he during the run-up to the 2004 election attended the Daytona 500 car race. A significant segment of those who vote for him are race-car drivers and the people who habitually attend car races or watch them on television. Car race computer games are of course an important subset of the genre. The ideologies of those who will lead the United States, at least until 2008, are steeped in the auto-mobile side of United States culture: our passion for fast cars, SUVs, 'peeckup trucks' (as they are sometimes called in California), Hummers, military tanks, and humvees.

Specialists in literary or culture studies have done much work investigating the way literary works, as a feature of capitalism (by way of the paper, book, and periodicals industries), have created, reinforced, and sometimes contested reigning ideologies. So many people now play computer games and have their beliefs, commitments, and political actions to some degree affected by them, that serious investigation of computer games urgently needs to be done by those in popular culture studies or in cultural studies. Playing computer games is the way a lot of people get a life these days. A provocative essay in *The New York Times* Technology section, Michael Erard's 'The Ivy-Covered Console' (2004), indicates in some detail how this new discipline is now being developed, with journals, websites, and conferences at places like Princeton University. Such study is one way academics might have of holding the surrounding culture of virtual automobility to some degree at arm's length, if they happen to want to do that. Such study could also be one form of possibly effective contestation.

Note

1 For information about SubSpace see www.subspacehq.com; and www.subspace.net.

References

Bukatman, S. (1993) *Terminal Identity: The Virtual Subject in Postmodern Science Fiction*. Durham, NC: Duke University Press.

Crystal, D. (2001) *Language and the Internet*. Cambridge: Cambridge University Press.

Derrida, J. and B. Stiegler (2002) *Echographies of Television: Filmed Interviews*, trans. J. Bajorek. Cambridge: Polity Press.

Derrida, J. (2005) 'Paper or Me, You Know ... (New Speculations on a Luxury of the Poor)' in *Paper Machine*, trans. R. Bowlby. Stanford: Stanford University Press, 40–69.

Dery, M. (1996) *Escape Velocity: Cyberculture at the End of the Century*. New York: Grove Press.

During, S. (2000) 'Literary subjectivity' *Ariel*, 31(1–2): 33–50.

During, S. (2002) *Modern Enchantments: The Cultural Power of Secular Magic*. Cambridge, MA: Harvard University Press.

Erard, M. (2004) 'The ivy-covered console' *The New York Times*, 2 Feburary, http://www.nytimes.com/2004/02/26/technology/circuits/26play.html.

Miller, J. H. (1999) *Black Holes*. Stanford: Stanford University Press.

Miller, J. H. (2002a) *On Literature*. London: Routledge.

Miller, J. H. (2002b) 'Will comparative literature survive the globalization of the university and the new regime of telecommunications?' *Tamkang Review*, 31(1): 1–21.

Negroponte, N. (1995) *Being Digital*. New York: Knopf.

Rickels, L. (1988) *Aberrations of Mourning*. Detroit: Wayne State University Press.

Rickels, L. (1989) 'Kafka and Freud on the telephone' *Modern Austrian Literature: Journal of the International Arthur Schnitzler Association*, 22(3–4): 211–225.

Ross, A. (1999) 'The Social Claim on Urban Ecology: an interview by Michael Bennett' in M. Bennett and D.W. Teague (eds) *The Nature of Cities: Ecocriticism and Urban Environments*. Tuscon, AZ: The University of Arizona Press, 13–30.

Trollope, A. (1996) *An Autobiography*, ed. D. Skilton. London: Penguin.

Turkle, S. (1997) *Life on the Screen: Identity in the Age of the Internet*. New York: Touchstone.

Werde, B. (2004) 'The war at home' *Wired*, 12(03): 104–105, http://www.wired.com/wired/archive/12.03/wargames.html.

Witmer, D. F. and S. L. Katzman (1997) 'On-line smiles: Does gender make a difference in the use of graphic accents?' *Journal of Computer-Mediated Communication*, 2(4), http://jcmc.indiana.edu/vol2/issue4/witmer1.html.

Bicycle messengers and the road to freedom

Ben Fincham

Introduction

The perception that automobility can be achieved through driving technologies is the primary motivator for the desirability of the motor-car (Urry, in this volume; Lomasky, 1997; Rajan, in this volume). As Böhm, Jones, Land and Paterson explain in the introduction to this collection, our belief in autonomy – the liberty to follow one's will – combined with the ability to be mobile permits the rationale that combines privacy, movement and the perception of progress to flourish in the shape of the motor-car. Loren Lomasky claims that autonomy and automobility are fundamental to understanding the desirability of the automobile and the needs of its user. The 'distinctively human capacity to be self-directing' is optimized by the motorcar (Lomasky, 1997: 7). The motorist is exercising the free choice that they have to do and go as they please, safe in the knowledge that the vehicle for their automobility is good for the purpose and good for the person driving. The Vice President for Research and Development and Planning at General Motors, Larry Burns, makes no bones about the positive connections between automobility, autonomy and the motorcar:

> Over time, vehicle ownership will increase dramatically . . . simply because automobility is an almost universal aspiration. An automobile gives me freedom – the autonomy to go anywhere I want, any time I want, with anyone I want, carrying whatever I require . . . (Burns, 2002)

In fact General Motors even launched a hydrogen-fuelled vehicle 'concept' called 'AUTOnomy' at the Detroit Auto Show in January 2002. Burns described it at the MIT Mobility Sustainability Symposium in May 2002:

> With a vehicle like AUTOnomy, everyone in the world has a better shot at vehicle ownership. Promises to extend freedom benefits of automobility to many more people, as we make vehicles dramatically cleaner and reduce the cost of advanced technologies like fuel cells and drive-by-wire, goes to the heart of the ownership equation – consumers will choose to buy a vehicle like this because of the exciting new features it offers and the passion it inspires. (Burns, 2002)

General Motors is obviously alive to the concerns of consumers with regard to fuel consumption, pollution and environmental degradation as well as recognizing automobility as 'an almost universal aspiration'. The ability to travel at speed in the direction that you want, with whom you want, when you want, does appear, on the surface, to confirm the optimistic view of the liberation of the individual from the constraints of inhibited mobility, lack of choices and restriction. People such as Lomasky argue that the motorcar can only enhance our social life by expanding the horizons we have to exercise our social selves. People may want to work miles from where they live, and people may be happy to spend time in their cars, either way the motorcar allows such people to make such choices. The link between the individual and the apparently *autonomous* nature of motorcar use are seductive elements to legitimizing its increased use.

The car as the provider of autonomy and speed has been the predominant idea supporting the positive benefits of their use. In advertising campaigns it is common to see the latest model speeding, unhindered, through the streets or roads of both the urban and rural landscape. As the deliverer of automobility the car embodies the spirit of freedom, privacy, movement, progress and auton-omy. But with car traffic in the UK 15 times the level that it was in 1950 (Trans-port 2000, 2002) the urban transport infrastructure appears to be creaking under its weight. The problems of congestion, delay and pollution are familiar to anybody who spends any time on Britain's roads. Even the Confederation of British Industry (CBI) freely admits that traffic congestion is a huge problem, costing the UK economy £20 bn per year (Transport 2000, 2002). The paradox is that the desire/need to be mobile is the major contributing factor to the motor-car being a source of immobility. A major qualitative study undertaken by the Department for Transport revealed that the driving public is aware of the major cause of congestion. It was reported that:

> The sheer volume of traffic is usually thought of as the main cause of congestion – and this is seen to be growing rapidly and inexorably.
>
> *'There can be nothing wrong with the road, absolutely nothing wrong between Heathrow and here, but you know as soon as the volume of traffic reaches a point of critical mass that it's going to start congesting, and when it starts congesting then every-thing builds up behind it.'*
>
> Other more immediate factors may be thought to trigger specific congestion episodes at specific points in time – which are important to motorists, and often the focus of irritation and criticism. However, at root the problem is mainly just put down to the growing number of vehicles. (Department for Transport, 2001)

Transport 2000 statistics also show that eight in ten people expect congestion to get worse in towns, cities and on the motorways over the next ten years. In its simplest incarnation the concept of automobility cannot be properly applied to motorcars. The idea of autonomy is confounded not only by congestion or grid-lock, but also by the simple fact of intense regimes of regulation through road traffic rules.

The principal aim of this chapter is to explore the complexities of the way that cycling can provide an apparent alternative to the motor-car as a provider of automobility in particular in urban environments. The role of bicycle use as a potential resolution to the 'motor-car and automobility' paradox, as either a direct alternative to the car, or as a beneficiary of the impossibilities of the car system, is becoming increasingly apparent. In 1999 the European Commission produced a report entitled 'Cycling: The Way Ahead for Towns and Cities'. The report acknowledged that the car had become a victim of its own success, and the most appropriate way of undermining the 'apocalyptic images of towns that had come to a complete standstill' is to promote and encourage increased bicycle use (European Commission, 1999: 10). By examining a group of cycle users I will illustrate the inherent tensions between cycling and driving, and argue that there has been an ongoing marginalization of cycling in terms of both urban infrastructure and public discourse. The source of the material for this work comes from a study conducted between 2001 and 2004 into the lives and working conditions of bicycle messengers in the UK. I conducted a questionnaire survey of messengers in the UK and Europe, followed by an 18-month period of participant observation during which I worked as a bicycle messenger in Cardiff, UK. The study was rounded off with 40 semi-structured interviews with messengers from Cardiff and London. This was not my first encounter with bicycle couriers, as I had worked as a messenger for a couple of years before the study. The study of bicycle messengers in relation to automobility raises an important question about types of cycle use as automobile. The fact that messengers cycle for money, rather than for recreation or commuting purposes, sets them apart from other cyclists in relation to autonomy. Although the general point is that the rationale for cycling in the city is speed and efficiency, as well as subsequent health and environmental benefits, messengers' behaviour is, to an extent, dictated by an economic necessity – the need to complete as many jobs as possible. As will be explored, the difficulty for messengers is that the challenge to car hegemony by the bicycle is tempered by the rationale for messengering being dependent on continued increased use of the motorcar, and the requirement to place themselves in danger to maximize their earning potential. It is widely acknowledged, however, that bicycle messengers are mobile in the world of the automobile. Whilst cars are idling in traffic queues, bicycle messengers are scooting up the outside, jumping lights, skipping pavements, going the wrong way up one-way streets – literally travelling door-to-door. The level of mobility experienced by messengers is one that could not be envisaged by the urban motorist. The bizarre reality is that the urban automobile is largely immobile, and it is this immobility that creates the space – and the demand – for bicycle messengers. Bicycle couriers are one of the finest examples we have of urban mobility. There is a price, however, and the unpleasant trade-off for enhanced mobility to messengers, and to other cyclists, is the risk of injury or death.

The problem with cyclists

There are many consequences for motorists of the failure of the motorcar to deliver the automobile dream. Incidences of road rage and general displeasure with the driving environment are well documented (Lupton, 1999; Marshall and Thomas, 2000). One symptom of the frustration of motorists, for whom the reality of car use does not match the advertising propaganda, is growing hostility to one class of road user who still seems to enjoy something resembling automobility: the cyclist. In recent years there has been a general shift in the perception of cyclists as being at best harmless and at worst irritating, to outright aggression from much of the driving public. A leader column in *The Guardian* newspaper articulated this shift in perception, in a piece entitled 'Mr Toad in Lycra: Cyclists are not all wonderful people' the newspaper charts the transformation of the cyclist from 'old maids, biking to holy communion through mists of an autumn morning' and 'children pedalling diligently to the school gate' to 'the helmeted Lycra-clad fanatic who rides wherever he chooses', 'hurling abuse at those who impede him' (*Guardian*, 2002: 17). The terms 'Lycra lout' (Bamber, 2002: 10) and 'bicycle guerrillas' have entered the language, and are frequently applied to bicycle couriers in particular. Also in *The Guardian*, an official from the Royal Automobile Club (RAC), when talking about proposed European legislation on insurance, is quoted:

> Many cyclists behave as if there were no legal constraints upon them, ignoring traffic lights, signs, one-way streets and pedestrian crossings, travelling as fast as possible with no lights or bell: they are bicycle guerrillas. (*Guardian*, 2002: 3)

On the same day in *The Sun* newspaper, Jeremy Clarkson wrote an article entitled 'The Lycra Nazis are Taking Over':

> When will people understand that roads are for cars and that there is no danger at all from speeding motorists if walkers and cyclists steer clear? (Clarkson, 2002)

There are also articles being written from a pseudo-sympathetic perspective, but where the onus of irresponsibility still lies firmly with the cyclists. In an article in *The Sunday Times* Bryan Appleyard paints a picture of a concerned driver who feels that he might kill a cyclist through no fault of his own:

> Your chic cyclist about town wears all black and rides a black bike. This makes him difficult to spot in traffic. Clever. He also likes to flaunt the superior mobility of his vehicle. Waiting at one set of lights I saw a cycle courier performing balletic figure eights in the junction in front, one hand on the handlebars and one clamping a phone to his ear. He could not see the lights and would only know they had changed by the cars moving forward. But we could not move forward; he was in the way. Meanwhile, he risked being hit by traffic coming in the other direction. But he did look really cool.
>
> For aggressive cycling style is all about courting risk. At most junctions in London you will see a cyclist cruising around the yellow grid, waiting for a chance to get across whether the lights change or not. If they're quick, they might make it, if they're not, they'll die. (Appleyard, 2002: 3)

There is a demonization of the cyclist, as an active agent in the disruption of the normal operation of the urban traffic network. Car drivers are now the

victims of 'louts' and 'guerrillas'. In examining the reasons for this scapegoat-
ing of sections of the cycling population as irresponsible and dangerous we are
being led into a discussion about 'risk'. Cyclists, so often complained about, are
either putting themselves or others at risk, and perhaps the exemplar of these
risk-inducing 'louts' and 'guerrillas' are cycle couriers. In an article in *Cycling
Plus* magazine, the journalist Cass Gilbert acknowledges this perception:

> The media's view of couriers, or messengers as they are known, has never been a lofty
> one. It's encapsulated by the image of a reckless male cyclist, in his twenties, adorned
> with tattoos, a nose-ring and plenty of attitude to boot. (Gilbert, 2003: 61)

As examples of risk taking or reckless cyclists, bicycle messengers are viewed
as extreme producers of the 'car driver as victim' sentiment. Through fieldwork
and interviews with messengers, however, the idea that car drivers are victims
falls away to reveal another set of motivations for complaining about cyclists in
general, and cycle messengers in particular.

Incidence of accident and injury in bicycle messengering

When discussing risk and risk-taking in relation to bicycle messengers, it is
important to establish levels of exposure to 'risk' – time spent on the road – and
rates of accident and injury. My research indicates that the distances travelled
by bicycle messengers – 45 to 70 miles a day, depending on the city being worked
– are far greater than those recreational cyclists and possibly many drivers –
people with less than a 25-mile car journey to work, for instance. With most
messengers working between 8 and 10 hours a day, it is testament to the skill of
messengers that rates of death appear to be so low. The only specific records of
messenger fatalities is an internet obituary board set up by the International
Federation of Bicycle Messenger Associations and occasional references in local
newspapers. As far as I can establish, through these sources and anecdotally,
there is about one messenger death every three to four years in the UK, although
the rate appears to be much higher in the US. One messenger reported that there
was at least one messenger death a year in New York alone, still a remarkably
low rate for a population estimated to be 2000 (IFBMA, 2004). The UK death
rate is mercifully low in the light of the rates of injury requiring hospital treatment reported by messengers. In the survey I conducted in 2002–3, 27 per cent
of messengers from the UK and Ireland (*n* = 96) reported that they had experienced one accident requiring hospital treatment and a further 34 per cent
reported experiencing two or more accidents that required hospital treatment.
In terms of rates of injury the findings in my survey have been broadly reflected
in similar research in the United States. In a study of injuries sustained by bicycle
messengers in Boston, USA, researchers found that

> 70% of working couriers have incurred an injury resulting in days away from work
> and in visits to a health-care professional or hospital (55%). Annual incidence rates
> were large at 51 injuries resulting in days away from work per 100 bike couriers. The

national average is 3 lost-work injuries per 100 workers, with the highest rate at 15 lost-work injuries per 100 workers in the meat packing industry. (Dennerlein and Meeker, 2002)

The types of accident were also very similar, with 'collisions and avoiding collisions with motor vehicles', being 'doored' and collisions with pedestrians accounting for 66 per cent of 'events leading to injury' (Dennerlein and Meeker, 2002).

The potential for death or injury appears to be statistically high for cyclists in general, as the road accident research suggests (Department for Transport, n.d. a). For bicycle couriers the statistics make even more startling reading. According to the Health and Safety Executive (HSE) the rates of non-fatal injury in the general working population is 1.2 per cent of workers per annum (HSE, 2002: 56). Although not a directly comparable figure the sample in my survey reported that in an average three-year period 62 per cent would end up with at least one injury that would require hospital treatment as a result of an accident at work.

Who then is the victim?

Many hours of cycling through 'the city' have led me to question the motivation for complaints about the behaviour of cyclists, and particularly messengers and the idea of the driver as a victim. I noted an incident in my field diary that illustrates this point perfectly. Having picked up a package I set off to deliver it:

> I rode at speed along the outside of the three lanes – towards the oncoming traffic – in order to avoid getting car doored [a collision with a car door that opens suddenly as the cyclist is riding past]. When I reached the end of the line of traffic, I swooped down in front of the cars being held at the light and joined the traffic passing in front. I would say that there was a good 20 yards between myself and the taxi coming at me, which then sped up as quickly as it possibly could and attempted to hit me. The driver was fuming. He sat on his horn and then gave chase. He was beeping me all the way along Duke Street, pulling up every now and again with the window down screaming 'That was a red light', when he next caught up with me a little further along he was purple and just screaming 'you fucking wanker!'. The interesting thing about this altercation is that at no point did he refer to 'safe' or 'dangerous' behaviour, in fact I don't think that his rage had anything to do with safety, more that he finds it genuinely annoying that I don't obey the same rules as him. (Field diary, 27 June 2002)

This opinion that people are more upset that cyclists are breaking the law, rather than a danger to themselves or anybody else is widely held in the courier community. I have had many conversations with riders who feel that they are easy targets for drivers' general frustration with the urban motor transport infrastructure. This general perception was summed up by a courier in an interview:

Or people get cross if you break the law, people get cross for . . . like you're breaking the law against them, even though they're not even affected by it . . . You're just pottering through an open junction and people do get a bit cross. I'm guessing that's because they use the road and they feel that because they're in a car they have to obey the rules but they feel . . . well I don't know . . . they feel like you ought to because they have to. (Messenger in Cardiff interview transcript, March 2002)

The general irritation with the state of the urban traffic infrastructure is understandable. I suppose it must be more frustrating for those who bought certain brands of vehicle on the evidence of advertisements depicting motorcars speeding along 'the open road' (Sofoulis, 2002) unhindered by obstacles to free movement. This frustration, however, spills over occasionally into acts of violence against perceived impediments. This point was illustrated in an interview with a London Messenger:

. . . the street I do ten, fifteen times a day, and it's got a chicane before it. You can get up to 30 miles an hour, it's one way and it's a really smooth surface, and it turns into Tottenham Court Road, so you've only got a left-hand turn. And this guy's behind me going RRR RRR [horn noise]. 'Get out of my fucking way!', you know, thirty metres from the Give Way. So I'm riding along and I eventually let him past and he overtook me, and he swerved twice and then hit the brake. I just went through his back window. (Messenger in London interview transcript, May 2003)

The idea that it is cyclists who are manufacturers of risk and that motorists are the victims of this manufacturing is a distortion of the proportional danger exacted upon any particular environment by the use of either technology. A cyclist, like *any* other distraction, may cause a motor vehicle to crash into something else – a wall or another motor vehicle – but a collision with a bike will hardly ever cause bodily harm to a motorist. Department for Transport (DfT) statistics show that in 1998:

Per kilometre travelled, pedal cyclists are 14 times more likely to be killed or seriously injured (KSI) in a road accident than car drivers. (Department for Transport, n.d. a)

It could be that assessing injury and death on a per kilometre basis is distorting an equitable comparison of the risk of death or injury between cyclists and motorists as car journeys tend to be further than those taken by bicycle. The distances travelled in cars, however, may not be as long as one might imagine; the National Transport Survey figures show that 1 in 4 car journeys were less than 2 miles in distance in 2001 (Transport 2000, 2002).

Perceptions of risk

Although the risk of injury, or even death, at work is greater in the bicycle couriering industry, the way in which couriers perceive and cope with 'risk' appears to be framed within quite specific understandings of what it means to be in danger or to behave dangerously. For instance, in an interview with a bicycle messenger firm manager in the UK the question of danger arose.

BF: You think there something like inherently dangerous about it?

FM: Yeah, I do. I think you need to be very . . . you need to concentrate and be aware of what's happening all the time and there's not many jobs where you could hurt yourself by being . . . by drifting off for a bit. You really have to concentrate on the road all the time and you know if you're just sat at the computer, well if you daydream for a few minutes no big deal. If you do that on the bike it could cause problems. So in terms of levels of concentration I think it's an issue. If you're careful you can stop yourself from causing any accidents.

I then suggested that it could well be that the courier's attentiveness may be worthless if an accident is caused by other road users behaving dangerously.

FM: Yes. Ok. It's an issue. Now whether you want to classify that as then a dangerous job. Now we've probably had a dozen actual incidents in the four years but how many . . .

BF: But what would you call an incident?

FM: Well when someone's actually been knocked off. A dozen? Maybe more. But certainly not as many as a dozen claims have gone in. But that's . . . I think you're looking at that more in terms of the sort of job where you're working with machinery or something like that that's incidents will always happen. (Firm manager interview transcript, March 2002)

This is an interesting passage for several reasons. The interviewee, whilst acknowledging that couriering *could* be a dangerous job, equates it with any other job where a worker uses machinery and needs to concentrate. Although this might be a point, statistically it appears as though bicycle couriering incurs more injuries than any other job scrutinized by the Health and Safety Executive in the UK and the Department of Environmental Health at Harvard in the United States. There are a couple of explanations emerging for the widely held attitude articulated in the above excerpt. One is possibly denial. The managers of many of the firms do not acknowledge that the job is in itself dangerous, preferring to explain that it is the behaviour of the individual riders themselves who are the major factor in accidents. Although it is possible to have a degree of sympathy with this view it is a contested description of the major factors in accidents or injury, and is a view disputed by bicycle messengers themselves. In fact when messengers apportion blame for accidents the vast majority report that they are not at fault. In my survey couriers describe 340 accidents where they felt fault or blame could be apportioned. A total of 10 per cent were described by respondents as 'all my fault', 22 per cent were described as 'partly my fault' and 68 per cent were described as 'not my fault'. Even if it is accepted that there is bound to be a reporting bias when it comes to apportioning blame for accidents, there is an obvious discrepancy between this particular manager's view of the risk of injury, as a by product of the activities of the riders who get injured, and the view that the activity itself is inherently dangerous.

Another reason for the interviewee's opinion might be that couriering is not inherently dangerous, and that the couriers are responsible for putting themselves at more risk than is necessary. By working as a bicycle messenger I have come to recognize that some people are comfortable with riding in a fashion that I might describe as 'risky'. I recorded in my field diary an example of the differences between people's riding styles and the differences in people's perceptions of risk:

> The day started quite strangely; when I left the house Alan 'Tiny' [another courier] was just along the road. I came up next to him at some traffic lights and said hello. After we had established that we were both working, the lights changed and he shot off. I'm not sure he was cycling like this before we met but I decided to tail him. We went from between 17 and 25 mph through the centre of the city. I never stop for red lights unless I think I will definitely get knocked off, but I do slow down! We flew through all of the lights and were just getting hooted by everything in sight. It was another reminder that I could be in a position of ignorance, because I simply do not *have* to ride like that. After he went across the enormous junction at the bottom of St Mary St I decided to let him go. He went a different way to me and was in the office when I arrived. I felt quite odd about the incident. I wondered whether he had been showing off, or needed to show me what type of a rider he is – hardcore courier – or whether he actually rides like that normally. I felt a bit wet for not riding quite so dangerously. (Field diary, 20 June 2002)

From this excerpt it might be reasonable to assume that some riders might be more likely to be involved in accidents than others, but another excerpt from the field diary illustrates the random distribution of dangerous situations.

> I was coming though a big roundabout with entrances onto it from a flyover, and I was going at a fair pace, when I noticed that a cement lorry wasn't slowing coming onto the road. I really stepped on as hard as I physically could and went across the front of the lorry, which just didn't stop. I reckon it missed me by half a metre. (Field diary, 9 May 2002)

There was another occasion on a dual carriageway when a car overtook me, stopped metres ahead and the passenger side door flew open. I rode straight into it, buckled my wheel and was thrown onto the pavement.

I would argue that the perception that accidents, and subsequent injuries, are the result of particular types of risk taking behaviour could, in part, be an element of a general mythologization of bicycle messengers. There are undoubtedly differences in the ways in which messengers ride and, when discussing 'risk', this will need to be borne in mind. The reporting by the workers themselves, however, and my own participation, reveal that having an accident is much more dependent on an array of circumstances rather than on the behaviour of couriers alone.

Symbolic compensation: collusion in image maintenance in a dangerous, poorly paid job

There are two major discourses in popular perceptions of bicycle messengers, and both serve to maintain an identity that is utilized and often enhanced by the messengers themselves. The first is derision and outright hostility and the second is a romanticized admiration. Both of these images are directly related to the subversion of the 'normalized' world of the motor-car by messengers – the role of danger, risk and law breaking are challenges to urban regulation. On the surface, the degree of mobility, freedom and autonomy exercised and celebrated by the messenger community might be perceived as true 'automobility'. The machine is powered by the individual, the barriers to spatial access are regulated only by the width of the bike, the temporal freedom is absolute – you can ride whenever you want, and if you are no respecter of the ancient and anachronistic laws of trespass, you can ride pretty much wherever you want. The subversive elements of law-breaking and risk are liberating to the extent that the impact of such behaviours are slight and individualized, whereas the ramifications of law-breaking and risk taking in a motor-car are likely to involve injury to others than the driver alone.

The idea of a romantic projection is something that begins to define bicycle messengers as something different from cyclists generally. Much of the commentary concerning bicycle messengers has a very strong romantic theme, and this romance is very much part of the 'culture' of couriering. The riders themselves engage in narratives of reflexive romanticization. Even when attempting to explain away the romance, many cannot avoid intensifying the preconceptions that the general population might have about the work itself and the people that do it. Bob McGlynn, a veteran New York messenger, provides an example:

> I remember once asking at a meeting of 50 bike messengers, 'has anyone here not had an accident?' No one raised their hands. Such is the reality of bicycle messengering beneath the human interest stories which romanticize 'those nonconformist free spirits, going for the big bucks'; and/or condemn us for murderous wild riding, 'law breaking,' 'bad attitudes . . . mental retardation,' etc. I find that many peoples' overcuriosity about bike messengers borders on the neurotic. 'You do that!? . . . Wow . . .' or (jealously) 'Well you've got some freedom but you can't do it all your life you know.' Perhaps they want/need a little of that 'free spirit' stuff: the relative frontier of the open street vis-à-vis [sic] the unnatural enclosedness of 9-to-5-land can be quite intriguing with its danger and autonomy. (McGlynn, 1985)

By documenting the harsh 'reality' of the life of a courier – the amount of accidents that occur in courier work – McGlynn claims to be exposing the 'reality' of the situation beneath the romantic image. It could be argued, however, that he is actually contributing to that image by presenting an occupation populated by people who expose themselves to high levels of risk every day. This simple story of the meeting conjures up images of bravery, bravado

217

and dedication. When he suggests that maybe people need to believe the 'free spirit' myth, there is the suspicion that he also needs to believe it. In an interview with an older messenger the bravura romance is once again articulated:

> MC1: You know if two cars pass very close, well it's rare that you haven't got 18 inches for you to fit into it, and if you can put yourself into that 18 inches even something pretty dodgy looking, you know, like turning into two lanes of oncoming traffic and going down the middle. It looks and sounds ridiculous, but you know the two cars are coming to you with plenty of room. Room for two of you to go through it, so you can always do it.
>
> BF: But isn't there always the chance that someone will swap lanes?
>
> MC1: Well . . . there is but . . . there's usually a gap and if you take one lane of traffic at a time there's always a bit where you can make yourself narrow and avoid being hit. (Messenger in Cardiff interview transcript, March 2002)

On the surface this extract appears to have little to do with the maintenance of a romantic image, but there are strong messages being transmitted by the description of riding. By explaining that there is nothing inherently dangerous about riding between two lanes of oncoming traffic, this behaviour is in some sense being both normalized and glamorized. It is normalized because, for this particular courier, if you are aware of the risks and understand traffic there is no reason to think that this is abnormally dangerous behaviour, and it is glamorized because the way in which the courier presents us with behaviour most of us would think of as recklessly dangerous is with a confidence which emphasizes the difference between a courier's idea of what constitutes 'risk' and anybody else's idea of what constitutes 'risk'. These elements of identity management contribute to an overall perception of bicycle messengers, which undoubtedly maintains a romantic, reckless 'outlaw' image.

The Atlantic magazine in the United States ran an article entitled 'Alleycat Couriers: Bicycle messengers, daredevil scofflaws every day, are holding tournaments to see who can get through tough traffic fastest' where the aura surrounding the industry and those who work in it was succinctly expressed.

> Bicycle messengers have existed for a hundred years in San Francisco and New York. They became cults of cool in the 1980s, when the number of messengers in New York reached a peak of around 5,000. E-mail and fax machines have attenuated their ranks (there are currently 1,000 to 2,000 New York messengers), but this has only added to the mystique. In an age when information travels around the world in a millisecond, these urban warriors still zip through the city on their own legpower to deliver legal documents, plane tickets, and other nondigital valuables. (Fisher, 1997)

During the working day, in the brief exchanges you might have with people working in offices, in studios or on industrial estates, there are often expressions of admiration, jealousy and, most frequently, curiosity about what the work entails and who does it. The danger associated with the work, the levels of physical fitness required to ride 60 to 70 miles a day and the weather make it easy to understand why there is a kind of edge to the job that is easy to romanticize.

There is a style, where affectations are adopted in order to mark yourself out on the road. Couriers tend to wear either very obvious practical cycling gear – with all of the paraphernalia required for couriering, making the worker distinct from other serious cyclists – or they will wear skate fashion – t-shirts, baggies and shades. It could be argued that these are just practical cycle wear, but in all of the interviews that I have conducted with riders, they have mentioned that the aura and the look of bicycle couriers was a contributing factor in attracting them to the industry – second to the need for a job, of course. The maintenance of this image serves to perpetuate the stereotype positively interpreted within messengering and often negatively interpreted outside of couriering. The maintenance of this image operates as an integral part of a cultural autonomy celebrated as messenger sub-culture.

Conclusions

There is a general perception that the roads are dangerous places to be if you are not in a car. The inhospitable landscape is accentuated by the expectation that the driving public will not be mindful to the safety requirements of non-drivers. The extensive reach of the consumption of car culture impacts on the ecological and social environment to devastating effect (Cubitt, 2001: 62). But the same reach makes it difficult to isolate the motorcar from considerations of social need. The discourse of the 'need' to drive is mobilized, creating the right to speed and consequently pollute as almost untouchable. The irony is, of course, that in the urban environment the access to speed is minimal, leaving only the right to pollute. The ideas of isolation from the outside world and abstraction from 'the weather and other people' are particularly important for developing a phenomenological understanding of the processes that permit us to make allowances for the increased use of a potentially destructive technology, and the preconceptions we have of our place in the world of the motorcar.

Merleau-Ponty points out that it 'is never our objective body that we move, but our phenomenal body' (Merleau-Ponty, 1964: 121). The driver creates a personalized, private, exclusive environment in the 'non-space' of their motorcars. It is from the inside of the car that the world is experienced as either a transitory blur or an endless queue of other people's exclusive personalized spaces. Urry highlights the privatized space as an insulating shell:

> Protected by seatbelts, airbags, 'crumple zones', 'roll bars' and 'bull bars', car-dwellers boost their own safety while leaving others to fend for themselves in a 'nasty, brutish and short' world of millions moving and crashing iron cages. As Adorno wrote as early as 1942: 'And which driver is not tempted, merely by the power of the engine, to wipe out the vermin of the streets, pedestrians, children and cyclists?' (Urry, in this volume: p. 23)

This sense of dislocation that drivers have from the outside world fuels the worries of potential cyclists that their safety is not a priority for those who could most easily kill them. The number of cyclists killed on the roads has been declining since 1959. In 1985, 286 deaths were recorded, by 1996 that figure had fallen to 203 – in 2003 there were 114 deaths of cyclists (Department for Transport, n.d. b). This figure, however, needs to be set against the dramatic decline in cycle use over the years in the UK. In the same period the number of journeys made by bicycle fell by 36 per cent, from 25 journeys per person per year in 1985/86 to 16 in 1996/97 (Sheffield Cycling Campaign, 2002). This is an analysis supported by Mayer Hillman:

> What is overlooked is that the level of casualties is only a partial measure of road safety, particularly where cyclists and pedestrians are concerned. A fall in their number can so obviously be explained by the greater danger from the rising volume and speed of traffic leading to fewer journeys being made by the non-motorized modes. (Hillman, 2000: 2–3)

The decline in the use of the bicycle in the urban environment has led to an increased marginalization of the activity as being reserved for the foolhardy and the reckless – the popular representation of the bicycle messenger.

The dangers are such that when cycling is a need – in the case of couriers an economic need – people do take to their bikes. The manner in which messengers ride, as has been illustrated, is popularly represented as irresponsible, dangerous or risky. I would argue, as would most couriers, that the way to ride swiftly and safely in dense urban traffic is with a degree of assertiveness, and maybe even aggression. My experiences as a messenger have shown that a certain amount of law-breaking and subversion of the 'normal' flow of motor traffic is essential for self-preservation. Examples of this are riding on the outside of traffic, often on the side of oncoming traffic, to avoid being 'doored', or making sure that, if you are not through red lights, that you are well ahead of the traffic about to go with the green simply so that they can see you. These sorts of behaviours are seen as aggressive but they are actually good practice. The organization of urban traffic, and the behaviour of many drivers, means that if people do take to their bicycles out of need they do so with a stark choice as to how best to ride. Either stick to the kerb and hope that nobody hits you, or assert yourself as a legitimate road user who will not be bullied.

What is therefore entailed in these arguments and developments is a challenge to the dominance of the motorcar as the provider of autonomy. It makes apparent that the car is auto-mobile, it needs a driver, and that the driver is auto-mobile, as the car cannot deliver automobility. The beneficial effects of cycling are obvious in terms of physical health, environmental impact and a sense of 'being-in-the-world'.

> Bicycles let people move with greater speed without taking up significant amounts of scarce space, energy or time. They can spend fewer hours on each mile and still travel more miles in a year. They can get the benefit of technological breakthroughs without putting undue claims on the schedules, energy or space of others. They become masters of their own movements without blocking those of their fellows. Their new tool creates only those demands which it can also satisfy. Every increase in motorized speed creates new demands on space and time. The use of the bicycle is self limiting.

It allows people to create a new relationship between their life-space and their life-time, between their territory and the pulse of their being, without destroying their inherited balance. The advantages of modern self-powered traffic is obvious, and ignored. That better traffic runs faster is asserted, but never proved. Before they ask people to pay for it, those who propose acceleration should try to display the evidence for their claim. (Illich, 1974: 74–5)

The tyranny of the motor-car is that there is an expectation that you should be prepared to drive, whether you like it or not. A frequent cry from drivers, when asked if they would give up their car, is that they would but they 'have to have it for work'. There is no choice, just a compulsion. All but one of the positive attributes that people ascribe to the motorcar in relation to autonomy and freedom are realized by the bicycle, the exception being that they sometimes don't go as fast, and therefore as far, in the same amount of time. Having said that, the average speed of traffic in London is 11 miles per hour (Greater London Authority, 2003), making it considerably quicker to cycle around the capital than drive. This chapter has shown that there are indeed other 'roads to freedom' than the motor car.

At the same time, what looking at cycle couriers (and arguably at cyclists more generally) suggests is not a project to end 'automobility' but rather the reverse, an attempt to reconstitute the principal object or technology through which it is to be understood. Hence, the instinctive reaction is to assert that the benefits of bicycle use are obvious for achieving the very things – mobility and autonomy – promised and undelivered by that most destructive of historical anachronisms, the motor-car.

But this entails both a reconstitution of how people see themselves as 'autonomously mobile', and a relationship between this 'new automobility' and the pre-existing complex centred on the car. One of the principal outcomes of this is the construction of the autonomy of the cycle courier precisely around the daily dangers they experience and the constant law-breaking, which is both rendered 'necessary' to their daily work and is the site at which they differentiate themselves from car drivers – the moment at which their autonomy is asserted as their 'right' to break traffic rules. In other words, while many of the concrete benefits of cycling are of course very real, the attempt to reconstitute automobility in terms of cycling creates its own contradictions.

References

Appleyard, B. (2002) 'One day i'll kill a lycra lout' *The Sunday Times*, July 28th 2002, Features: News Review: 3.
Bamber, D. (2002) 'Lycra louts' face curbs in new cycle crackdown' *The Sunday Telegraph* Sunday June 30th, 2002: 10.
Burns, L. (2002) 'Autonomy: Reinventing the automobile' Address to the MIT Sustainable Mobility Symposium, May 3rd, http://www.gm.com/company/gmability/sustainability/news_issues/speeches/autonomy_050602.html, accessed 11 November 2002.
Clarkson, J. (2002) 'The lycra nazis are taking over' *The Sun*, August 5th 2002.

Cubitt, S. (2001) *Simulation and Social Theory*. London: Sage.

Dennerlein, J. and Meeker, J. (2002) 'Occupational injuries among Boston bicycle messengers', http://www.hsph.harvard.edu/ergonomics/bike, accessed 13 February 2002.

Department for Transport (2001) *Perceptions of Congestion: Report on qualitative research findings*. 10.12.2001, http://www.dft.gov.uk/itwp/congestion/04.htm, accessed 27 November 2002.

Department for Transport (no date a) 'Pedal cyclists in road accidents: Great Britain 1998', http://www.dft.gov.uk/stellent/groups/dft_transstats/documents/source/dft_transstats_source_505 544.doc, accessed 13 February 2004.

Department for Transport (no date b) 'Road accidents and casualties 1950–2003', http://www.dft.gov.uk/stellent/groups/dft_transstats/documents/page/dft_transstats_031761.xls, accessed 16 March 2005.

European Commission (1999) *Cycling: The Way Ahead for Towns and Cities' Office for Official Publications of the European Communities*, http://europa.eu.int/comm/environment/cycling/cycling_en.pdf, accessed 9 February 2004.

Fisher, M. J. (1997) 'Alleycat couriers' *The Atlantic online*, http://theatlantic.com/issues/97jul/couriers.htm, accessed 26 June 2002.

Gilbert, C. (2003) 'Kings* of the Road: *and queens too' *Cycling Plus*, 147(August): 60–5.

Greater London Authority (2003) 'Press Release 6.6.2003', http://www.london.gov.uk/view_press_release.jsp?releaseid=1770, accessed 13 February 2004.

Guardian (2002) 'Mr Toad in lycra: Cyclists are not all wonderful people' *The Guardian*, August 5th, leader column.

Health and Safety Executive (2002) *Health and Safety Statistics 2000/01. Part One: Statistics of workplace injury, gas safety, dangerous occurrences and enforcement action*, http://www.hse.gov.uk/statistics/2001/hsspt1.pdf, accessed 30 June 2002.

Hillman, M. (2000) *Cycling at the Top of the Policy Agenda*, http://www.eeca.govt.nz/content/sustainable_transport/cycle/hillman.pdf, accessed 27 November 2002.

Illich, I. (1974) *Energy and Equity*. London: Calder and Boyars.

International Federation of Bike Messenger Associations (2004) 'IFBMA City Guide/Statistics – New York', http://www.messengers.org/travel/new_york.html, accessed 13 February 2004.

Lomasky, L. (1997) 'Autonomy and automobility' *The Independent Review*, 2: 5–28.

Lupton, D. (1999) 'Monsters in metal cocoons: "Road rage" and cyborg bodies' *Body and Society*, 5: 57–72.

Marshall, E. and Thomas, N. (2000) 'Traffic calming: The reality of road "rage"', http://www.homeoffice.gov.uk/rds/prgpdfs/brf1200.pdf, accessed 22 November 2002.

McGlynn, B. (1985) 'Road warriors and road worriers – NYC bike messenger tale of toil', http://www.processedworld.com/Issues/issue15/15nyc_bike.htm, accessed 18 October 2001.

Merleau-Ponty, M. (1962) *Phenomenology of Perception*. London: Routledge and Kegan Paul.

Sheffield Cycling Campaign (2002) 'The pedal pushers statistics page', http://www.pedalpushers.org.uk/stats.html#_Recent_trends_in_cycling, accessed 22 November 2002.

Sofoulis, Z. (2002) 'The open road' Paper presented at Automobility Conference, Keele University, 8th September, 2002.

Transport 2000 (2002) 'The national environmental transport body, "Facts and Figures"', http://www.transport2000.org, accessed 26 November 2002.

'Always crashing in the same car': a head-on collision with the technosphere[1]

Mark Dery

The turn of the millennium may have come and gone, but the Mazda Millenia [sic] is still with us. Hyped in a 1994 ad as 'so advanced, it required a whole factory', the Millenia is a determinedly futuristic (and orthographically challenged) luxury sedan.[2] Ads for the Millenia update the snob appeal that has been a mainstay of luxury car advertising for decades, retrofitting it with geek-appeal technobabble – a tacit acknowledgement of the cyborging of the automobile in recent years, as electronic components have infiltrated braking, steering, and suspension systems. The automobile industry is accelerating onto Bill Gates's Road Ahead, literally as well as figuratively.

To be sure, the bullying SUV and its even nastier, more brutish successor, the Hummer – two giant steps backward for fuel efficiency, passenger safety, and inconspicuous consumption – are the undisputed Kings of the Road in America. Even so, visions of smart cars still dance in tech heads. In late 2004, Honda debuted the 2005 Acura RL and the Odyssey, both of which combine navigation systems, voice-recognition technology, and text-to-speech programmes to create cars that 'converse' with their drivers, talking them to their destinations, one turn at a time (Gartner, 2004). In a similar vein, MIT's Media Lab is experimenting with a prototype smart car that DaimlerChrysler hopes will anticipate the driver's needs 'as intelligently as a horse, which is intelligent enough to compensate momentary inattention on the part of the driver' (High Tech Report, 2002; cf. Howard, 2003). Fitted with sensors and dash-mounted video cameras that monitor the driver's actions, the Chrysler 300M IT-Edition is intended to prevent accidents by guarding against driver distraction. The goal, says DaimlerChrysler, is accident-free driving 'through an improved human-machine interface' (High Tech Report, 2002). Ironically, the company's smartmobile musters a high-tech arsenal to combat the sensory assault of too much technology – the cell phones, dashboard instrumentation, and electronic signage clamouring for our attention.

The most futuristic of the 300M's technologies is 'affective computing' – a touchy-feely species of artificial intelligence intended to 'sense the emotional state and stress levels of the operator (in this case, the driver)' and react accordingly (High Tech Report, 2002). According to DaimlerChrysler, the empathic car of the future will respond 'to different types of drivers, their driving style and their emotional state at the time' (High Tech Report, 2002). Its cameras and sensors will tell it if you're holding the gearshift calmly or gripping it with white-knuckled tension; if you're scanning your surroundings, indicating alertness, or if you're gazing fixedly with a thousand-yard stare, the sure sign of a tired or wandering mind. 'Based on the perception of the momentary driving situation', notes DaimlerChrysler,

> the 300M IT-Edition can act like spouse or co-pilot, providing information to the driver appropriately. [. . .] So if the phone rings while the driver is changing lanes on a busy freeway, the 300M IT-Edition suppresses the ringing tone, diverts the call to voicemail, and informs the driver when it is safe to do so. [. . .] Because the 300M IT-Edition monitors driver activity so closely, it is also able to help the driver avoid poten-tially hazardous developments. If, for example, it detects that the driver has not glanced at the side mirrors for an extended period, the computer causes an LED in the mirror to blink, attracting the driver's attention in a very non-intrusive way. (High Tech Report, 2002)

The obvious endpoint of this trajectory is the development of an artificially intelligent car that acts not only as helpful spouse or steed but shrink as well, providing push-button psychoanalysis in the anodyne tones of *2001*'s HAL. ('Look, Dave, I can see you're really upset about that Range Rover cutting you off. I honestly think you ought to take a stress pill and think things over.') During uneventful stretches of midwestern highway or big-city traffic jams, smart cars could analyse their drivers, exploring the depth psychology of the American motorist: the Electra Complex haunting her fetish for big, swinging SUVs; the sadism inherent in her tendency to tailgate slow-moving subcom-pacts, bearing down on them in her Hummer like the Exterminating Angel; the death drive lurking in her devotion to her Ford Explorer, rollovers be damned.

Of course, advertisers have courted male buyers by extolling the technical sweetness of this year's model virtually since the car entered the public imagi-nation. With the dawn of the Digital Age, ad copywriters have increasingly tar-geted the cash-flush, gadget-happy nerdoisie, who until the dotcom flameout had money to burn on boy toys like that electronic tape measure with the LCD readout in the Hammacher Schlemmer catalogue. A 1993 ad for the Mazda 929 touted it as 'a luxury sedan that thinks like a human . . . thanks to its advanced "fuzzy logic" computer', which automatically adjusted cruise control, air con-ditioning, and ventilation. By 1997, the Nissan Infiniti Q45 – ballyhooed in an earlier ad as 'one of the most intelligent automobiles ever conceived' – was not only artificially intelligent, but possessed of a divine spark as well.[3] 'Introduc-ing the new Infiniti Q45', trumpeted the campaign. 'Everything changes but the soul.'[4] Any who doubted that the Infiniti's gleaming hood concealed the soul of a new machine were exhorted to take the car out for a test drive to 'see why the soul is eternal'. Ascending even further into the empyrean, an ad for the Toyota Avalon showed the car sailing through Sistine Chapel clouds, over the tagline, 'Experience the tranquility' – a somewhat ominous enticement, given Avalon's original status, in Arthurian legend, as a hereafter for fallen heroes.

Introducing the new Infiniti Q45. Everything changes but the soul.

Figure 1: The Soul of the New Machine: The ultimate factory add-on for the Smart Car that has Everything – conciousness. © Infiniti; reprinted under Fair Rights clause of U.S. copyright law.

Then again, the association of auto and thanatos makes perfect sense, in light of the overlapping vocabularies of car and casket advertising, with their shared emphasis on gracious living – or dying, as the case may be. The language of the luxury car ad is echoed in trade publications for the funeral industry: in *The American Way of Death*, Jessica Mitford quotes an ad for the 'Monaco' model casket, a deluxe vehicle that features 'Sea Mist Polished Finish' and an interior 'richly lined in . . . velvet, magnificently quilted and shirred' (Mitford, 1979: 57). Of course, the connection between car and coffin runs deeper than polished finish; both are abject objects in the sense that they remind us of our own mortality.[5] They infect life with death, and in so doing unsettle the neat distinction we make between the two. Seen not as a gleaming totem of unbridled freedom but as a steel-paneled, leather-upholstered coffin, ready to receive its roadkill-to-be, the car flickers disconcertingly between meanings, and thus becomes abject. But, as the Critical Art Ensemble points out in its essay, 'Human sacrifice in a rational economy', awareness of the car's status as a death trap is crowded out of the conscious mind: 'Recognition of the car as an abject object is extremely temporary ... Signs of safety abound – traffic laws, safety inspections, the highway code – and so the auto is disassociated even further from death' (Critical Art Ensemble, 1996: 101). At the same time, the authors note, 'we know that more than 50,000 will die in the US this year in motor vehicle mishaps' (1996: 101).

The Freudian question looms, dead ahead: Is our motorphilia rooted in suicidal impulses? Who among us hasn't flirted, if only for an instant, with the fantasy harbored by Annie's abnormally normal brother Duane (Christopher Walken) in *Annie Hall* (1977):

> Can I confess something? I tell you this because, as an artist, I think you'll understand. Sometimes when I'm driving on the road at night, I see two headlights coming toward me, fast. I have this sudden impulse to turn the wheel quickly, head on, into the oncoming car. I can anticipate the explosion, the sound of shattering glass, the flames rising out of the flowing gasoline.

(*That, Virginia, is why they call it the death drive.*) Risking bathos, we can read Duane's monologue (delivered in a hilariously edgy deadpan by Walken) as a comic take on the psychic collision of eros and thanatos (definitively theorized by Georges Bataille in *Erotism: Death and Sensuality*). Here, accelerating into the oncoming headlights of certain death culminates in the ecstatic (if fatal) release of psychic tensions, in fulfillment of the Freudian death instinct. Extinguishing the self in a fiery car crash is synonymous, in Duane's fantasy, with that *other* consummation devoutly to be wished, the ego-obliterating orgasm, which in French slang is known, tellingly, as 'the little death'. (As we shall see in a few pages, the SF writer J.G. Ballard improvises virtuosically on this theme in his novel *Crash*.) The delicious anticipation, the ejaculatory 'explosion' followed by the 'shattering' climax, the flow of post-coital juices: Duane merely makes manifest the latent content of all those car chases that are a staple of Hollywood action movies. With their immersive, videogame-like P.O.V. and their adrenalin-pumping footage of rear-ending, sideswiping vehicles, car chases put our reptilian hindbrains in the driver's seat. And they tease our desire, crescendoing in fiery wipeouts that are the action-movie version of porn's 'money shot'.

Then, too, the fantasy of swerving, suddenly, into an oncoming car offers cathartic release, venting the repressed awareness that, every time we climb into a car, we stand a chance of dying. (According to the National Highway Traffic Safety Administration, motor vehicle crashes were the eighth leading cause of all deaths in 2001, when vehicular accidents killed 42,196 Americans. They were the number one cause of deaths for Americans from age four through 33, that year.)[6] As the tension of waiting for our seemingly unavoidable date with death mounts, the perverse fantasy of taking control of our destinies by choosing the time and place of our *autos-da-fé* grows increasingly seductive.

Some drivers cross the double yellow line between wish-fulfillment fantasy and deadly reality. Whether they do so to break the unbearable tension of waiting to become another one of the NHTSA's grim statistics, as a sacrifice to the psychopathology of everyday life (specifically, the death drive), or as a final solution to their problems can never be known, in many cases. According to the cultural critic Mikita Brottman, in her introduction to the essay collection *Car Crash Culture*, 'investigators have speculated that a certain percentage of the single-vehicle car crashes that happen every year may in fact be deliberate suicides, disguised as accidents either because of the social stigma frequently attached to suicide or in order to let surviving relatives claim substantial insurance policies' (Brottman, 2001). In 'Suicide and homicide by automobile', the psychiatrist John M. MacDonald mentions several incidents straight out of Duane's suicidal ideation: 'A middle-aged woman while driving down a highway suddenly swerved her car into the path of a large semi-trailer truck and was killed. There were no skid marks, and she had made no effort to avoid collision' (MacDonald, 2001: 92). 'A young sociopath drove into the path of an oncoming car whose driver swerved into the wrong lane to avoid collision. This evasive action was not successful, as the sociopath corrected his aim and both cars were badly damaged' (MacDonald, 2001: 94–5).

Naturally, death is the last thing on the minds of car advertisers, who conjure images of gravity defied and immortality attained, draping their product in the macho myth of the *Top Gun* pilot or the rocket jock with the Right Stuff. Such imagery draws on a tradition of four-wheeled futurism as old as the tailfins of the 1948 Cadillac, famously inspired by General Motors designer Harley Earl's tour of a Lockheed hanger, where a test model of the viciously cool twin-tailed P-38 Lightning fighter plane took his breath away. Earl's jet-age streamlining and the mythic language it spoke still reverberate, loud and clear, in ad campaigns such as the one for the 1997 Acura NSK, whose 'sweeping lines and forward-poised cockpit' mimic the design of the F-16, mythologizing the car as a spacecraft for Major Dad, guaranteed not to 'burn up on reentry'. Likewise, Chrysler's Eagle Talon was hyped as a 'rocket full of miracles . . . ungodly good at flying on the ground'.

Rocket-sled fantasies for wannabe flyboys may have peaked in the high-flying, tech-crazy '90s, but they live on, somewhat more discreetly, in those stealth ads passing as product reviews that *The New York Times* sneaks into its 'Automobiles' section, where a puff piece on the Mercedes-Benz SL500 ('one of the world's most technologically competent and complicated cars') worshipped the $100,000 'touring machine' as 'the four-wheeled, leather-upholstered equivalent of a private Gulfstream IV jet' (Martin, 2002: 1). Likewise, a 2002 ad for the Lexus ES 300 announced, 'Rain-sensing windshield wipers. Even Jules Verne didn't see this one coming.' The copy swooned over the car's sensors, which detect raindrops on the windshield (can someone, *anyone*, explain why any driver not drunk or asleep at the wheel would need to be *told* that it's raining?), as well as its Navigation System, which can 'verbally direct you to any destination within the contiguous United States'. (A footnote, in microscopic print, advised, 'Rely upon your common sense to decide whether or not to follow a specified route', an admonition that conjures sick-funny visions, in cynical minds, of Lexuses hurtling confidently off half-built freeway ramps.)

With their microchip implants and post-Moderne streamlining (the 'blob' aesthetic made possible by computer modeling and popularized by product designer Karim Rashid), the RoboCars of ad myth and pop-science journalism invoke a sleek, technocratic Tomorrow. Nonetheless, despite the ministrations of overworked ad agencies, the automobile remains a supreme anachronism: a metal box on wheels, propelled by an engine that guzzles fossil fuels and spews toxic effluvia. In an age consecrated to escape velocity, when scientists have already begun to chafe at the speed-of-light barrier that limits the millions of operations per second a computer can perform, the near-permanent congestion around many big cities dramatizes the contrast between data traffic streaking along the Information Superhighway and rush-hour traffic crawling along real-world freeways. 'To the telematic nomad, a car is pure nostalgia, a sign of lost time', argues the semiotician Marshall Blonsky (1992: 27), improvising in the key of Baudrillard. At a time when cell phones, laptops, and the wiring of the world have made a mockery of time and geography, the car is a nagging reminder that we still haven't figured out how to zap our Darwinian luggage – the body – from here to there, in *Star Trek*'s transporter.

Of course, the car crash, which will kill one of every 75 Americans and is the US's leading cause of untimely death, is the cruellest reminder of that fact – a whiplash reality check to cyberbole like the Progress and Freedom Foundation's now laughably dated 'Magna Carta for the Knowledge Age' (1994), which proclaimed that 'the central event of the 20th century is the overthrow of matter . . . The powers of mind are everywhere ascendant over the brute force of things' (quoted in Seabrook, 1997: 274). Undoubtedly, the manipulation of symbols is fast superseding heavy manufacturing as the economic engine of post-industrial culture. Nonetheless, the messy reality of what happens when flesh and metal collide at high speed is a powerful reminder, to those of us who spend entirely too much time online, that 'the powers of mind' are not *everywhere* ascendant.

The car is a Second Wave totem: ever-present reminder of the assembly line that made industrial modernity possible, Ur-commodity at the heart of postwar consumer culture, essential ingredient in the rise of suburbia and the dereliction of the nation's inner cities, prime mover behind the strip-malling of America. 'The road is now like television, violent and tawdry', writes James Howard Kunstler in *The Geography of Nowhere*. 'The landscape it runs through is littered with cartoon buildings and commercial messages . . . There is little sense of having arrived anywhere, because everyplace looks like noplace in particular' (Knustler, 1993: 131). The car (specifically, American consumers' insistence on cheap, plentiful gas) was a primary impetus behind the Persian Gulf War, a self-evident truth acknowledged at both extremes of the political spectrum, from Jello Biafra's patriot-baiting punk rock song, 'Die for Oil, Sucker', to the pugnacious slogan popular with the pro-war faction, 'Kick their ass, take their gas'.

Although in Madison Avenue myth it sings the song of the open road, conjuring all-American visions of unbounded freedom and ceaseless progress, the automobile has in truth been an implacable foe of progress in the broadest social

Figure 2: Futurrific! Selling the car – an industrial throwback if ever there was one – as a Vision of Things to Come. © Lexus; reprinted under Fair Rights clause of U.S. copyright law.

sense. In its 'Futurama' exhibit at the 1939 World's Fair, General Motors supplanted the monorails of pulp SF with teardrop-shaped cars that zipped along fourteen-lane expressways – a science-fiction echo of its covert campaign, then well under way, to derail mass transportation by buying up streetcar lines and scrapping them (Klein and Olson, n.d.).

* * *

'"In my humble opinion," said Rick Schmidt, founder of the International Hummer Owners Group, "the [Hummer] H-2 is an American icon . . . it's a symbol of what we all hold so dearly above all else, the fact we have the freedom of choice, the freedom of happiness, the freedom of adventure and discovery, and the ultimate freedom of expression. Those who deface a Hummer in words or deed deface the American flag and what it stands for."' (quoted in Weinberger, 2005: 116)

The most potent symbol of everything that's wrong with car culture, and the gasoholic, environmentally toxic mentality behind it, is of course the SUV, the huge – and, in this country, hugely popular – 'light truck' that embodies Imperial America, early in the twentyfirst century. Like too many of us, it is a four-wheeled monument to morbid obesity. According to Greg Critser's (2003) book *Fat Land*, Americans now enjoy the unenviable distinction of being the fattest people in the world (one-fifth of us are obese), a status that is partly the result of federal subsidies for agribusiness, which make food cheap and plentiful, and partly the result of the marketing genius that hooked Americans on 'supersized' portions (the Big Gulp, the Big Mac).

As the Last Remaining Superpower[tm], we have a lot of military and economic weight to throw around, too – a fact of geopolitical life that is making our allies increasingly uneasy about the 7,000-pound Hummer in the middle of the room. And well they should be: the foreign-policy road map in the Bush administration's glove compartment is *Rebuilding America's Defenses: Strategy, Forces, and Resources for a New Century*, a spooky, Strangelove-ian report issued in September 2000 (in other words, *before* the 9/11 terror attacks, instructively) by the Project for the New American Century, a conservative brain trust.[7] Many of the report's recommendations – that the administration repudiate the anti-ballistic missile treaty, embark on the creation of a global missile defense system, pump up defense spending, and cast the net of American military power around the planet – have been taken to heart by the administration. Dreaming of empire, George II and his post-cold warriors imagine a Pax Americana – a global lockdown ensured by an America unafraid to administer a little rough justice, nuclear or otherwise, in the performance of what the report wryly calls its

Figure 3: The Subtext That Speaks the Truth: Our fossil-fueled habit of riding roughshod over the natural world is on a collision course with the disaster-movie reality of global warnning. In a near-future world where tsunamis and hurricanes will turn the pump-and-dump schemes of coastal developers into Donald Trump's idea of Atlantis, even Infiniti will have its limits. © Infiniti; reprinted under Fair Rights clause of U.S. copyright law.

Figure 4: My Way or the Highway: In the Age of Bush, even nature cowers before the Last Action Superpower. A geopolitical parable for the New American Century. © Lexus; reprinted under Fair Rights clause of U.S. copyright law.

Figure 5: Ecology of Fear: Through the smoked glass window of my GPS-equipped SUV, exurban sprawl, species extinction, and extreme weather are mere mirages, conjured by calamity-howling liberals. Who needs nature when you've got culture? © Lexus; reprinted under Fair Rights clause of U.S. copyright law.

'constabulary duties', duties that necessarily 'demand American political leadership rather than that of the United Nations' (Bookman, 2002). Call it SUV foreign policy, a my-way-or-the-highway attitude toward what Defence Secretary Donald Rumsfeld likes to refer to as 'Old Europe', not to mention the irrelevant ragtag and bobtail offstage, somewhere in the developing world.

And it is a policy with consequences, as our Beloved Leader likes to say, when in finger-wagging mode. There's a zigzagging but unbroken line, here: it begins with our love affair with the hideously fuel-inefficient 'light trucks' (sport utility vehicles, pickups, and minivans) and leads, naturally, to off-the-charts profits for Detroit automakers and a what, me-worry? attitude, among American voters, toward oil addiction. From there, it's but a minute's drive to the US government's all-too-happy willingness to exempt such engines of job creation, stock inflation, and consumer confidence from Federal standards for pollution and fuel-consumption. (Light trucks are becoming 'the fastest-growing source of global warming gases in the United States, exceeding the increase in all industrial emissions combined', according to an Environmental Protection Agency researcher (Bradsher, 1997: 42). In such a political climate, our industry-friendly refusal to sign off on environmental agreements such as the Kyoto Accords is a no-brainer. Meanwhile, our dependence on oil mandates a growingly interventionist role in the Middle East, a 'constabulary' role that inflames the blood-and-soil jihadi, who would rather die than suffer the presence of hated infidels in their sacred lands. Righteously angry at US military support for Israel's collateral damage-heavy suppression of the Palestinian uprising and America's historical role as the cosy bedfellow of authoritarian regimes throughout the Middle East, the jihadi will happily kamikaze US planes into Trade Towers, Pentagons, and other symbols of the Great Satan. Granted, the United States's refusal to swerve in its global game of chicken with bin Laden, barrelling head-on into the bearded one's demented dream of a pan-Islamic Caliphate, may have something to do with fundamentalist ire. But long before the rise of the House of Saud's answer to Dr. Evil, America's colonial presence in the region, aiding and abetting human-rights abusers in Israel, Iran, Egypt, Saudi Arabia, and, irony of ironies, Iraq, sewed the dragon's teeth from which bin Laden's shock troops have sprung. Plagued by historical blindspots and prone to geopolitical rollover, the SUV world-view is unsafe at any speed.

* * *

Paradoxically, we can also read the automobile not as some Second Wave holdover but as a premonition of the slow-motion collision of biology and technology that began with the Industrial Revolution and accelerated with the Information Age (transistor, integrated circuit, microchip, network), skidding out of control in the wired 1990s. Now, the point of impact, in which organic and synthetic meet (at least metaphorically, though increasingly literally, in genetic engineering and bionic medicine), seems only split-seconds away, in an age of cloned sheep, bacterial computing, pigs with human hemoglobin, and artificially intelligent cyberpets, such as the Sony Aibo. In retrospect, the car seems a likely candidate for the bifurcation between the born and the 'borged', a clunky presentiment of myoelectric prostheses, teleoperation, and the Holy Grail of cyberpunk SF, the brain jack that would dissolve the membrane between mind and machine altogether. 'When driving a car, one's nervous system becomes linked with the vehicle in a very basic way', writes David Paul, in his essay, 'Man a Machine'. In a sense, Paul argues, 'the car is the driver's body and is directly controlled by the driver's brain and central nervous system. The driver "feels" other objects external to the vehicle and judges distances from the car in a manner crudely analogous to the operations involved in judging one's environment from the physical body' (Paul, 1987: 169).

Paul isn't the only one to note the cyborgian nature of car and driver, a relationship immortalized in Enzo Ferrari's maxim that 'between man and machine there exists a perfect equation: fifty per cent machine and fifty per cent man' (cited in Bayley, 1986: 34). Here is professional driver Lyn St. James on her relationship to her racecar: 'You're strapped in so tightly that you end up wearing it. You become one with the car . . . This is where . . . I'm in my most powerful form' (Leiber, 1993: 55). Jacques Villeneuve, who won the 1995 Indy 500 in a sensor-studded, microprocessor-enhanced machine that looks more like a cruise missile than a car, seconds her emotion: 'You forget that it's a separate thing. You feel everything. You feel what is happening to the car through the steering wheel, your hands, your feet, your butt, and your back . . . [O]nce you get used to it, it feels natural . . . like walking . . .' (cited in Lapin, 1995: 130). Even at a mere 110 miles per hour – a veritable crawl compared to the 220-plus speeds clocked by Villeneuve – the car columnist Lesley Hazleton bonded with her Porsche 911: 'It was as though I became the car, or the car became me . . . Road, driver, and machine were blended into a single entity, an unholy union of asphalt and steel and flesh' (Hazleton, 1992: 22).

Hazleton's 'unholy union' will become a fixture of Tomorrowland's fourteen-lane expressways if technoscience starts spawning drivers like Cowboy, the cyborged road warrior, in Walter Jon Williams's cyberpunk novel *Hardwired*, who 'drives without the use of hands or feet, his mind living in the cool neural interface that exists somewhere between the swift images that pass before his windscreen and the electric awareness that is the alloy body and liquid crystal heart of the Maserati' (Williams, 1987). Recalling 'an experimental automobile braking system which was to be engaged by simply lifting an eyebrow', David Paul (1987: 169) speculates that 'we appear to be approaching a time when "willing" a machine into action will be relatively common'. J.G. Ballard imagined just such an interface when he told me, in an interview, 'It's possible that the driver will not just put on his seatbelt but will also put on some sort of cranial harness so that the onboard computer of the car will pick up various responses by the driver – brain waves, blood pressure, you name it – to the terrain. There will no longer be an accelerator, because the car will respond to the driver's instructions before he's even realized that he's made them.'[8]

For the immediate future, however, the Futurist poet F.T. Marinetti's fist-banging declaration that 'we will conquer the seemingly unconquerable hostility that separates our human flesh from the metal of motors' remains a posthumanist pipe dream (cited in Mackintosh, 1992: 12). The tension generated by this seemingly unresolvable situation seeks release in the car crash, in which man and machine are conjoined, once and for all.

Intriguingly, Jacob Kulowski's 1960 study, *Crash Injuries: The Integrated Medical Aspects of Automobile Injuries and Deaths*, is tinged with the influence of cybernetics and human engineering, both of which are concerned, to varying degrees, with optimizing the man-machine interface. 'I believe it to be true that crash-impact engineering' – elsewhere defined as 'the distinctive art of delethalizing automobiles' – 'is a mirror image of human engineering', writes Kulowski, who calls human engineering 'the field of activities wherein special emphasis is placed on determining optimum mode of interaction between man and machine systems *of which he is a part*' (Kulowski, 1960: xxi; xix; xx, emphasis added). The phrase is instructive, presuming as it does that the human is an organic component in a larger technological system – the proverbial 'cog in the machine' – rather than a co-evolutionary factor in an environment that is equal parts organism and mechanism.

Tellingly, *Crash Injuries* is shadowed by vague forebodings about the fate of the human in an ever more technological landscape, betrayed in Kulowski's tragicomic observation that the 'mechanical efficiency of the human body is a refreshing commentary on man's . . . supremacy over at least some elements of [the] mechanical environment' (1960: 14). Elsewhere, he notes, tellingly, that 'the epidemic frequency of these accidental injuries and deaths is thought to derive from . . . stress-strain patterns of behaviour peculiar to the age of power and speed in which we live, work and play' (1960: vii).

In mythic terms, the car crash – memorably defined by one of Kulowski's sources as 'an extremely complicated phenomenon of a very brief duration ending in destruction' – is at once a precognitive dream of our fusion with our machines and a ritualized enactment of the moment when we lose control of them. Obviously, the escalating number of fiery rollovers, head-on collisions, and multiple-car pileups in action-adventure movies is a concession to the Lowest Common Denominator in a channel-surfing culture afflicted with Attention-Deficit Disorder. But on the more profound level of science-fiction myth, the liberation of special effects from what McLuhan might call the 'Gutenbergian' constraints of narratives rooted in Oedipal psychology suggests the first stirrings of sedition in the technosphere – the machine kingdom's dream of taking the human out of the loop altogether, the moment when SkyNet becomes self-aware.[9]

Ironically, the car crash (again, considered mythically, as opposed to matter-of-factually) also recalls us to our humanity. Deadened and decentered by the ceaseless shocks and jolts of consumer culture and the mass media, more and more of us have come to resemble crash test dummies, existentially speaking. In this light, the crash functions as a bracing blow that re-connects us with our own bodies and other people at a time when our interaction with the world around us consists, increasingly, of headfirst immersion in machines with screens or human contact squeezed through wires, whether they're connected to phones, fax machines, or networked computers. In Ballard's novel *Crash*, the terminally numb narrator is jolted out of his postmodern autism by a collision, 'the only real experience I had been through for years' (1985: 39). He reflects, 'For the first time I was in physical confrontation with my own body, an inexhaustible encyclopedia of pains and discharges, with the hostile gaze of other people, and with the fact of the dead man.'

Inspired in part by *Crash Injuries*, *Crash* is among other things a science-fiction response to what the author calls 'the most terrifying casualty of the [20th] century: the death of affect' (1985: 1). In the detached, exact language of the forensic pathologist and the engineer, Ballard shadows forth a 'sexuality born from a perverse technology', a new entry for Krafft-Ebing's *Psychopathia Sexualis* written in the mutilations of *Crash*'s protagonists, 'her uterus pierced by the heraldic beak of the manufacturer's medallion, his semen emptying across the luminescent dials that registered forever the last temperature and fuel levels of the engine' (1985: 8). Vaughan, the car-crash fetishist around whom the plot revolves, savors the pornography of slow-motion collisions in technical films and dreams of dying, at the moment of orgasm, in a spectacular accident with Elizabeth Taylor's limousine.

Violent and passionless, beyond ego psychology or social mores, this is a posthuman sexuality 'without referentiality and without limits', as Jean Baudrillard puts it in his essay on *Crash* (1991: 313). Alienated from a body that seems, more and more, like a preindustrial artifact, it fetishizes urban desolation, televised disasters, celebrities, and commodities, above all the automobile.

In *Crash*, sex happens almost entirely in cars; removed from that context, it loses its appeal. The body is erotic only when it intersects with technology or the built environment, either literally (punctured by door handles, impaled on steering-columns) or figuratively ('[t]he untouched, rectilinear volumes of this building fused in my mind with the contours of her calves and thighs pressed against the vinyl seating' (Ballard, 1985: 74)).

Here, as in SF films such as *2001* and *Blade Runner*, humans are dispassionate mannequins while the technology around them is disconcertingly anthropomorphic: the 'grotesque overhang of an instrument panel forced on to a driver's crotch' in an accident conjures a 'calibrated act of machine fellatio', while the 'elegant aluminized air-vents' in a hospital 'beckon as invitingly as the warmest organic orifice' (Ballard, 1985: 12, 41). In the depraved geometry of *Crash*, semen and engine coolant, crotches and chromium instrument heads are congruent. 'I believe that organic sex, body against body, skin area against skin area, is becoming no longer possible', said Ballard, in a 1970 interview, 'simply because if anything is to have any meaning for us it must take place in terms of the values and experiences of the media landscape' (in Vale and Juno, 1984: 157).

Crash refracts human psychology through the fractured windshield of postmodern culture, with its flattened affect, celebrity worship, obsessive documentation of every lived moment, and psychotic confusion of subjective experience and filmic fiction. Like David Cronenberg's *Videodrome*, Don

DeLillo's *White Noise*, and Ballard's own *Atrocity Exhibition*, the novel represents a poetic attempt to psychoanalyse the cybernetic subjectivity borne of the late twentieth century – a century characterized by speed and sensory overload, by the supersession of embodied experience by media simulation, and by the over-arching dynamics of disembodiment and dematerialization. Ballard has long maintained that the psychology of the mainstream novel – introspective and solipsistic, an artifact of the book – is a remnant of the nineteenth century, and that science fiction is the only literature capable of making sense of the moment we live in. It is a moment whose psychological torque is centripetal, not centrifugal – a moment where 'social relationships are no longer as important as the individual's relationship with the technological landscape', which is another way of saying that interpersonal psychology has been displaced by a new, cyborgian psychology: the feedback loop between human and machine (Ballard, 1996: 205).

As *Crash* brilliantly illustrates, the relationship between car and driver offers a convenient metaphor for our present psychological (and, increasingly, physiological) symbiosis with our machines. Moreover, the image of freeway drivers jockeying for position, each sealed in his or her climate-controlled conveyance, reminds us of the increasingly atomized nature of our society, where many among the growing ranks of the self-employed live wired lives, communing virtually while physically isolated in their electronic cocoons.

But, as argued earlier, the car–driver relationship is more than a handy metaphor; it is an ubiquitous example, hidden in plain sight, of our everyday psychological symbiosis with our machines. As Deleuze and Guattari argue in *A Thousand Plateaus*, 'tools exist only in relation to the interminglings they make possible or that make them possible. The stirrup entails a new man-horse symbiosis that at the same time entails new weapons and new instruments. Tools are inseparable from symbioses or amalgamations defining a Nature-Society machinic assemblage . . . a society is defined by its amalgamations, not by its tools' (Deleuze and Guattari, 1987: 90).

Incredibly, over a century after the invention of the automobile, we have only begun to scratch the surface of the psychological relationship between driver and car, or driver and driver. Deborah Lupton's (1999) 'Monsters in metal cocoons: "Road rage" and cyborg bodies' (in which the author argues that car and driver fuse, psychologically, to form a cyborg body); Jörg Beckmann's 'Mobility and safety' (a meditation on traffic accidents highlighting the role of the car–driver hybrid), Mimi Sheller's 'Automotive emotions: Feeling the car' (which straddles the phenomenology of car use and the sociology of emotions), Mike Featherstone's inquiry into the 'car-driver-software assemblage', and Tim Dant's 'The Driver-car' (an analysis of the sociological aspects of that cyborgian assemblage, the 'driver-car'), all of which appear in the *Automobilities* issue of *Theory, Culture & Society* (Featherstone, Thrift and Urry, 2004), John Urry's *Sociology Beyond Societies: Mobilities for the Twenty-First Century*; and the essays collected in Brottman's (2001) *Car Crash Culture*, as well as those in this anthology, most notably Peter Merriman's '"Mirror, signal, manoeuvre": assembling and governing the motorway driver in late fifties Britain' (in this volume), have opened the discursive territory of the cyberpsychology of the car-driver hybrid, but only just.

We might begin our inquiries into the cyberpsychology of car and driver by asking: do other drivers subconsciously perceive our grilles and headlights as our faces? Are fender-benders assaults on our metallized bodies? Is the rear-ender sublimated sodomy? Most important, what is the precise psychological mechanism that enables us to 'feel' the boundaries of our cars when negotiating tricky maneuvers such as parallel parking?

This last question goes to the heart of human–machine interaction. Describing the eerie sensation of 'telepresence' experienced when operating a rocket launcher with the aid of virtual-reality goggles that give the operator a weapon's-eye view of the target, machine artist Mark Pauline noted, 'The depth perception is incredible, and once you get all the little adjustments right, you just sink into it. You start to imagine your body in different ways just like you do when you're in an isolation tank; it becomes transparent, really, because of the comfort level, which is the key feature in any of these input devices. Once you achieve transparency, interesting things start to occur. It doesn't take much, because the mind is looking for these things, actively trying to meld with anything' (quoted in Dery, 1995: 52).

Understanding the phenomena Pauline describes – the seeming mutability of the body image in the mind's eye, our eagerness to project ourselves into our technological interfaces (amply evidenced in the widespread experience of virtual spaces such as chat rooms and online role-playing games as 'places') – will yield a skeleton key to the emerging psychology of the Information Age. We've caught fleeting glimpses of the cybernetic self in McLuhan's *Understanding Media* and Sherry Turkle's *Life on the Screen*; in Fredric Jameson's visions of the 'psychic fragmentation', decentering, and death of the subject; and in Scott Bukatman's 'terminal identity' ('an unmistakably doubled articulation in which we find both the end of the subject and a new subjectivity constructed at the computer station or television screen' (Bukatman, 1993: 9).

But sustained scrutiny is imperative if we're going to understand the cultural g-force warping and buckling the bounded, coherent psyche of modernist humanism and Enlightenment rationalism. Since few of us use teleoperated rocket-launchers, the car–driver relationship suggests itself as a more suitable locus of inquiry. Obviously, the psychosexual subtext of automobile design and advertising has been exhaustively mined, most notably in *Crash*, Marshall McLuhan's *The Mechanical Bride: Folklore of Industrial Man*, Stephen Bayley's *Sex, Drink, and Fast Cars*, and Kenneth Anger's underground classic of auto erotica, *Kustom Kar Kommandos*.[10] But the latent sexual content of car styling is only the most prominent landmark in a much larger territory – the cyborg psychology of the car-driver hybrid, a territory that has lain largely hidden from view, until recently. Now, one of the great remaining terra incognitas of inner space awaits the Sigmund Freud of the driver's-side air bag and the C.G. Jung of the anti-locking brake.

Notes

1 The title is taken from David Bowie's song of the same name, on his album *Low*.
2 Mazda ad, 1994.
3 Infiniti ad, 1993.
4 Infiniti ad, 1997.
5 The 'abject', as theorized by Julia Kristeva in *Powers of Horror: An Essay on Abjection*, is that which unsettles us by destabilizing the philosophical dualisms, or binary oppositions, that structure the Western world-view – specifically, the distinction between subject and object, and self and other. Shit, sewage, and especially corpses, the abject object *par excellence*, force us to confront what we 'permanently thrust aside in order to live', argues Kristeva (1982: 3).
6 See 'Top 10 Leading Causes of Death in the United States for 2001, by Age Group', National Highway Traffic Safety Administration website, http://nhtsa.gov/people/Crash/LCOD/RNote-LeadingCausesDeath2001/pages/page2.html.
7 See The Project for the New American Century, Rebuilding America's Defenses: Strategy, Forces, and Resources for a New Century – A Report of The Project For the New American Century, http://www.informationclearinghouse.info/pdf/RebuildingAmericasDefenses.pdf.
8 Unpublished excerpt from a 1989 interview with the author.
9 For non-geek readers, SkyNet is the SDI-like military computer network in *Terminator 2: Judgment Day*. According to the hunter-killer 'terminator' cyborg (played by Arnold Schwarzenegger), 'The system goes online on August 4th, 1997. Human decisions are removed from strategic defense. SkyNet begins to learn at a geometric rate. It becomes self-aware at 2:14 A.M. Eastern time, August 29th.'
10 Not to mention, at the risk of immodesty, my chapter 'Sex times technology equals the future' in *Escape Velocity* (Dery, 1996).

References

Ballard, J.G. (1985) *Crash*. New York: Vintage Books.
Ballard, J.G. (1996) *A User's Guide to the Millennium*. New York: Picador.
Baudrillard, J. (1991) 'Two Essays' *Science-Fiction Studies*, #55, 18(3): http://www.depauw.edu/sfs/backissues/55/baudrillard55art.htm.
Bayley, S. (1986) *Sex, Drink and Fast Cars*. New York: Pantheon.
Blonsky, M. (1992) *American Mythologies*. New York: Oxford University Press.
Bookman, J. (2002) 'The President's real goal In Iraq' *The Atlanta Journal-Constitution*, 29th September: archived at the Information Clearing House, http://www.informationclearinghouse.info/article2319.htm.
Bradsher, K. (1997) 'Light trucks increase profits but foul air more than cars' *The New York Times*, 30th November, 'National' section: 42.
Brottman, M. (2001) 'Introduction' in M. Brottman (ed.) *Car Crash Culture*. New York: Palgrave.
Bukatman, S. (1993) *Terminal Identity: The Virtual Subject in Postmodern Science Fiction*. Durham, NC: Duke University Press.
Critical Art Ensemble (1996) *Electronic Civil Disobedience*. Brooklyn: Autonomedia.
Critser, G. (2003) *Fat Land: How Americans Became the Fattest People in the World*. New York: Houghton Mifflin.
Deleuze, G. and F. Guattari (1987) *A Thousand Plateaus*. Minneapolis: University of Minnesota Press.
Dery, M. (1995) 'Deus ex Machina' *21.C*, 3
Dery, M. (1996) *Escape Velocity: Cyberculture at the End of the Century*. New York: Grove Atlantic.
Featherstone, M., N. Thrift and J. Urry (eds) (2004) 'Automobilities' Special issue of *Theory, Culture and Society*, 21(4–5).

Gartner, J. (2004) 'Finally, a car that talks back' *Wired News*, 2nd September, http://www.wired.com/news/autotech/0,2554,64809,00.html.

Hazleton, L. (1992) *'Confessions of a Fast Woman' American Way* 15th December.

High Tech Report (2002) 'Cars that anticipate needs – just like a horse' *High Tech Report: Research and Technology,* Issue 2, http://www.daimlerchrysler.com/index_e.htm?/research/htr2002-2/htr2002-2_medialab_e.htm.

Howard, B. (2003) 'Smart car: The Chrysler 300M cruising through Cambridge, Massachusetts, with a trunk full of computer gear' *PC Magazine*, 1st February: 26.

Jameson, F. (1992) *Postmodernism, or, the Cultural Logic of Late Capitalism.* Durham, NC: Duke University Press.

Klein, J. and M. Olson (no date) 'Taken for a Ride' *Culture Change*, 10, http://www.culturechange.org/issue10/taken-for-a-ride.htm.

Kulowski, J. (1960) *Crash Injuries: The Integrated Medical Aspects of Automobile Injuries and Deaths.* Springfield, IL: Charles C. Thomas.

Kunstler, J.H. (1993) *The Geography of Nowhere.* New York: Simon & Schuster.

Kristeva, J. (1982) *Powers of Horror: An Essay on Abjection*, trans. L.S. Roudiez. New York: Columbia University Press.

Lappin, T. (1995) 'The ultimate man-machine interface' *Wired*, October.

Lieber, J. (1993) 'A road less taken' *Sports Illustrated*, 3rd May: 55.

Lupton, D. (1999) 'Monsters in metal cocoons: 'Road rage' and cyborg bodies' *Body & Society*, 5(1): 57–72.

MacDonald, J.M. (2001) 'Suicide and homicide by automobile' in M. Brottman (ed.) *Car Crash Culture.* New York: Palgrave.

Mackintosh, J. (1992) 'An ode to cyborgs' *Adbusters*, 2(2 – Summer/Fall).

Martin, K. (2002) 'That six-figure swagger: A personal jet minus the wings' *The New York Times*, 14th July, Section 12: 1.

Mitford, J. (1979) *The American Way of Death.* New York: Fawcett Crest.

Paul, D. (1987) 'Man a machine' in A. Parfrey (ed.) *Apocalypse Culture.* New York: Amok Press.

Seabrook, J. (1997) *Deeper.* New York: Simon and Schuster.

Vale, V. and A. Juno (eds) (1984) *Re/Search #8/9: J.G. Ballard.* San Francisco: Re/Search Publishing.

Weinberg, Eliot (2005) *What Happended Here: Bush Chronicles.* New York: New Directions.

Williams, W.J. (1987) *Hardwired.* New York: Tor Books, http://www.scorpiusdigital.com/teasers/hardwired_x.html.

Notes on contributors

Steffen Böhm is Lecturer in Management at the University of Essex. He is a member of the editorial collective of *ephemera: theory & politics in organization* (www.ephemeraweb.org) and co-editor of mayflybooks (www.mayflybooks.org). He has been co-organizing conferences and conference streams on themes such as sound and silence, literature and organization, art and organization, and automobility. His book *Repositioning Organization Theory: Impossibilities and Strategies* is out with Palgrave. He is active in the social forum movement and has been involved with a number of Radical Theory Forums and knowledgelabs (www.knowledgelab.org.uk). He doesn't own a car, commutes to work by train and bike, and can occasionally be seen at Critical Mass cycle rides in London.

Jennifer Bonham has a background in Human Geography and is an Adjunct Research Fellow in the Transport Systems Centre at the University of South Australia. In the past ten years, her research has focused upon street life and the mechanisms which shape street space and the practice of urban travel. She has authored a number of papers which examine the relationship between spaces, bodies, and practices of mobility. Jennifer has also co-authored papers on transport policy, road space as a site of public art, and changing mobility and meanings of travel amongst older citizens. She is currently undertaking research on the cycling body.

Mark Dery ⟨markdery@optonline.net⟩ is a cultural critic. He is the author of *Escape Velocity: Cyberculture at the End of the Century* (1996) and *The Pyrotechnic Insanitarium: American Culture on the Brink* (1999) ⟨www.levity.com/markdery⟩. His seminal essay, 'Culture Jamming: Hacking, Slashing, and Sniping in the Empire of Signs' popularized the guerrilla media tactic known as 'culture jamming'; widely republished on the Web, 'Culture Jamming' remains the definitive theorization of that subcultural phenomenon. In *Flame Wars: The Discourse of Cyberculture* (1993), an academic anthology he edited, Dery coined the term 'Afrofuturism' and kick-started the academic interest in black technoculture, and cyberstudies in general. He's at work on *Don Henley Must Die*, a book about the cultural psyche of San Diego, where he grew up in the 1970s, amid the borderlands and badlands of its suburban sprawl. Dery teaches journalism and media criticism in the Department of Journalism, at New York University, and writes a blog, 'The Gilded Hack,' at http://www.markdery.com/blog.html.

Ben Fincham is a research associate in the Cardiff School of Social Sciences. He has passed his driving test but prefers to cycle.

Per-Anders Forstorp is a senior lecturer and teaches communication studies at the Royal Institute of Technology in Stockholm, Sweden. Recent research include studies in moral and political discourse, the theory, practice and methodology of ethics and discourse in connection with public controversies and risk. The present chapter is a contribution to a project on Vision Zero, the traffic safety campaign in Sweden. His interests are also in the wider field of communication and knowledge, its theories and practices. Forthcoming work include the development of an interdisciplinary approach to communication studies based on the philosophy of Emmanuel Levinas.

Campbell Jones is Director of the Centre for Philosophy and Political Economy and Senior Lecturer in Critical Theory and Business Ethics at the University of Leicester, UK. His recent work includes *For Business Ethics* (2005, Routledge), *Manifestos for the Business School of Tomorrow* (2005, Dvalin, www.dvalin.org), *Contemporary Organization Theory* (2005, Blackwell) and *Philosophy and Organization* (forthcoming, Routledge). He walks a lot.

Chris Land now teaches at the University of Essex. His research has predominantly been concerned with the constitutive role of technology in producing human subjectivity. In the course of researching automobility he has ridden and repaired a number of human powered vehicles. In order to maintain a fair and balanced, academically objective perspective on the question of automobility, however, he has spent the last year driving a huge diesel powered MPV and towing a 24ft caravan around the British Isles whilst working as a mobile, autonomous, freelance lecturer and researcher. This experience has, frankly, disillusioned him with the whole valorization of mobility and fluidity so prevalent in contemporary society and he is in the process of researching a book on precarity as the counterpoint to mobility.

Joanna Latimer draws together issues of power/knowledge with ideas about identity and culture to research the medical domain. She questions why those with the most complex health and social needs are also the most problematic to modern health services. Her ethnography, *The Conduct of Care* unpicks the politics of modern health care and its enactment at the bedside. Her current research examines the social significance of genetic categorizing. As well as teaching social theory and medical sociology in the School of Social Sciences at Cardiff University, Joanna is Associate Editor of *Gender, Work and Organization* and a founder member of the Centre for Social Theory and Technology at Keele University. She is writing a new book, *The gene, the clinic and the family: diagnosing dysmorphology, reviving medical dominance*.

David Martin-Jones is Lecturer in Film Studies at the University of St Andrews. He is the author of Deleuze, Cinema and National Identity (Edinburgh University Press, 2006) and the co-author of Why Deleuze? (I. B. Taurus, forthcoming). He has published articles in various international journals, and is on the editorial board of the international salon-journal Film-Philosophy. His research focuses on questions of national identity, primarily using Deleuze, but also by examining representations of Scotland, and various Asian Cinemas.

Peter Merriman is a lecturer in the Institute of Geography and Earth Sciences at The University of Wales, Aberystwyth. He completed his doctoral research on the cultural geographies of England's M1 motorway at the University of Nottingham, and between 2000 and June 2005 he was a lecturer in human geography at The University of Reading. His research focuses on the themes of mobility, space and social theory; cultures of landscape in twentieth century Britain; and music, sound and space. His articles have appeared in the *Journal of Historical Geography*, *Environment and Planning D: Society and Space*, *Cultural Geographies* and *Theory, Culture and Society*. He is currently completing *Driving Spaces* (Blackwell, forthcoming).

J. Hillis Miller was educated at Oberlin College and Harvard University, where he received his PhD in 1952. After teaching for a year at Williams College, he joined the faculty of The Johns Hopkins University, where he taught for nineteen years. That was followed by fourteen years at Yale University. He has been teaching at the University of California at Irvine since 1986 and is now UCI Distinguished Research Professor of English and Comparative Literature there. He now lives most of the year in Maine. He has lectured in many countries and is the author of numerous books and essays on nineteenth and twentieth-century literature and on literary theory. His most recent books are *Others* (Princeton: 2001), *Speech Acts in Literature* (Stanford: 2002), *On Literature* (Routledge: 2002), and *Literature as Conduct: Speech Acts in Henry James* (Fordham: 2005). A *J. Hillis Miller Reader* came out from Edinburgh in 2005. He gives a 'mini-seminar' for the Critical Theory Emphasis at Irvine each spring.

Rolland Munro is Professor of Organization Theory at Keele University and Director of the Centre for Culture, Social Theory & Technology. He has published in a wide range of journals on topics such as accountability, identity, organization and culture and co-edited two previous sociological review monographs *Ideas of Difference* and *The Consumption of Mass*.

Matthew Paterson is Associate Professor of Political Science at the University of Ottawa, Canada. His main research interests are the politics of global warming, ecological perspectives on global politics, and the political economy of global environmental change. His main publications are *Global Warming and Global Politics* (1996) *and Understanding Global Environmental Politics: Domination, Accumulation, Resistance* (2000). He is close to the completion of a monograph entitled *Automobile Politics: Ecology and Cultural Political Economy*, to be published by Cambridge University Press. Having moved to the continent of enforced automobility, he is now no longer car-free, although the bike remains his drug of choice.

Chella Rajan's academic career began with training as an aeronautical engineer, followed by postgraduate work in meteorology and environmental studies at UCLA. While trying to make numerous ends meet, including developing a meaningful research topic for his dissertation, he drove fifty miles a day to and from his job at the California Air Resources Board, a state agency that regulates motor vehicle pollution. His thesis was subsequently published as *Enigma of Automobility* (University of Pittsburgh Press, 1996), after which he moved into work in energy research and advocacy, living variously in Bangalore, New York and London. He is currently a Senior Fellow at Tellus Institute, where he leads its Programme on Global Politics and Institutions. His current research focuses on the social and institutional conditions needed to form a global political community with a common 'we' identity and a clearly articulated collective interest in the environment, equity, and human development.

Nicole Shukin is currently a Postdoctoral Fellow in the Department of English at the University of Western Ontario, Canada. She first theorized 'rendering' in her doctoral dissertation, *Animal Capital: The Material Politics of Rendeirng, Mimesis, and Mobility*, implicating technologies of representation/mimesis in the material violence of cultures of capital. Interested in intersecting biopolitical constructions of race and species, her other work has taken up Heidegger, Derrida, and Deleuze and Guattari to interrogate western discourses of nature and of animality. In her contribution to *Deleuze and Feminist Theory* (Edinburgh University Press, 2000), texts of Deleuze are confronted with a semiotics of 'meat' which subliminally encodes them. Her current postdoctoral project, *Forest Product: Manufacturing a Natural, National, and Transnational Resource*, continues to interrogate traffics in material signs of 'nature' in their specific currency as cultural and economic capital.

Andrew Thacker is Senior Research Fellow in the School of English at De Montfort University, Leicester. Previously he has taught at the University of Wolverhampton and the University of Ulster. He is the author of *Moving Through Modernity: Space and Geography in Modernism* (2003) and the co-editor of *The Impact of Michel Foucault on the Social Sciences and Humanities* (1997) and *Geographies of Modernism: Literatures, Cultures, Spaces* (2005). He is also an editor of the journal, *Literature and History*. His undergraduate degree was in English and Philosophy at Keele, and his MA and PhD at the University of Southampton. His main research interests are in modernism and Michel Foucault. He is currently completing a short book on the Imagist poets, and commencing a large project on Modernist Magazines.

John Urry, Professor of Sociology and Director of the Centre for Mobilities Research, Lancaster University. Chair RAE Sociology Panel 1996, 2001. Founding-Academician of the Academy of Learned Societies in the Social Sciences. Editor of the *International Library of Sociology*, Routledge. Recent books include *Sociology In the New Millennium*, special double issue of the *British Journal of Sociology* (2000), *Sociology Beyond Societies* (2000), *Bodies of Nature* (2001, co-edited with P Macnaghten), *The Tourist Gaze*, Second Edition (2002), *Global Complexity* (2003), *Presence-Absence*, special issue of *Society and Space* (2003, with M Callon and J Law), *Automobilities* (2005, with M Featherston, N Thrift), *Complexity*, special issue of *Theory, Culture and Society* (2005), and *Mobile Technologies of the City* (2006, with Mimi Sheller). Co-editor of the new journal *Mobilities*.

Index

Douglas, M. 37, 40, 43, 49
Driscoll, B. 6
driver 8, 10, 12, 18, 19, 20, 21, 23–5, 27, 41
  aids 224, 227
  and high speed 122, 126
  and space 185
  as victim 212, 213
  autonomous 186
  controller of movement 176
  danger 120
  future 233
  inattention 223
  infringing rights 119, 121
  isolation of 185
  motorway 82–9, 237
  racing 84
  smart cars 193
  subject 115
drivers' licences 66
driving
  as engrossment 33, 43–5, 47
  as immoral activity 119
Dumm, T. 124, 125
du Maurier, D. 18
Dunn, J. 3, 127n
During, S. 196, 201
Durkheim, E. 33, 35, 38, 42, 43, 48, 49, 50n
dwelling 18, 19, 22–30, 38, 40–1, 47, 48, 82, 99

Earl, H. 158, 227
Eason Gibson, J. 82
Eastman, G. 156, 157
Economist 113, 118
Edison, T. 156, 157
Education Gazette 65, 66, 67, 68
efficiency 58, 71
elicitation 34, 39, 42–3, 48
Eliot, T.S. 178
Elliott, S. 136
Ellis, H. F. 77
Ellmann, R. 178
Enlightenment 117, 123, 128n, 134, 237
environment 99, 127
  and cycling 210, 220
  antagonism 10
  consequences for 5, 13

costs to 13, 118, 119
degradation 9–10, 208
justice 119
problems 10
resources 5
risks 121
see also climate change; greenhouse gases; pollution
equality 117–18
Erard, M. 206
Espinosa, J.G. 147
European Commission 210
European Union 96
Ewald, F. 98
expert knowledge 65–6, 67, 69
extension 24, 34, 39–40, 40–2, 48
  producing relations 42–3
extrusion 38, 45–6, 47
Exxon Valdez 163
eye-contact 21–2
Eyerman, R. 18, 27

Fabian, J. 162
Fairclough, N. 110
families
  and road safety 68–9
family life 35
  automobilization of 25–6
Faulkner, W.C. 205
Featherstone, M. 4, 17, 123, 236
Ferrari, E. 233
Ferretti, D. 71
fetish 164, 224
fetishism 167
film audiences 134
films 4, 205
  Coen brothers 133, 134, 136, 144, 146
  political content 147–8
  2001 224, 235
  Alice Doesn't Live Here Anymore 27
  Annie Hall 226
  Badlands 27
  Barton Fink 133
  Big Lebowski, The 133, 135–8, 140–8
  Big Sleep, The 147
  Blade Runner 235
  Bonnie and Clyde 27, 137
  Bowling for Columbine 134, 146
  Citizen Kane 147